KANT'S COSMOPOLITAN THEORY OF LAW AND PEACE

Kant is widely acknowledged for his critique of theoretical reason, his universalistic ethics, and his aesthetics. Scholars, however, often ignore his achievements in the philosophy of law and government. At least four innovations that are still relevant can be attributed to Kant. He is the first thinker, and to date the only great thinker, to have elevated the concept of peace to the status of a foundational concept of philosophy. Kant links this concept to the political innovation of his time, a republic devoted to human rights. He extends the concept by adding to it the right of nations and cosmopolitan law. Finally, Kant democratizes Plato's notion of philosopher-kings with a concept of "kingly people." This book examines all aspects of this important, but neglected, body of Kant's writings.

Otfried Höffe is professor of philosophy at Eberhard-Karls-Universität, Tübingen, and Director of the Research Center for Political Philosophy. He is a Fellow of the Heidelberger Akademie der Wissenschaften and a member of the Collegium Europeanum Jenense. In 2002 he received the Karl-Vossler-Preis of the Bavarian Ministry for Science and Culture. He is the author of many books, most recently *Gerechtigkeit. Eine philosophische Einführung, Medizin ohne Ethik?* and *Kant's Kritik der reinen Vernunft,* and he sits on the editorial boards of many scholarly journals.

Alexandra Newton is a Ph.D. candidate in philosophy at the University of Pittsburgh.

D0905581

KANT'S COSMOPOLITAN
THEORY OF LAW AND PEACE

OTFRIED HÖFFE
Eberhard-Karls-Universität, Tübingen

Translated by Alexandra Newton

CAMBRIDGE
UNIVERSITY PRESS

CAMBRIDGE UNIVERSITY PRESS
Cambridge, New York, Melbourne, Madrid, Cape Town, Singapore, São Paulo

Cambridge University Press
40 West 20th Street, New York, NY 10011-4211, USA

www.cambridge.org
Information on this title: www.cambridge.org/9780521826761

Königliche Völker. Zu Kants Kosmopolitischer Rechts- und Friedenstheorie
© Suhrkamp Verlag Frankfurt am Main 2001
© Translation Cambridge University Press 2006

German edition first published 2001
English edition first published 2006

Printed in the United States of America

A catalog record for this publication is available from the British Library.

Library of Congress Cataloging in Publication Data
Höffe, Otfried.
[Königliche Völker. English]
Kant's cosmopolitan theory of law and peace / Otfried Höffe.
p. cm. – (Modern European philosophy)
Includes bibliographical references and index.
ISBN 0-521-82676-4 (hardcover) – ISBN 0-521-53408-9 (pbk.)
1. Law – Philosophy. 2. Law and ethics. 3. Peace – Philosophy.
4. Kant, Immanuel, 1724–1804. I. Title. II. Series.
K457.K3H6413 2006
340'.112 – dc22 2005016095

ISBN-13 978-0-521-82676-1 hardback
ISBN-10 0-521-82676-4 hardback

ISBN-13 978-0-521-53408-6 paperback
ISBN-10 0-521 53408-9 paperback

CONTENTS

ABBREVIATIONS

Works by Kant

Anthropology	*Anthropology from a Pragmatic Point of View* (*Anthropologie in pragmatischer Hinsicht,* VII:117–334)
CJ	*Critique of Judgment* (V:165–485)
"Common Saying"	"On the Common Saying: That May Be Correct in Theory, but It Is of No Use in Practice" ("Über den Gemeinspruch: Das mag in der Theorie richtig sein, taugt aber nicht für die Praxis," VIII:273–313)
Conflict	*The Conflict of the Faculties* (*Der Streit der Fakultäten,* VII:1–116)
"Conjectures"	"Conjectures on the Beginning of Human History" ("Mutmaßlicher Anfang der Menschengeschichte," VIII:107–123)
Correspondence	*Kant's Correspondence* (X–XIII)
CPR	*Critique of Pure Reason* (A: IV:1–252; B: III:1–552)
CPrR	*Critique of Practical Reason* (V:1–163)
DR	*Metaphysical First Principles of the Doctrine of Right* (*Metaphysische Anfangsgründe der Rechtslehre,* first part of the *Metaphysics of Morals,* VI:203–372)
DV	*Metaphysical First Principles of the Doctrine of Virtue* (*Metaphysische Anfangsgründe der Tugendlehre,* second part of the *Metaphysics of Morals,* VI:373–492)

GMM   *Groundwork of the Metaphysics of Morals*
                        (IV:385–464)
"Idea"   "Idea for a Universal History with a
                        Cosmopolitan Purpose" ("Idee zu einer
                        allgemeinen Geschichte in
                        weltbürgerlicher Absicht," VIII:15–31)
Logic   *Logic. A Handbook for Lectures* (*Logik, Ein
                        Handbuch zu Vorlesungen*, ed. G. B. Jäsche,
                        IX:1–150)
MFS   *Metaphysical Foundations of Natural Science*
                        (*Metaphysische Anfangsgründe der
                        Naturwissenschaft*, IV:465–565)
Peace   *Toward Perpetual Peace* (*Zum ewigen Frieden*,
                        VIII:341–386)
Prolegomena   *Prolegomena to Any Future Metaphysics That
                        Will Be Able to Come Forward as Science*
                        (IV:253–384)
Religion   *Religion within the Boundaries of Mere Reason*
                        (*Die Religion innerhalb der Grenzen der bloßen
                        Vernunft*, VI:1–202)
"Supposed Right"   "On a Supposed Right to Lie from
                        Philanthropy" ("Über ein vermeintes
                        Recht aus Menschenliebe zu lügen,"
                        VIII:423–430)
"What Is Enlightenment?" "An Answer to the Question: What Is
                        Enlightenment?" (VIII:33–42)

                        Works by Others

EN   Aristotle, *Ethica Nicomachea/Nicomachean
                        Ethics*
SC   Rousseau, *Social Contract*

TRANSLATOR'S PREFACE

Kant's Cosmopolitan Theory of Right and Peace: The German title of this book is a phrase taken from Kant's treatise on peace: "Königliche Völker." Mary Gregor's translation of the phrase as "royal peoples" in the context of Kant's work does not bring out the importance of Kant's point for the purposes of this study. The phrase, literally translated as "kingly people," poignantly captures Kant's democratic response to Plato's philosopher-kings: The state should be ruled by an "enlightened" people, rather than by an elite society of philosophers.

Otfried Höffe's rewarding study of Kant's cosmopolitan theory of law and of peace has long deserved to be read and discussed in English-speaking countries. In my translation, I have relied on former renditions of Höffe's work into English on related topics, especially Marshall Farrier's translation of *Immanuel Kant* and Mark Migotti's translation of *Categorical Principles of Law*. These have been particularly helpful in translating important terms that have no clear counterpart in English.

I should like to take this opportunity to express my thanks to Henry Pickford for his kindness in revising and indexing the manuscript and to Jochen Bojanowski for many valuable suggestions. Any infelicities that remain are entirely my own responsibility. I should also like to thank the Fritz Thyssen Stiftung for the generous grant that made this translation possible.

PREFACE

To the educated, Kant is known as the author of a critique of reason who tears down traditional metaphysics to create a new edifice on its ruins. They acknowledge his moral philosophy and perhaps his theory of art, but not his philosophy of law and of government. Despite dispersed acclaim, Kant's *Doctrine of Right* does not, even in scholarship on legal and political theory, attain the status of that narrow canon comprising Plato's *Republic*, Aristotle's *Politics*, Augustine's *City of God (De civitate dei)*, Machiavelli's *Il principe*, Hobbes's *Leviathan*, Locke's *Second Treatise on Government*, Rousseau's *Social Contract*, and Hegel's *Philosophy of Right*. Kant's treatise on *Perpetual Peace* might play a prominent role in contemporary peace debates, but it is not fully acknowledged as an attempt to provide a foundation for a comprehensive philosophy of right and law that is linked to a doctrine of political prudence and a philosophy of history. It thereby yields no fewer than four innovations that still remain relevant today: (1) Kant is the first thinker and to date the only great thinker to have elevated the concept of peace to the status of a foundational concept of philosophy. (2) He links this concept to the political innovation of his time, a republic devoted to human rights. (3) He extends it with a cosmopolitan perspective by adding the right of nations and cosmopolitan law. (4) Finally, Plato's notion of philosopher-kings receives a republican bent with the concept of a "kingly people." Kings are not a separate elite, the philosophers, but rather the people themselves, insofar as they rule "themselves according to laws of equality."

The reasons accounting for the decline of Kant's influence are more contingent than philosophically substantive, such as the replacement of his innovations by Hegel's philosophy of right, which quickly became predominant. But as exemplified by the following study, Kant's legal and state philosophy, emerging at the intellectual peak of the European Enlightenment, is no less innovative than that of Machiavelli, Hobbes, Rousseau, or Hegel. Prejudices that are neither philosophically nor politically convincing do enter his political philosophy, such as the excessive importance placed on the protection of property in the justification of the state, the priority of men over women, the discrimination against wage laborers, and the defense of castration as a legal penalty. But methodological considerations show that few of these statements are intended as expressions of principles, which are Kant's professed concern. Therefore, if one focuses on the central purpose of the legitimation of right and state on the basis of a priori concepts, then Kant ranks among the classical thinkers of legal and political theory. Due to his aforementioned innovations, his theory is even more future-oriented than most alternatives. A political philosophy of freedom is indispensable in an age of weaponry that endangers the entire human race. And in an age of globalization, this philosophy should not confine itself to the borders of nations. Nor is a worldwide order of peace conceivable without the extension of the right of nations by cosmopolitan law.

Peace does not become a foundational concept of philosophy merely by its occurrence in the title of a significant text that addresses issues still relevant today. It must also have a bearing on and even be central to larger areas of discussion. For Kant, peace belongs mainly, but not exclusively, to right and law, which in turn are an important domain of morals: Kant's philosophy of right and law, of the state, and of peace is an *ethics* of right and law, of the state, and of peace. Consequently, we should first elucidate the foundation of Kant's philosophy of peace, namely, the moral concept itself. Following introductory remarks on the current relevance and challenge of Kant's theory (chapter 1), this study will turn to reflections on morals (part I), then consider the moral concept of right and law (part II) and the relation between peace and legal morals (part III).

In philosophical interpretation, it has become fashionable to place classical texts on the dock, following the North American model of criminal trials, in order to reveal the ambiguity of their concepts, the fallacies of their arguments, the contradictions in their claims, and even the deceptive character of their basic intuitions. The primary task of providing a consistent interpretation often recedes behind this objective of revealing inconsistencies. A closer reading of the texts urges the contrary. It is rather facile criticism that should be placed on the dock, not out of compassion, as of late suggested by the "principle of charity," but rather out of estimation for Kant's insights. This study will not settle for an interpretation unless it can rationally account for the meaning of Kant's line of thought. Only thereafter is criticism appropriate. This is especially exigent with respect to two elements of Kant's ethics of peace, namely, the alleged peaceableness of republics and his indecisiveness with respect to the alternative between a "federation of peoples or world republic." However, this is a matter for a "fine-grained debate with Kant." His general cosmopolitan approach still remains convincing.

The studies here pursue not only hermeneutical, but also systematic interests. For this reason, the three topics – morals, right, and peace – are not treated as comprehensively as in Kant himself. Guided by the intuition that debates on perpetual issues may profit from Kant's inspiration, only relevant factors have been chosen for inquiry (for a methodical outline, see Höffe 2002a).

The substantive question of part I concerning the epochal difference between classical antiquity and modernity is preliminary. Are the two paradigms of occidental ethics, namely, Aristotelian ethics with its principle of eudaemonism and the preponderance of virtue, on the one hand, and Kantian ethics with its principle of autonomy and the preponderance of principles, on the other, in fact incompatible alternatives, such that it is unproblematic today to adhere to Aristotle instead of Kant? A positive answer would considerably weaken the persuasiveness of Kant, for his philosophy of right and law, and of peace, would be relativized in the face of an alternative ethics. However, if considered more closely, the putative discrepancy may be moderated, Aristotle awarded his due, and the superiority of Kant acknowledged on a more fundamental level (chapter 2: "Aristotle Instead of Kant?"). The faculty of judgment, which is indispensable to a legal and state ethics, and is often only accredited to Aristotle, is not absent in Kant. He even extends it with a fundamentally new dimension. Whereas Aristotle only acknowledges a moral-practical faculty of judgment, Kant additionally introduces a genuinely moral faculty of judgment. Both the lasting significance of a moral-practical faculty of judgment and its expansion by a genuinely moral dimension are preliminary to Kant's novel interpretation of philosopher-kings (chapter 3: "Universalistic Ethics and the Faculty of Judgment"). Further, the problem of evil is to be regained as an issue that was recognized as deeply problematic by Kant and was already discussed in Aristotle as various stages of vice (*kakia*). Strangely, it is missing in contemporary Kantian ethics, such as in Apel and Habermas, whereas it plays a role for Kant both in his legal theory and in the theory of peace (chapter 4: "On Evil").

Part II demonstrates in an exemplary fashion why a fundamental moral philosophy should not neglect right and law, and conversely, why a fundamental legal theory should not neglect morals. Their interconnectedness should play a part in determining the relationship between law and morals (chapter 5: "Kant's More Nuanced Approach" and chapter 6: "The Moral Concept of Right and Law") and their principles, the "Categorical Imperatives of Right According to Ulpian" (chapter 7).

Part III shows that moral law culminates in a theory of public right, which leads to the theory of a peaceful global juridical order. It is precisely for this reason that peace becomes a foundational concept of philosophy in Kant (chapter 8) and that his philosophy of history is developed from a global perspective out of a legal ethics of peace (chapter 9). Two elements, however, demand further critical inquiry: "Are Republics Peaceable?" (chapter 10) and which option is more convincing in the face of the alternative "Federation of Peoples or World Republic" (chapter 11)? Finally, a novel political reading of the *Critique of Pure Reason* shows that the cosmopolitan concept of peace, relevant to Kant's entire philosophy, has implications even for what continues to be his most renowned work, the first *Critique*. Contrary to the popular contention that Kant's theoretical philosophy resembles a monologue, it in fact has both a republican and a world citizen character. In certain respects, this is already shown by Kant's innovative interpretation of the Platonic principle of the philosopher-king, namely, the idea of a kingly people (chapter 12).

Several chapters have been written expressly for this book. Others are taken from essays already published, but they have been changed to such an extent that they often do not resemble the original. I thank my students and colleagues, especially Dr. Alessandro Pinzani and Philipp Brüllmann, for their suggestions and help.

Tübingen, July 2000

KANT'S CHALLENGE
AND RELEVANCE TODAY

1.1. The More Fundamental Theory

Kant's relevance to the philosophy of right and law and to political philosophy was first shown not by the four innovations mentioned in the preface. It had already become evident in three dimensions of the fundamental character of his theory, although these in turn are partly responsible for the innovations. Compared with most alternatives, Kant's thought on right and law and on the state is more extensive and substantial in its inquiry, more finely nuanced in its conceptual relations, and at once more adroit and radical in its argumentation.

Among the reasons for this precedence is the "measured respiration" of Kant's development. Already as a young philosopher, he was concerned with questions of law and right; in the early 1740s, he attended lectures by Martin Knutzen (1713–51), a follower of Wolff. In the 1760s, he began to study works on juridical science and the philosophy of right and law. In the summer semester of 1767, he also began to lecture on "natural law." But Kant did not consider his philosophical reflections on right and law and on the state as sufficiently matured for publication until after he wrote the *Groundwork* as a prolegomenon to practical philosophy and the second *Critique*. Because he saw the foundation of his political philosophy in morals, he exposed the former to the public only after he gained reasonable clarification on the grounding of the latter.

(1) To begin with, his inquiry covers a great deal of ground. Critics still like to contend that Kant's moral philosophy amounts to a "single-principle-ethics" (*Ein-Satz-Ethik*; Marquard 1987, 111), that it is mere formalism (Scheler 2000), and that it falls victim to "the impotence of ought" (Hegel, *Werke* II 444, 460 f., 464; III 448; VII 252f.). If one takes

a look at Kant's systematic moral philosophy, *The Metaphysics of Morals*, these objections prove to be unfounded, rendering their broad influence inexplicable. Within the first part of the book, the *Doctrine of Right*, Kant begins by elucidating the foundational concepts of practical philosophy in general, namely, freedom and the faculty of choice, person, accountability, guilt, and crime ("Introduction to the Metaphysics of Morals"). He then presents the foundational concepts of the philosophy of right and law in particular: right and law, natural and positive law, the authorization to use coercion, private and public right, along with separate phenomena such as equity and the right of necessity ("Introduction to the Doctrine of Right"). But even this diverse array of issues is only preliminary to the larger project of developing a theory of fundamental legal institutions. These include a primitive right to which all human beings are entitled by virtue of their humanity, along with property and its various basic forms; further, the division of power, forms of government, penal law, and the right to resist, although Kant repudiates the latter.

Unlike other modern legal and political philosophers, Kant divides public right into its only three conceivable areas: state law, the right of nations, and cosmopolitan law. With respect to the right of nations, he concedes to both the right to peace and to war and distinguishes in the latter among the right to go to war, right during a war, and right after a war. The domain of public right also comprises specific questions concerning public duties (taxes, customs duties), the statute of limitations, amnesty, and the right to emigrate, along with authorship rights (copyright), state liability toward the poor and orphanages, and the relationship between church and state. Finally, we may discern a scathing criticism of colonialism in Kant's writings.

These observations provide a *first* reason for the challenge and relevance of Kant today. Both compared with prominent predecessors such as Hobbes, Locke, and Rousseau, and with many successors, including Hegel and particularly contemporary legal and political philosophers, the scope of Kant's thought is decidedly more substantial. The "application" of the categorical imperative to right and the state and to their specific tasks leads to a legal and state ethics that recognizes the authorization to use coercion as an integral element of right and law, develops the principle of human rights, and grounds the basic institutions such as property and criminal punishment. Above all, it overcomes the prevailing tendency to restrict legal and political philosophy to the "national" level, and responds to its concentration on single communities with a global and cosmopolitan perspective. Two further innovations lie within Kant's expanded horizon of inquiry: the expansion of a legal and state ethics by an ethics of peace and by the theory/practice debate surrounding his democratic revision of Plato's principle of the philosopher-king.

(2) The conceptual precision of Kant's arguments with respect to all of these issues is, for a thinker of his caliber, self-explanatory. An example may be singled out to begin with: Without harping on conflicting views, Kant demonstrates that the contract consists in a relationship between persons and not between persons and things. The nevertheless subsisting relationship with things is mediated by the personal relationship: "By a contract I therefore acquire another's promise (not what he promised), and yet something is added to my external belongings" (VI 274).

Our examination of these issues in exemplary fashion (chapter 5) will not address this particular example, since it has – unfortunately – migrated from philosophy to the merely juridical theory of right and law. We will address the relationship between morals and right or law, as it is still discussed by philosophers (albeit rarely with the same discrimination and keen awareness of the problem as in Kant). (a) From a legal standpoint, Kant distinguishes between law that has positive validity ("what is laid down as right?") and law that has moral validity ("what is right": natural law). (b) He acknowledges two groups of duties within morals: the legal duties that each owes to one another under authorized coercion, and those duties that go beyond what is owed and are not enforced, namely, the duties of virtue. The latter do not belong in the province of right and law or of the state. (c) At least two components belong to legal duties: the mere conformity with duty or *legality* and the recognition of duty for its own sake, acting from duty or *morality*. Armed with this twofold distinction, Kant is able to avoid two forms of moralizing: both a philanthropic concept of law that aims at enforcing duties of virtue, such as beneficence, and a disposition-based concept of law (*Gesinnungsrecht*) that is not satisfied with legality even with respect to genuine legal duties, but additionally demands inner recognition.

It is tempting to apply the distinction between legality and morality not merely to legal duties, but also to duties of virtue. The *Groundwork* confirms this conjecture, for it spells out in exemplary fashion the difference between "in conformity with duty" and "from duty" for those four types of duties (perfect and imperfect duties, both to oneself and to others) that cover the entire scope of moral duties. Whereas the *Groundwork* acknowledges that such uncontroversial duties of virtue as beneficence may be the product of incentives such as "the inclination to honor" (IV 398), the "Introduction to the Metaphysics of Morals" calls the lawgiving involved in duties of virtue ethical. In contrast to juridical lawgiving, ethical lawgiving makes "duty the incentive" (DR VI 219 l. 46). This leads to the following problem: If ethical lawgiving is to correspond to the duties of virtue, then duty will be made an incentive, thus leading to morality and, *ab ovo*, excluding legality. Only a thorough interpretation of the text can show whether Kant indeed infringes on his own criterion from the *Groundwork*, that of the "common idea of duty" (IV 389). For beneficence apparently does not always follow from duty; it can also result from inclination, as when there is an interest in honor.

(3) The radicalism of Kant's questions and the thoroughness of their elucidation have more bearing philosophically than the broad scope and conceptual precision of his theory. This provides a *second* reason for the provocation and relevance of Kant today. Under the influence of Critical Theory, the idea of "freedom from hegemony" or from "domination" ["*Herrschaft*"] held sway for a long period of time – admittedly in German more than in Anglophone debates. Since then, social philosophy has again opened up to legal and state theories and has already turned to normative speculation on justice and liberal democracy. However, the preliminary question of why people should at all be regulated by law, that is, subject to authorized enforcement, is still not fully acknowledged. Kant evidently provides a more thorough legitimation of the existence of the state and is therefore a more radical thinker (chapter 6). Many theories today limit themselves to a hermeneutics of Western democracy in a gesture of modesty. They thereby overlook the specific task of legitimation that has arisen in an age of globalization and of growing sense of identity among non-Western cultures: the justification of a form of social self-organization that is valid for all people of all cultures. The *third* reason for Kant's provocation and relevance today lies in the Kantian perception that neglecting this task of legitimation cannot be defended on philosophical or political grounds.

Kant often gives more radical answers to his more radical questions. Arthur Schopenhauer, otherwise an admirer of Kant, sees Kant's whole theory of law to be "a strange tangle of errors, one leading to the next," which he can explain only by "Kant's feebleness through old age" (*The World as Will and Representation*, book 4, sec. 62). He criticizes in particular Kant's general principle of external acquisition. In truth, however, Kant's *Doctrine of Right* is generally more finely grained in its concepts and more sensitive to the issues at hand than his earlier works, so that possible errors cannot be explained as the product of the author's enfeeblement due to old age. In other respects, precise reflection is conjoined with well-thought and convincing argumentation through extended passages of Kant's text. Paragraphs 15 (VI 265) and 17 (268f.), for example, contain a wholesale attack on the theories of property grounded in evolutionary formation and labor relations advocated by Locke and later reprised by Schopenhauer. Kant's more radical thought is demonstrated most clearly in his novel interpretation of the three (pseudo-)Ulpian legal rules [*Rechtsregeln*]: *honeste vive, neminem laede,* and *suum cuique tribue* (236f.). Kant's understanding is deeper than that of common interpretations and reveals an unusual, possibly contradictory duty. A *fourth* challenge of Kant's theory lies in the question of whether the justification of right and law presupposes a notion of duty that has systematically been driven out of philosophies of right and law and that seems to exceed the scope of the concepts of right and law: This is the notion of a duty to *oneself* that nevertheless signifies a legal duty (chapter 7).

1.2. Natural Law and Metaphysics

It is widely understood today that Kant advocates a cognitivist ethics of right and law and of peace that does not concern facts ("Is": "It is/is not the case, that p"), but rather obligations ("Ought": "It is right/wrong that one should do/refrain from a"). But even the latter do not comprise subjective attitudes or convictions to the extent that they imply contingent approval or disapproval, but rather demand rigorous objectivity. Within the large family of cognitivist (legal) ethics, Kant explicitly rejects the family of meta-ethical naturalists prominent today (e.g., Brink 1989 and Schaber 1997). He does not agree that the capacity for truth in moral assertions can be taken in an empirical or general descriptive sense. For Kant, moral principles cannot be traced back to assertions about the world alone, neither to those concerning the eternal world nor to those about the "inner world." The latter describe needs, interests, and their optimal fulfillment, happiness, along with their minimal fulfillment, self-preservation. Equally insufficient are assertions about the serviceability of the external world for the internal world or any combination of these three categories of descriptive assertions.

The plausibility of "antinaturalistic cognitivism" is immediately apparent if one considers the Is/Ought fallacy, a component of theories of argumentation according to which a moral Ought does not follow from a mere descriptive Is. Kant's antinaturalism, however, rests on two assumptions that, from a contemporary viewpoint, pay much too high a cost: It binds a legal ethics to metaphysical and natural law theories. This contemporary verdict is perhaps the unavoidable result of presupposed concepts that are overly narrow and demanding. Be that as it may, more emphatically modest concepts do not entail that Kant's metaphysical (concept of) natural law is "already a priori a failure," as will become clear in the following.

In the seventeenth and eighteenth centuries, natural law was viewed as the nonempirical counterpart to empirical political science. This leads us to refute a *first* skeptical worry that natural law is committed to religious or theological assumptions not shared by secular and pluralistic societies. In the Enlightenment, natural law was a discipline grounded exclusively on reason and independently of doctrinal elements. As a section of practical philosophy and a propaedeutic to positive juridical science, it belonged both to the faculty of jurisprudence and to that of philosophy. It was also advocated by members of both faculties, both by philosophically competent jurists, such as Hugo Grotius, Samuel Pufendorf, Christian Thomasius, Gottfried Achenwall, and Gottlieb Hufeland, and by philosophers versed in jurisprudence such as Thomas Hobbes, John Locke, and Jean-Jacques Rousseau. In Kant's time, a generation of "intellectual leaders" in natural law migrated from jurisprudence to philosophy. Kant's legal philosophy of natural law, as presented already in the "Idea" and the "Common Saying," is followed by the publication of Fichte's *Foundations of Natural Right* (1796), then by *Kant's Doctrine of Right* one year later, and at the start of the next century, by Hegel's work on *The Scientific Ways of Treating Natural Law* (1802). Hegel's subsequent work entitled *Elements of the Philosophy of Right* (1821) carries the subtitle "Or Natural Law and Political Science in Outline." Not long after Hegel, however, the "opinion leaders" of the philosophy of natural law and legitimacy theories of right and law came to their demise. Inspired by Kant's *Critique of Pure Reason*, and even before his publication of the *Doctrine of Right*, Gustav Hugo, in the *Lehrbuch des Naturrechts als einer Philosophie des positiven Rechts* (1789), advocates the view, still widely supported today, that natural law cannot be separated from positive law. One generation later, in the 1820s, the historical school of law, led by Friedrich Carl von Savigny, gained victory over the philosophical school of law. And around 1840, it became commonplace in Germany to speak of the "nullity of natural law." One aim pursued by the present study is to confront this commonplace still in force today with a theory that upholds natural law in the sense of rational law.

Prior to Kant, natural law was developed by philosophers and jurists in such a way that it was grounded in reason, but not exclusively in pure reason. Kant here forges ahead with a methodically decisive improvement indebted to the critical turn. Hence, we may refute the *second* critical worry that Kant's ethics of right and law and his ethics of peace belong to a pre-critical theory of natural law. This view is already weakened by the fact that Kant dealt with natural law at an early date but refrained from publications on this matter before he succeeded in providing a new, critical-transcendental foundation of philosophy. The systematic legal and peace ethics presented in the *Doctrine of Right* is, as a section of the *Metaphysics of Morals*, no longer a critique of practical reason, but it presupposes the insights achieved by the latter. With respect to content, Kant adopts two insights from his predecessors: "Hobbes' Ideal that it is necessary to leave the state of nature" (*Reflections* XIX 99; cf. DR p. 44) and to establish a legally and politically instituted state, and Rousseau's criterion necessary for reaching this state: the "ideal of state law" (XIX 99). With respect to the methodical determination of these and other elements of his theory, however, he proceeds on the level of his new critical foundation of morals and in this way overcomes the precritical, dogmatic notion of natural law.

The novel notion of critically examined natural law becomes manifest in two ways: First, it opposes the frequent conflation of heterogeneous Biblical and rational arguments or of empirical and historical arguments. Second, it instead follows the principle of the "Preface" to the *Groundwork*; it "[carefully separates] the empirical part . . . from the rational part" (IV 388) and reduces the ethics of right and law and the ethics of peace to their pure constituents. The leading concept of these ethics, namely, right as a "pure" concept, can be accommodated only by pure reason (VI 205). Now such a concept has a metaphysical character, thus providing the grounds for the *fifth* challenge: Kant questions a (common) dogma of contemporary philosophy and commits a foundational ethics of right and law to a certain degree of natural law and metaphysics.

The argument Kant presents for his case is not prima facie implausible. Moral obligations that are binding "for everyone" cannot be derived "from observing [man] himself and his animal nature" nor "from perceiving the ways of the world, what happens and how we behave" (VI 216). Since experience is disqualified as their ultimate source, this – *e contrario* – leaves only what transcends experience, namely, meta-physics. Moreover, Kant's natural law and metaphysics turn out to be agreeably modest.

First, Kant places a supreme normative-critical criterion on all pos-itive legislation. But contrary to an inflated rationalism that aims at deriving positive law from reason, he reduces the domain of philoso-phy to that small division of "first principles" mentioned in the title, the concepts of which must first be determined. At the same time, this defuses yet a *further worry*. As a science independent of experience, nat-ural law replaces not the legislator nor the judge nor the legal expert. However, all three *rely* on the justification of legal principles, for oth-erwise they could not demonstrate that the constitution and the legal system are reasonable and just.

As elements of pure practical reason, the principles do have meta-physical characteristics, yet they turn out to be modest to the extent that only their practical aspects are pertinent, not their theoretical aspects. Since the ultimate concern is the overcoming of natural drives and not the human drives themselves, namely, inclination or the desire for hap-piness, the theory does contain a supernatural or metaphysical element: an element of pure reason. This deflationary metaphysics nevertheless covers a great deal of ground. Kant does not rest content with the fundamental concept of right, but shows its indispensability for basic institutions such as those of external objects that are yours or mine. The fundamental institution of property can in fact be conceived as a legal claim only independently of physical possession. Stolen goods do not belong to their factual possessor, the thief, but rather to the per-son bearing a legal entitlement. Kant thus reasons that legal possession is not physical, but intellectual; it consists in a nonsensory, noumenal, that is, metaphysical relationship. The moral foundation of all legal contracts, namely, the obligation to keep one's promises, is similarly independent of "all sensory conditions of space and time" and is in this sense metaphysical. By the same token, the state can be justified only by an original contract, that is, a purely rational and, contrary to Locke and Hume, nonempirical element.

According to Kant, the basic institutions of property, state, and crim-inal penalty cannot be derived from the human experience of oneself or of the world. For experience is not only variable, but also highly disputable. If one attempts to derive moral principles from experience, one "run[s] the risk of the grossest and most pernicious errors" (VI 215). The blunder is thus twofold: at once theoretical ("grossest errors") and moral ("pernicious errors"). Whoever like Hume takes right and law to consist solely in rules of instrumentality and convention falls victim to the theoretical deficit of failing to perceive their claim to binding validity, and thus likewise stumbles into the moral problem of simply wishing away such binding validity.

However, Kant's metaphysical theory of natural law does not venture beyond the basic institutions of law and right. It does not, for example, specify an order of ownership, let alone a complete system of private right. On the contrary, the basic institutions and their principles are open to individual and cultural differences and for this very reason call upon the faculty of judgment; they give ample leeway to the legislator and to diverse cultures. The self-limitation of philosophy inherent in its focus on basic institutions and principles is appropriate not only philosophically, but also in the face of cultural diversity.

1.3. False Estimations

A circumspect assessment of Kantian ethics of right and law cannot overlook major false estimations. Three already merit our attention here.

(*1*) *The Right to Resist.* Although Kant's metaphysical elements carry conviction "in principle," isolated cases may invite suspicion. In particular, the "General Remark" of the *Doctrine of Right* and its elaboration on the right to resist (section A) raise doubts as to whether the boundary line is drawn correctly between the metaphysical (noumenal) and empirical (phenomenal) realms. Kant here is concerned no longer with the idea of reason itself, but rather with a person's empirical use of reason; he thus already broaches on the phenomenal sphere. In §51 of the *Doctrine of Right*, Kant himself distinguishes between "the idea of a head of state" and a "physical person," who "represent[s] the supreme authority in the state and make[s] this idea effective on the people's will" (VI 338). If this person distorts his or her assigned task and acts counter to the idea, instead of contributing to its realization, then this weakens the moral legitimacy of his or her action. It does not in any way mean that he or she has *carte blanche*, but rather amounts to a normative criterion that bears the power of legitimation. Moral invulnerability, the fulcrum on which Kant's refutation of the right to resist rests, is primarily granted only to the noumenal (metaphysical), not to the phenomenal (empirical) head of state. Therefore, the abuse of its power by a physical person is not unrestrictedly rightful to the extent that every resistance is *eo ipso* illegitimate.

One can also articulate this criterion as a question. How tyrannical may a despot be to still count as an authority that knows no resistance and obliges a people "to put up with even what is held to be an unbearable abuse of supreme authority" (VI 320)? Without doubt, Kant's counterarguments should be taken seriously. On the one hand, the person who claims the right to resist acts as a judge of him- or herself, thereby contravening a fundamental demand of public right, namely, the impartial arbitration of disputes. On the other hand, the concept of the sovereign power would involve a contradiction, for its dependence on the judgment of those concerned would run contrary to its sovereignty. Both arguments draw attention to grave difficulties that must be solved by a theory of the right to resist. However, they do not invalidate the claim that the empirical personification of the idea of reason does not have the same moral status as the moral idea itself.

According to Kant's own understanding of right and law, the status of an end-in-itself is not bestowed on the state or its ruler. Right and law merely serve toward the realization of private right concerning what is internally and externally mine or yours, which otherwise remains provisional and is not law in the full sense. As long as private demands still rely on individual interpretations and on private capacities to execute them, they lack reality. This can be remedied only by powers that are no longer private, but public. The sum total of these powers, the state, is nevertheless a secondary and subsidiary institution in comparison with private right, and it dissolves its own legitimacy by severely violating its tasks over a long period of time. The philosophical social contract still commits the state to the consent of those affected, albeit not to their factual consent but to the worthiness of consent. The state undoubtedly forfeits the worthiness of consent in the event of continued massive infringement of the law.

(2) Human Rights in the Plural. Kant began thinking about right and law during the period of the Prussian king Frederick II the Great (1740–1786). This prominent advocate of enlightened absolutism resumed what his predecessor, the soldier king Frederick William I (1713–1740), had initiated: the development of an authoritarian welfare state. Its objective was to maintain a strong army in accordance with a mercantile economic policy and to introduce a modern bureaucracy on the basis of both a rigid tax system and a highly commendable legal code at

the time. Owing to the drastic reformation of law and right, including the penitentiary system (torture, for example, was abolished in 1754) and law schools, Prussia was transformed into a constitutional state with a clear division of power and became one of the most modern polities of the epoch. Its progressive foreign policy was also notable: Prussia was the first European state to sign an agreement with the United States and thereby acknowledge its newly won independence. Long before, beginning with the great prince elector Frederick William, Prussia cultivated confessional tolerance and welcomed religious refugees such as the Huguenots from France (1685) and Lutherans from Bohemia and Moravia (starting already in 1623) and from Salzburg (1732). Jews also were not excluded from state tolerance. Following the *Universal Prussian Law of the Land* [*Das prussische allgemeine Landrecht*] (1794), thus markedly before the French civil code (*Code Napoléon*) of 1804, no person was to be perturbed, made accountable, held in derision or persecuted due to his or her religious beliefs (Theil II., Titel XI., §§1–6, here §4). The degree of religious freedom achieved by these legal proceedings was, however, again reduced by an edict of religion issued under Frederick William II.

Kant acknowledged the value of Prussia's relative progressiveness, particularly the tolerance under Frederick II (VI 329 and VIII 40). But he opposed both aristocratic privilege (VI 329 and 36f.) and the serfdom of farmers (283) and rejected state-decreed religious faith (368, cf. XXIII 133). On an international and general level, not merely restricted to his native country, Prussia, he attacked policies of war, armament, and conquest (VI 364ff.), colonialism (§§15 and 58) and slavery (283, cf. 348). And as a safeguard of inalienable human rights, he advocated the right of public criticism: The "freedom of the pen" ("Common Saying" VIII 304) should be an instrument for urging the leader toward reforms in the name of justice.

At least several of these aspects accord with our understanding of human rights today. In the *Doctrine of Right*, however, Kant mentions only one human right, characterized as the "only original right belonging to every man by virtue of his humanity." This is the right to "freedom (independence from being constrained by another's choice), insofar as it can coexist with the freedom of every other in accordance with a universal law" (VI 237). Kant thereby places a single criterion on all human rights, but does not further consider the possibility of human rights in the plural (discussion of this possibility emerges in the *Perpetual Peace*).

Kant was an enthusiastic supporter of the American independence movement and the French revolution. It is uncertain whether he was familiar with the first declaration of human rights, the *Virginia Bill of Rights* (1776), but one may assume that he was acquainted with the French declaration of human and civil rights. Despite this, he does not provide a catalogue of human rights, nor does he marshal arguments against their possibility or expediency. But he de facto acknowledges a certain plurality to the extent that he speaks of an innate right or of the foundation of its legitimacy for every man "by virtue of his humanity" (VI 237) in the "Introduction" to the *Doctrine of Right* and elsewhere. Analogous formulations also occur in "Private Right," where of the four passages, at least two make reference to human rights. In addition, relevant passages appear in "The Right of Nations" (see also section 6.5).

First, in paragraph 11, "the humanity in his own person" is invoked as an argument against the view that man is "his own possession." A subjective obligation toward others does belong to the concept of human rights, but here Kant is concerned only with the duty to oneself.

Second, according to paragraph 24, an "unnatural use" of sexual organs "does wrong to humanity in our own person" (VI 277). Here, too, subjective obligations toward others are not at issue, but only a duty to oneself.

Third, a subjective obligation first appears in the "natural permissive law." It follows from "the right of humanity in our own person" (276) and consists in the right to a household, along with marriage right, parental right, and the right of a head of the household. Marriage right in a subjective sense, that is, the demand that one be allowed to marry, is a specification of the single innate right to enter a specific type of situation. Kant thereby sets foot on more concrete terrain that opens the floodgates to a whole range of human rights and relativizes the singularity of innate right (237). Strictly speaking, Kant should have said that only the criterion is singular, whereas a plurality of rights fulfill this criterion. However, our emendation has the unfortunate consequence that human rights would require treatment not only in the prolegomena, the "Introduction" to the *Doctrine of Right*, but also in the *Doctrine of Right* itself, in part under the heading of private right and in part under that of public right.

Fourth, even the right of children "to the care of their parents until they are able to look after themselves" – which by no means has become obsolete today – is for Kant "an original innate (not acquired) right"

(280). It thus belongs in a catalogue of human rights and reinforces the possibility of human rights in the plural.

Finally, a further human right emerges in the sphere of the right of nations. Kant asserts that "human beings, especially as members of a state . . . must always be regarded as co-legislating members of a state," and he elucidates this demand by means of the end-in-itself formulation of the categorical imperative: "not merely as means, but also as ends in themselves" (VI 345). The right to participation in legislation thus has a moral standing and hence a human rights character. But this character is qualified by Kant's distinction between the active and passive citizen (VI 314). Two years later, in *Common Saying*, Kant maintains that even participants of the community who lack independence are not citizens, but merely "co-beneficiaries of this protection" (VIII 294).

(3) The Right to Life and Limb. The *Doctrine of Right* strangely does not immediately discuss the right to life and limb, despite its fundamental character. In his treatment of penal law, Kant maintains that murder is a capital crime that can be atoned for only by the death penalty (VI 333), thereby tacitly consenting to life as a legally protected cardinal right, perhaps even as a human right. Even more odd, his system of right and law does not accommodate concern for life. This cannot be due to the apparent fact that the right to life is self-evident. Perhaps it is missing because it is cumbersome to subsume it under one of the headings considered: It cannot be categorized under what is internally mine or yours, nor is it a standard external mine or yours. Kant does not consider the fact that questionably free beings are unquestionably living, corporeal beings and, consequently, that external rights are real only if the beings retain their life.

1.4. The Cosmopolitan *Leitmotif*

The modern age does not suffer a lack of theories of right and law or of the state, yet it harbors a surprising deficit. From Hobbes, Locke, and Rousseau to Hegel, and to some degree also to Marx, and in the twentieth century from Kelsen and Hart to John Rawls, up through Dworkin and Habermas, the prominent texts deal almost exclusively with the juridical order of a single state. A *sixth* reason for the relevance of Kant today and for the challenge of his thinking lies in the fact that he makes room for an international and even global perspective. Two of three sections of "Public Right" in *The Metaphysics of Morals* are dedicated to the right of nations and cosmopolitan law. Together they manifest Kant's world citizen or cosmopolitan perspective.

The ideal of world citizenry or of cosmopolitanism has a long tradition in the Occident, but for the large part without political ramifications. More than one generation before Plato, Democritus had already anticipated globalization, understood as the consciousness of a common world: "The entire world is open to the wise man; the universe is the home of the good soul" (Diels and Kranz, *Die Fragmente der Vorsokratiker*, 59B8). Cosmopolitanism itself first appears later, although it does not appear in the works of the two eminent political philosophers of antiquity, Plato and Aristotle, despite Cicero's disclaimer that the expression *kosmou politês*, world citizen, can be traced back to Socrates (*Tusculanae disputations* V 8). There is unambiguous evidence that the term was used by Socrates' follower, the cynic Diogenes of Sinope (Diogenes Laertius, *Lives and Opinions of Eminent Philosophers*, VI 63). When he who is banned from his homeland refers to himself as a world citizen, his world citizenship takes the place of his "national" citizenship; Diogenes' notion of cosmopolitanism is thus exclusive, not complementary. In addition to this, he places emphasis on the cosmos, not the polis, since there is no mention in his oeuvre of global institutions or of a common human legal consciousness. The contrary is true of Zeno of Citium, the founder of Stoicism. According to his teaching, all people are fellow citizens; together, they constitute a herd that does not merely convene in self-nourishment, but also shares common rights and laws (*Stoicorum veterum fragmenta*, ed. H. v. Arnim, I 54, 60f., 133, and 262).

With the second founder of Stoicism, Chrysippus, this political cosmopolitanism again degenerated to an essentially apolitical form. The cosmos may be the common polis of all people, but it is not the sum total of a community regulated by law. It is rather a living space without a specific political contour. Even Cicero, who revitalized theories of right and law and of the state, endorses not political cosmopolitanism, but rather a somewhat indiscriminate version of epistemic cosmopolitanism – he speaks of a common epistemic world of reason, along with a moral cosmopolitanism, since he is concerned with a shared world of morals. Only in Marcus Aurelius do we encounter again a political world order that is a multilayered state and thus genuinely signals complementary cosmopolitanism. Due to the commonality of reason (*nous*) among all people, and thus to an epistemic cosmopolitanism, Marcus Aurelius espouses the ideal of a unity of mankind that transcends the borders of all states and peoples. In the global polis, the philosopher on the king's throne allows for the existence of the common poleis "as though they were separate houses" (*Meditations* 3, II, 2).

This is not the place to discuss in more detail a conceptual history of cosmopolitanism (for a short outline, see Busch and Horstmann 1976 and Höffe 2002a, chap. 8). However, the few clues provided allow us to present a profile of Kantian cosmopolitanism under three headings. First, a subsidiary motive becomes a main theme in Kant's philosophy. Second, Kant develops it in a thorough and finely nuanced manner. Third, his intention is that of expanding the theme, or even universalizing it, since he applies the concept of world citizen to his entire philosophy. Even the *Critique of Pure Reason* contains a cosmopolitan perspective, along with Kant's pedagogy ("the basis of a scheme of education must be cosmopolitan," IX 448) and his moral philosophy, since its rigorous universalistic approach can be interpreted as cosmopolitanism (cf. section 2.2). Further, the kingdom of ends corroborates moral cosmopolitanism (rightly, according to Herman 1997) – but it should be stressed that the latter is, as such, apolitical, for it contains no elements of right and law or of the state. Far more political is the cosmopolitanism of *criticism* (section 12). Political cosmopolitanism in a more narrow and strict sense first appears in legal and peace ethics, including its historical part (section 8–11).

The arguments Kant puts forward for cosmopolitanism go beyond the merely external fact that intergovernmental and supranational legal tasks exist. The leading task of right and law, the replacement of private arbitration through laws that adhere to moral principles, can be completely fulfilled only when private force yields to public right both within states and among them, and finally among the private spheres (individuals, companies, etc.) of diverse states. This enables us to specify the sixth reason for Kant's relevance today: At least five component arguments speak for his theory of a world juridical order. Regarding the first argument, it should be recalled that extensive ("global") and lasting ("eternal") peace is among the oldest visions of humanity and yet does not become a foundational concept of philosophy until Kant. Kant's predecessors even frequently praised war. Second, Kant links unqualified or eternal peace to the principle of modern politics, namely, a democracy committed to human rights and to the division of power, at his time referred to as a republic. Kant, in confrontation with Plato, integrates the republic in his portrait of a "kingly people." However, whether republics or kingly people are as peaceable as Kant and his followers in contemporary political science assume has yet to be tested.

The idea that the world juridical order is subjected to the ideal of a single state or republic and that it is to be established as a world republic with a homogenous state invites weighty objections. The fact that Kant confronts them and thereby anticipates contemporary debates to a large extent is a third component argument for his relevance today. But it is hard to see how Kant's suggestions are compatible with the foundational tenets of his own state theory. By Kant's own lights, the universally accepted element of peremptory law, namely, the public and sovereign power, is not supposed to be necessary on a global level. Both in the "Idea" and in the *Perpetual Peace*, Kant rests content with an institution that is even less than a minimal world state: the idea of a federation of peoples. He conceives this federation as an association that does not need any sovereign powers and "can be broken up at any time," thus thwarting the purpose of that global rule of law, in which, as maintained in the *Doctrine of Right*, nations "decid[e] their disputes in a civil way, as if by a lawsuit, rather than in a barbarous way (the way of savages), namely by war" (§61: VI 351). However, the consideration that "reason, from the throne of the highest morally legislative power, delivers an absolute condemnation of war as a procedure for determining rights" (VIII 356) has become anything but obsolete in an age of globalization. With respect to the particular means that serve to achieve the envisioned end, one can still make use of Kant in order to go beyond Kant. One cannot expect philosophy to provide a detailed account of a world legal order, nor of a constitution, nor even of the codes of law for a single state or for a global order.

Models of a global order in political science tend to assert that the role of the states in the world has been diminishing. To put it in slightly drastic terms, a social world has been taking over the former world of the state. This implies an oversimplification that is avoided by Kant's twofold division of international law into the right of nations and cosmopolitan law. Already a fourth contributing argument for the current relevance of Kant's world juridical order becomes apparent: The mutual exclusivity of the world of the state and that of society is overcome by integrating both state and society into an inclusive whole. Kant's right of nations stands for a world of states that is legally instituted, whereas cosmopolitan law represents, among other things, a world of societies that is likewise instituted by law.

A fifth component argument for the relevance of Kant's ethics of both global right and law and of world peace assumes that many Europeans during the Enlightenment understood themselves to be members of "civilized races" that look down with contempt on the indigenous people of America, the "savages," because they "struggle unceasingly" (VIII 354, l. 17). Kant opposes both positive self-complacency and negative judgment of the foreign (cf. section 11.4). Because he rejects all arrogant European-centered perspectives on the basis of impartiality, he proves to be a committed world citizen. This is shown not only by his overall motivation, but also in relatively concrete judgments. Moreover, among the greatest philosophers, Kant still remains the only cosmopolitan not only in a political, but also in a philosophical sense.

PART I

MORALS

Kant did not develop his philosophy of right and law and of peace haphazardly. It forms an integral component of his entire thought and, as an ethics of law and peace, is founded on his general ethics. The persuasiveness of the latter is patently undermined in recent attempts to reintroduce Aristotelian perspectives into ethics. These attempts are carried out on a broad front and urge the question of whether Kant's ethics can hold its ground in the face of Aristotle's ethics, its most prominent philosophical rival. The question itself, however, presupposes that Kant and Aristotle in most respects constitute an either/or alternative that demands opting for one over the other. In fact they share a diverse array of commonalities. And despite remaining differences, Kant's view on morals can be shown to be more fundamental (section 2).

Even those who generally do not give preference to Aristotle's ethics, who on the contrary consider Kant's concept of the will and principle of freedom to be superior to the Aristotelian concept of striving and principle of happiness, nevertheless tend to favor Aristotle with respect to a particular task. This task is by no means peripheral to a legal ethics and ethics of peace. It concerns the mediation of the general with the specific through the faculty of judgment. An unbiased view of Kant's ethics, however, once again reveals both similarities with Aristotle and a radicalization of the task allotted to the faculty of judgment. This leads to the novel faculty of pure practical judgment (section 3).

Strangely, even Kantians in contemporary ethics are silent about evil, a concept that Kant himself considered indispensable to ethics. It is neglected even in significant reinterpretations of Kant. This has a counterpart in neo-Aristotelian theories, for these divert their attention away from the concept of *kakia*, vice or viciousness. Since evil also plays a role in Kant's ethics of peace, one should ask whether this concept should be regained for both general ethics and a legal and peace ethics (chapter 4).

2

ARISTOTLE INSTEAD OF KANT?

More recent moral theories tend to engage in foundational debates following the guidelines of two major figures, Aristotle and Kant, and to place these under Muirhead's (1932) alternative headings of teleological and deontological ethics. Whereas some consider Aristotle's teleological or, more specifically, eudaemonistic ethics as fundamentally discredited or as a *via antiqua* that is simply outdated as a result of Kant's *via moderna*, an ethics of autonomy, others view Aristotle's ethics as the only viable alternative up to the present day. Neo-Aristotelian ethical theories naturally do not share a common core, but do display family similarities.

To the extent that the communitarians appeal to Aristotle, they are partially interested in a criticism of modernity or are distrustful of the Enlightenment and of liberalism (especially MacIntyre 1985/1987; 1988; and in less extreme form Walzer 1983). Skeptical toward the possibility of a universal moral justification independent of history and culture, they plead for the naturally evolved life forms of a community and thus consider Aristotle to be their progenitor, for he attaches importance to education and friendship between citizens, speaks of common goods of the polis, and sees virtues as an expression of what is handed down by tradition. Against the Frankfurt School, which consigns tradition to oblivion, Odo Marquard (1986, 122ff.) also presents an apology for traditions or conventions that stand the test of time, but his arguments differ and are mostly influenced by Hegel's thoughts on substantial morality [*Sittlichkeit*]. In essence, they accord with Wolfgang Kluxen's plea for an "ethics of the ethos" (1974). A third form of neo-Aristotelianism, virtue ethics (e.g., Trianosky 1990; Beiner 1992), emphasizes the importance of a stable character (see Chapman and Galston 1992; Höffe and Rapp 1999). Finally, some thinkers champion a theory of the good life or of the art of living in countering Kant's ethics of duty (see Crisp and Slote 1997; Wolf 1999; and Rippe and Schaber 1999).

One who reads Aristotle himself will have difficulties with many of these motives. Aristotle was not a communitarian, nor a proponent of ethos-ethics, nor an anti-Kantian *avant la lettre*. He acknowledges as self-evident those substantial distinguishing features of the Enlightenment such as the renunciation of the theological justification of morals. Furthermore, he qualifies the traditions of his own society; he never defends conventions that have not been measured against general obligations. One may also encounter deontological elements in his theory. Conversely, the good life is not foreign to Kant and reliable attitudes or virtues play a vital part in his theory. He even does not exclude reflection on consequences, a teleological element.

The popular antithesis – either Kant or Aristotle – thus should be dismissed. (For first attempts, see Engstrom and Whiting 1996; Sherman 1997; and, in a different fashion, O'Neill 1996.) To the extent that Kant adopts substantial insights from Aristotle, he is himself Aristotelian (section 2.1). Even in virtue ethics, Aristotle and Kant share a great deal of common ground (section 2.3). With regard to decisive differences, however, Aristotle can still be seen not as a viable rival to Kant, but rather as a thinker who is qualified by Kant's more radical reflections (sections 2.4 and 2.5).

2.1. Kant as a Follower of Aristotle

To begin with, Kant proves to be a follower of Aristotle through a series of commonalities. This is first shown by the fact that he tacitly consents to Aristotle's idea of practical philosophy (see Höffe 1996b, Teil I).

According to an image that is intimated in Aeschylus (*Agamemnon* V 628), later reprised by Plato in the central passage of the analogy of the cave (*Republic* VII 519 c), and colorfully illustrated by Aristotle, man is like an archer who hits his target with the aid of ethics (EN I 1, 1094a22–24). Turning from the image to the concept as the proper medium of philosophy, the catchword reads as follows: "*to telos estin ou gnosis alla praxis*" (1095a5f.), or to provide a short translation: the end is not theoretical knowledge (not even that of practical philosophy) but practical action. Kant, too, does not take moral theory to be an end in itself in the *Groundwork* and the *Critique of Practical Reason*, nor in the *Metaphysics of Morals*, and even less in the treatises "Common Saying,"

Toward Perpetual Peace, and *The Conflict of the Faculties*. His moral theory does not, that is, search only for "the purely theoretical clarification of the conditions for the possibility of morality" (Bien 1981, 70).

Kant explicitly asserts in the "Preface" to the *Groundwork* that he wants to establish "a pure philosophy of morals" because "morals themselves remain subject to all sorts of corruption" (IV 390). In criticizing the conflation of genuine moral principles with empirical elements, Kant intends to ensure both "certitude" and "purity" (DV 509/VI 376). On the one hand, his aim is to achieve more than merely "very contingent" conformity with duty and, on the other hand, to reveal "the moral law in its purity and genuineness" (IV 390); a pure philosophy of morals thus serves the purposes of legality and morality, respectively. In both respects, a "completely isolated metaphysics of morals" is valid not only as "an indispensable substratum of all theoretical... cognition," but also as "a desideratum of utmost importance to the actual fulfillment of their precepts" (IV 410).

The moral-practical character of Kant's theory is clearly unearthed in the categorical imperative. For this is not a morally neutral measure of morals or a "moralometer" that leaves the agent free to decide whether to conform to morals. On the contrary, the categorical imperative commands commensurate action. Even the notion of a "fact of reason" reveals Kant's moral-practical interest. Because we would conceivably refuse to "give false testimony against an honorable man," even "on pain of... immediate execution" (CPrR §6 Remark: V 30), we declare that the "love of life" is surmountable and deny that pure practical reason or morality is an unrealizable "ought."

Kant's moral-practical interest is also demonstrated by his belief that the philosophy of right and law is the highest form of science in this domain, but that it is prey to shortcomings in legal expertise or prudence (see section 6.2). Finally, his moral-practical concern is revealed in the "Casuistical Questions" of the *Doctrine of Virtue*, as in the treatise on peace, which begins with a discussion of the moral principles of a peaceful order and closes with the proof of how politics can come to adopt these principles.

Second, like Aristotle, Kant discusses practical philosophy within two disciplines, which despite shared foundational concepts remain relatively independent of one another. In Aristotle, these disciplines are ethics and politics; in Kant, the *Doctrine of Virtue* and the *Doctrine of Right*. In their execution, Kant *thirdly* makes use of Aristotle's epistemological notion of draft-sketch or outline (*typô*) knowledge (see Höffe 1996b, part II). Accordingly, he presents only normative principles, but leaves open how they are to be concretely fulfilled.

Furthermore, the refutation of a theonomic morality posited by God, as enunciated by some theologians, stems not from Kant, but is already taken for granted in Aristotle; the latter does not even take it into consideration. *Lastly*, both philosophers oppose restricting morals to relations between coexisting agents. Kant is familiar with duties to oneself, and Aristotle discusses self-referential virtues such as temperance.

2.2. Aristotle's Ethics Is Universalistic

With regard to the question of whether Aristotle's ethics is an ancestor of universalism, it is important to distinguish between universalism in moral theory and moral universalism. According to Kant, ethics must be cleansed of everything anthropological for the sake of the purity of morals ("Preface" to the *Groundwork*). Kant here supports "transhuman universalism" for reasons pertaining to moral theory. Just as some basic statements in contemporary ontology are true "in all possible worlds," the validity of morals transcends the bounds of our human species and pertains to all rational beings, in all rational worlds. Kant's universalism, a genuine cosmopolitanism not of a political but of a moral kind, is supported by significant arguments. Kant rightly asserts in the preface to the *Groundwork*: "[T]he command 'thou shalt not lie' does not hold only for human beings, as if other rational beings did not have to heed it." The prohibition against lying, namely, is justified not by human particularities but by the very "concept of the action in itself" (IV 402). The justification may proceed as follows: Speaking to someone does not merely involve an assertion, but also involves the claim that one's assertion expresses one's own conviction. Whereas propositional truth is at stake in the mere assertion "that p," it is one's claim about one's assertion that is relevant to the prohibition against lying. The latter claim is a matter of pragmatic truth, for it is a claim to uprightness: "I claim that I am personally convinced that p." One who lies declares something to be his conviction of which he is not convinced. It is possible in singular cases to contradict oneself through this additional claim – otherwise the prohibition against lying would be superfluous. However, the additional claim would be annihilated in a world constructed in such a way that it is invariably false. If one's declaration of a conviction constantly contravenes one's own conviction, the conviction ceases to be a declaration at all. Thus, no claim to pragmatic truth or truthfulness is made, and a world in which one is invariantly dishonest cannot even be conceived.

Although the more precise vindication of the prohibition against lying remains controversial (for a suggested reconstruction, see Höffe 1999b, 206–233), there is consent over one point. If the justification is to be persuasive, it must appeal to the concept of lying and not to particularities of our living space or of species-related features of our biological kind. Our specific linguistic capacity may be an exception, but it is conceivable for this capacity to be found in other species. If other living beings do exist that are gifted with language, they are subject to the same duty, the prohibition against lying, notwithstanding their divergent biological makeup and different natural surroundings.

Aristotle likewise claims transhuman validity, despite his appeal to an *ergon (tou) anthrôpou*, the characteristic activity of the human being (EN I 6, 1097b24ff.). This activity consists in an element indispensable to moral adeptness: an activity of the soul in accordance with *logos*, reason and language. Transhuman validity also pertains to Aristotle's formal determination of happiness as an absolutely supreme goal and to the normative concept of virtue, if it carries any conviction at all, as a mean between excess and deficiency. The conditions governing the application of single virtues, such as danger as a condition for courage, exist not only for humans, but also for beings of *logos* on other planets.

Since it is implausible that humans commune with rational beings or with pure spirits ("angels"), today's ethics takes only the human being into consideration as "a being that has reason and a will" (GMM IV 295). As a consequence, it is restricted to a "species-specific universalism," according to which morals, unbound by culture, tradition, or community, do not stop at the limits of political, religious, or linguistic communities. A stubborn prejudice prohibits the coherence of this universalism with a clear commitment to a specific community or with the intermixing of culture-specific elements in morals. Kant, as a model for ethical universalism, supports an international juridical community without calling for the dissolution of single states (see chapters 10 and 11; for a substantial discussion, see Höffe 2002a). And universalism is incompatible with culture-specific elements only if it extends to relatively concrete rules. Kant, however, rejects this extreme universalism and advocates a more moderate form of principle universalism, which, because it allows for heterogeneous applications, is open to various traditions and contexts.

Both an analogous principle universalism and an openness to diverse traditions and contexts can be found in Aristotle. Moreover, universal validity is a feature of the leading principle of eudaemonism and of its formal determinations as a perfect and autarkic end. If at all applicable, the claim that all human action is goal-directed pursuit applies to every human being of all cultures and epochs. This pursuit does not appear "fruitless and vain" so long as there is an end "that we want for its own sake, and everything else we want is for the sake of this end" (EN I 1, 1094a18f.). This end is happiness.

The material determination of happiness is equally universal. One might expect Aristotle to present a normative, substantial conception of human nature, an "anthropological" or "humanistic essentialism," which pluralistic societies today can no longer accommodate. However, Aristotle's definition is clearly more modest. Even if the activity of the soul in accordance with reason (*kata logon*) or not without reason (EN I 6) is understood not as "transhuman," but only as "species-specific universalism," it is smoothly compatible with the pluralism of modernity. The fact that Aristotle does not consider all humans to be equal, but excludes women, slaves, and barbarians, may speak against this universalistic reading. This exclusion, however, concerns not the fundamental elements of his ethics, but "only" their application on the basis of additional empirical assumptions. *If* Aristotle's assumption is correct that slaves exhibit fundamental deficiencies of reason, then their economic subordination, as endorsed in the *Politics* (Book I), is not absolutely fallacious. One may still object, however, that the deficiencies are not as frequent and fundamental as he purports them to be and, more important, that an economical subordination does not entail legal subordination. Here, Aristotle erroneously draws nonuniversalizable conclusions from his own universalistic approach.

The concept of a life-form plays a prominent role in the antiuniversalistic ethics of communitarianism (MacIntyre 1984, 91; Taylor 1989, 29; Walzer 1983, 65). It understands a life-form to be culture-specific and community-bound; for example, an ancient life-form may be distinguished from a modern life-form, to which the North American form may be said to belong. Aristotle's corresponding concept *bios*, on the contrary, is related to fundamental given realities of humanity in general. The corresponding life-forms (EN I 2) may thus be found not only in the Athens of classical antiquity, but also in the myriad societies of the most diverse epochs. Aristotle's arguments against two life-forms, against the life of enjoyment (*bios apolaustikos*) and the life of making money (*bios chrêmatistês*), likewise maintain their validity across cultures. This also holds for his criticism of a third life-form, the political life, if it is defined merely in terms of honor (*timê*) and not of virtue (*arête*). Aristotle further presents nonparticularist arguments for the remaining life-forms that are conducive to happiness, namely, the political life that observes virtue (the moral-political life), and the life of contemplation.

2.3. An Outline for an Aristotelian-Kantian Virtue Ethics

The concept of virtue does not bear directly on Kant's ethics of law and peace. However, the concept rounds off the comparison between Aristotle and Kant and, more important, is preparatory for determining the elements that actually divide Aristotle's and Kant's universalism.

Aristotle defines the crucial notion of ethical virtue or virtue of character (*aretê ethikê*) as usual through genus and species difference. (On the complementary dianoetic or intellectual virtue of prudence, see chapter 3.) According to its genus, the virtue of character is a disposition (*hexis*) and according to its species a mean for us (*meson pros hêmas*). Whoever has the disposition acts, as he or she acts, not by accident or from an auspicious temperament, but rather from a firm component of his or her personality and thus in a reliable manner. Although there is a natural predisposition or proclivity to this disposition (EN VI 13, 1144b1f.), the virtue itself is acquired through nontheoretical learning. In avoidance of misunderstanding over this point, Aristotle does not grow weary of emphasizing that one becomes virtuous not through philosophy, but through practical activity: One becomes just through just action, temperate through temperate action, and so on (EN II 4, 1105b9, etc.).

In agreement with his general line of thought, Kant acknowledges the importance of a reliable attitude (for a provisional comparison of Aristotle and Kant with regard to virtue, see Sherman 1997). Like Aristotle, he defines virtue as "a considered and firm resolution" (DV VI 409). He polemicizes only against a view that does not stem from Aristotle. Virtue, he argues, cannot be seen as mere aptitude or habit, for then it would have something mechanical about it (*Anthropology* VII 147) and would at best elicit actions conforming to duty, but not action from duty (*Religion* VI 14). Kant does qualify this slightly, for human nature, which is affected by inclinations, cannot ever "settle down in peace and quiet" with virtue (VI 409). However, this qualification concerns only the possibility of fully realizing virtue. Kant does not call the importance of virtue into question, nor does he doubt the priority of evaluating the person over the action with respect to morality. The issue of whether an action follows from duty is resolved by maxims that are manifested in the character of a person or, in the case of moral maxims, in virtue, defined as the "moral strength of one's maxims" (DV §22). The duty toward one's own perfection even demands that one cultivate one's will "up to the purest virtuous disposition" (VI 387). Due to the frailty of human nature, however, duty is only "wide and imperfect in terms of its degree"; one's duty is only "to *strive* for . . . perfection, but not to *reach* it" (DV §22). The consolidation of virtue in a reliable disposition [*Haltung*] to the extent that one cannot succumb to any conflicting inclinations is possible only for a holy being, in not only a practical but "ontological" sense, that is, a pure being of reason, which man, as a sensible being, cannot ever become. Thus, virtue is a "moral disposition *in conflict*, and not *holiness* in the supposed possession of a complete *purity* of dispositions of the will" (CPrR V 84).

Kant distinguishes between two concepts in the *Religion* in order to trace a profile of his position. Whereas virtue in its empirical character or phenomenal virtue ("*virtus phaenomenon*") is "acquired little by little . . . through gradual reformation of conduct" (*Religion* VI 47), virtue in its intelligible character or intelligible virtue ("*virtus noumenon*") can be had only by one who "recognize[s] a duty" and is "in need of no other incentive . . . except the representation of duty itself." This kind of virtue – Kant rightly maintains – cannot be acquired piecemeal. It is affected by a "revolution in the disposition of the human being," a single "decision," which gives rise to a new human being, namely, one who distances himself from all inclinations (VI 48; this idea, incidentally, is reminiscent of Plato's analogy of the cave, according to which one acquires insight into the ideas and into the idea of the good only after a "turning of the soul" (*Republic*, VII 515c)). And only this "revolutionary" man is " 'free,' 'healthy,' 'rich,' 'a king,' and so forth" (DV VI 405; see section 8.2).

Kant may have captured moral reality more accurately than Aristotle. Socrates was a living example of someone who remains true to his convictions in the face of an unjust death penalty – as Kant agrees in his elucidation of the "fact of reason" (CPrR §7, Remark following Corollary: V 32). Because this remains a rare and exceptional case, however, Kant's dictum that even the virtuous person is endangered by his propensity to evil is not vulnerable to criticism (see chapter 4). This propensity is overcome only in intelligible virtue, which cannot ever be ascertained of a phenomenal human being.

Kant rejects the second component of Aristotle's definition of character virtue, the concept of the mean for us. However, he here falls victim to mistaking this for a "middle way" or a sort of compromise "between opposing vices" (DV, "Introduction," section XIII). In truth, virtue and vice for Aristotle do not merely differ in degree. This is because for Aristotle and classical antiquity in general, the mean does not merely have a mathematical significance, but also refers to perfection. The two superlative expressions that Aristotle uses to determine virtues – the quality of acting in the best way (EN 3, 1104b28) and excellence (EN II 6, 1107a7) – clearly show that what matters to him is a difference not of degree but of kind, a mean in the sense of a supreme form of human existence. Aristotle is concerned with humanity in an emphatic sense, the perfection of human being. He thus consistently qualifies both the good and the bad not by comparative expressions but by a grammatical positive, which here amounts to a superlative expression: Lying is strictly and unqualifiedly mean and culpable [*aischros*], while truth is morally good (*kalon*: fine) and worthy of praise. These qualities belong to falsehood and truthfulness "in themselves" (*kath' hauto*: EN 1127a 28ff.).

With the exception of justice, this supreme form cannot be objectively determined. It depends on individual particularities, along with the respective situation in which the individual is involved. Aristotle determines it as the *meson pros hêmas*, the mean for us, which differs from the objective *meson pragmatos*. His argument is also tenable; a wealthy person who wants to be generous must sacrifice far more than a pauper. Aristotle does not confound "morals and worldly wisdom," as his Kantian translator Daniel Jenisch maintains (1791, 195, Remark). He rather considers both equally important, but deserving of methodical differentiation.

It is well known that moral virtues can be instrumentalized. Because honesty, for example, yields credit (Weber 1904–1905), it is not always sought for its own sake. For the complete realization of morals, precisely that intensification is needed that Kant himself introduces using the example of honesty (GMM, Section I), namely, the transition from external conformity with duty to inner consent, morality. Kantians who labor under the delusion of the alternative "Aristotle or Kant" tend to acknowledge this intensification only in Kant. Fixated on the alternative "duty or virtue ethics," their opponents, the exponents of virtue ethics, pride themselves on seeing the primary reference for moral evaluation in the agent, in his character. In truth, attitude or character is also of great importance to Kant's morality. Conversely, the transition from the weaker condition of legality to the stronger condition of morality can already be found in Aristotle, who demands that the virtue of character be sought for its own sake, not as a means to striving for an end external to ethics. Like Kant, he thereby acknowledges the "purity and rigor" of virtue. This is already suggested by the aforementioned superlative expressions; and it is revealed most clearly at the beginning of the treatise on justice, where Aristotle ascribes three functions to justice. By means of three clear stages of transition, he declares that justice is a disposition that makes people (a) capable of just things, (b) act justly, and (c) wish for what is just (EN, 1129a8f., V 10–13).

For Aristotle, then, more belongs to justice than mere conformity to what is just. Free consent is needed over and beyond mere "legality" to transform acting rightly into a disposition to right or morality. Analogously, with respect to injustice, one acts unjustly more than in a merely incidental way when one acts on the basis of having a certain character (EN V 11, 1137a22f.). Further, it does not suffice that one acts correctly with regularity; one must also do so out of free consent (EN II 2, 1104b3ff.). Only then does one act not merely knowingly, but also on the grounds of a decision and hence for the sake of the end itself. One is then reliable in one's action and does not waver (II 3, 1105a28–33; cf. VI 13, 1144a16ff.). If it is characteristic of the courageous to act courageously for the sole reason that this is morally good and its contrary morally reprehensible (III 12, 1117a17), then he or she does what is morally good not to obtain an external end but for its own sake; he or she thus defines him- or herself through Kantian morality. (*To kalon*, literally translated as "the beautiful," thus corresponds to the morally good to the extent that it refers to what attracts without any concern for what is useful; *kalon* is the good-in-itself.)

Because the virtuous person performs the good action for its own sake, there is an element of pleasure in his motivation. This element does not provoke a word of protest from Kant as Korsgaard assumes (1996a, 245f.). For example, Aristotle's statement that among all activities in conformity with virtue, an activity in accordance with wisdom is the most pleasant (EN X 7, 1177a23f.) is not subject to Kant's criticism of pleasure as a determining ground. Kant, to be sure, levels his criticism not merely against the pleasure of the senses, but also against that of the understanding (cf. CPrR §3 Remark I: V 22f.). But the pleasure that Aristotle enunciates is not the determining ground of activity in accordance with wisdom or *theôria*, although it is a determining ground for activity in the life of enjoyment. According to the second treatise on pleasure (EN X 1–5), this pleasure is rather an element that perfects an activity (X 4, 1174b23; on Aristotle's doctrine of pleasure, see Bostock 1988 and Ricken 1995). The pleasure here indicates inner consent – or execution of the respective action for its own sake – and does not go missing in Kant. Contrary to early criticism of Kant's alleged rigorism (e.g., already F. Schiller, *On Gracefulness and Dignity*, 1793, 283f.), a truly virtuous disposition is expressed in a joyous frame of mind, "without which one is never certain of having gained also a love for the good, i.e. of having incorporated the good into one's maxim" (*Religion* IV 24).

Kant's concept of morality achieves final completion in Aristotle's *spoudaios* or excellent character. The latter, namely, does not just have both the virtue of character and the prudence that goes along with it. The excellent character does what is good only because it is good. The transition from legality to morality is also suggested in the concluding chapter of the *Nicomachean Ethics*, where the enhancement of "virtue through laws" that corresponds to legality is only valid as a alternative backup to virtue (EN X 9, 1179b4ff.; in more recent publications, Korsgaard 1996a rightly sees no discrepancy between Aristotle and Kant on this point).

A further point of convergence with Aristotle is revealed by Kant's twofold distinction between duties of right, the recognition of which humans owe to one another, and duties of virtue that are not owed, but merited. Ignorant of these expressions, Aristotle nevertheless is familiar with the distinction. Within the framework of justice, namely, he speaks of an *allotrion agathon* (EN V3, 1130a3; cf. V 10, 1134b5), the "good of another" that is to be understood as a good that the other lays claim to because it belongs to him. The demands of justice thus appear to be owed, whereas virtues that are not owed, such as generosity, exceed the realm of justice.

The question of whether Aristotle's doctrine of virtue is to be read as universalistic or particularistic may be divided into three subquestions. (1) Two examples should suffice to demonstrate that the characteristic situation types for each virtue depend not on specifically Greek but on general human conditions: Courage is requisite because dangers (against life and limb) appear in every culture, and generosity, because commerce and fortune exist almost everywhere, along with the danger of wasteful or miserly conduct that go along with them. Even the catalogues of virtue developed in Greek philosophy are not merely valid for a specific culture. This explains similar catalogues found in other cultures. They are less the product of a particular tradition than schematizations of certain types of passions or domains of action that can be found in virtually all traditions.

(2) Courage, generosity, and other virtues may be given more definitive shape by the relevant community and its mores. The basic form of virtue, however, is independent of these: It is the overcoming of primitive reactions such as the inclination to cowardice or rashness, to wastefulness or miserliness, and their replacement by circumspect action. In this way, *kata logon zên* replaces *kata pathos zên*. And because this alternative is formal (EN I 1, 1095a8, a10), Aristotle proves here as well, with respect to so-called formalism, not to be a mere antipode to Kant. On the contrary, his formal determinations suggest that he would be an important voice in intercultural ethical debates.

According to MacIntyre (1988), an influential neo-Aristotelian, but less prominent interpreter of Aristotle, there are no universally valid principles of justice. This is not consonant with Aristotle's quasi-mathematical definition of justice as "a mean" that is concerned with a mean (*meson pragmatos*). Besides this, Aristotle distinguishes within the domain of political (polis) right (*to politikon dikaion*) among suprapositive, "natural" (*physikon*), and positive (*nomikon*) components and emphasizes that what is natural has "the same force everywhere and does not depend on people's thinking" (EN V 10, 1134b18ff.). Furthermore, although he does not put forward a catalogue of basic or human rights, he does plead indirectly for the rights of property, protection of life and limb, and the right to a good reputation, which correspond to his prohibition against theft and robbery, treacherous murder and manslaughter, maltreatment, wrongful detention, and slander (V 5, 1131a6–9). Besides this, he thinks the right to political participation is self-evident. Furthermore, he appeals to the principle of mutual benefit as an elementary principle of justice at the beginning of the *Politics* (I 2, 1252a26ff.), where the principle is shown to be fundamental to the social union of male and female and of ruler and subject (see Höffe 1994, chap. 7). Finally, the "good of a community" also does not show marks of antiuniversalism. What matters to Aristotle is the common good, that is, a vague, but universalistic criterion. He rejects tyranny and supports both a moderate and mixed form of the state, the polity (*politeia*), which approaches a democratic rule of law with a division of powers.

Aristotle's emphasis on the praiseworthy character of virtues and the reprehensible character of vices could be adduced in arguments to support the communitarian, particularistic interpretation. These arguments are tenable, however, only on the assumption that the grounds for public recognition or reprehension lie in the particularities of a single society. But this sort of relativistic belief that what one society praises is what another society reproves is foreign to Aristotle. In the first evaluation of the *bios politicos*, he even dismisses public recognition as a much too superficial criterion. What matters is not (particular) recognition but rather (universalistic) virtue (EN I 3, 1095b22–31).

(3) In support of its antiuniversalistic core, communitarianism usually appeals to the fact that one learns virtues not in an abstract world society but within one's own community. This observation, however, points only to the moral value of a concrete society but does not mean that learning virtues amounts to settling in with the customs of one's own society. It is not morality that is particular, including moral principles or virtues, but rather only the appropriation of morality. Communitarians confuse the community-bound, very particular way of acquiring virtues with their universal concept and core. Aristotle's thesis that virtues are learned only within one's own community has a different thrust. Against the view that man acts morally from birth, it insists that one can and must first learn moral action.

All three elements of Aristotle's doctrine of virtue thus rely on arguments that are independent of tradition: (1) the challenges faced by each virtue (contact with danger, fortune, etc.) arise from the general human spheres of affection and existence. (2) The response to these challenges follows from the final end of all human beings, namely, happiness, and from reason as that which is particular to the human species. (3) The internalization and stabilization of the response arise from further general human elements: Practical reason must be learned and the threat posed by the passions stabilized. (On the nonrelative character of virtues, cf. Nussbaum 1993.) This has made evident *pars pro toto* that at least the core of the common good for the *polis* is not bound to the particularities of the *polis*. One could object that no Spartan would deliberate about the best form of government for the Scythians (EN III 5, 1112a28f.). But this claim speaks for the communitarians only to the extent that Spartans and Scythians have divergent views on a good form of government. Aristotle is saying something different: The

Scythian constitution is not to be subsumed under the competence of the Spartans. The ideals of state themselves do not differ, although the competences of each do.

2.4. An Ethics of Striving or an Ethics of the Will

The common ground shared by Aristotle and Kant even extends to the concept of morals. The same superlative underlies both Kant's principle of autonomy and Aristotle's principle of eudaemonism: the concept of the absolute good formed *via eminentiae.*

A semantic criterion is embedded in Kant's famous introductory sentence to the *Groundwork*: "Morally good" means "good without limitation" or "unconditionally good"; it is in itself (intrinsically) good and has the character of an end in itself. Moreover, this sentence lays claim to exclusivity: The criterion can be fulfilled only by a good will. Aristotle has similar claims concerning happiness. Happiness has a distinctively superlative character as an end that we desire for its own sake and for the sake of which we want everything else (EN 1094a18f.), as the highest of all good things to be done or of all practical goods (1095a16f.), as something that is self-sufficient, or worthy of choice and lacking in nothing (1097b14ff.), and above all as an end that is an end in the fullest sense, or most complete (*telos teleiotaton*, 1097a30). As in Kant, happiness is the condition for all supposedly good things to become truly good, meaning that they are not in any way only conditionally good (1097a34ff.). In this sense it is a superlative in the primary sense of an unconditional end in itself. This is a quality that exclusively pertains to happiness.

The highest end may be interpreted in two ways. It is either something monolithic, a homogenous end that towers above and dominates all other ends (e.g., Heinaman 1988; Kenny 1992), or it is something that is manifold in itself, as an end that inclusively encompasses all other ends (Ackrill 1974). Both interpretations accord with Aristotle's concept of happiness, but only under certain restrictions. To the extent that happiness is logically prior to the ordinary ends, it does have a dominant character, but one that has eluded customary interpretations. Among the ordinary final ends, Aristotle thinks that knowledge is more worthy of choice ("more dominant") than honor, and honor combined with knowledge more worthy of choice than knowledge alone. Happiness, by contrast, is a unique end that does not become more worthy of choice through an addition of such ends as knowledge, honor, or pleasure; for it is as such absolutely worth choosing (1097b17; cf. 1172b31, and Topic III). This singular dominance follows from the inclusive character of happiness. It synthesizes several alternatives provided by ordinary "final ends." In particular, pleasure as a kind of of completion is an indispensable component of happiness. In the course of the *Ethics*, Aristotle deals with virtually all common Greek ideas of happiness that were cited in the *Rhetoric* (I 5, 1360b19–24). But he does not claim that happiness rests on the convergence of all of these ideas. On the contrary, several of them are dispensable in the second highest life form, the *bios politikos*, and in the life form that is most suitable for happiness, the *bios theôrêtikos*. The inclusive character of happiness is for this reason subject to restrictions.

Aristotle's concept of happiness is reminiscent of the ontological concept of god. Anselm's statements (*Proslogion* II) about being (*ens*), such as that god is that of which nothing greater can be conceived – *aliquid quo nihil maius cogitari possit* – are here valid with respect to the good or end of action. As a *telos teleiotaton*, happiness is an end that is realized as an end in an unsurpassable, highest sense. And since this end is on a higher level than ordinary ends but can be attained only from "within" these ends, it has a transcendental character. Aristotle does not identify a synthetic a priori here, as Kant would require; but he does fulfill the demand of indicating a "fundamental condition for the possibility of x": Happiness is the condition that decides on the validity of all ends as ends for action; only those ends that contribute to happiness in the sense of *eudaimonia* are worthy of pursuit.

According to the popular contemporary antithesis, Aristotle advocates an end-oriented, teleological ethics, whereas Kant stands for a deontological ethics characterized by duty. In truth, Aristotle's ethics is not free from elements of duty and obligation. For example, he often uses terms such as *to deon* or *(hôs) dei*, which mean far more than is considered appropriate in conventional interpretations. To the extent that these terms are understood as an obligation without qualification, a deontological moment is present even in the concept of happiness; for Aristotle's concept of happiness is not subjective but objective. There are instances in which Aristotle qualifies the principle of happiness, but only de facto. Although a virtue such as bravery occasionally damages one's own happiness, since one can perish because of it (EN 1094b18f.), Aristotle does not allow it to be suspended in the name of happiness. Virtuous action is commanded in any situation whatsoever, that is, it is commanded categorically. Aristotle does not draw the consequence this entails for moral theory, namely, that the comprehensive leading principle of ethics cannot lie in happiness.

Conversely, a teleological moment enters Kant's theory with the idea of the absolute good. Aristotle shows that assessing practical activity involves asking questions that lead to the idea of the absolute or unsurpassable good. This is shown in the intensification from an arbitrary given end [*telos*] to a pure end [*monon teleion*], to a (absolutely) complete end (*teleiotaton*, 1097a25ff.). In this way, the complete end becomes the ultimate end of human assessment. The same holds for Kant's proof that the rational assessment of action begins with technical reason or rationality. Assessment then naturally proceeds first to pragmatic and finally to pure practical reason or categorical rationality, which can no longer be surpassed.

Both in Aristotle's and in Kant's ethics, teleology brings along a metaphysical element. But we are dealing here with a practical and modest metaphysics (see Höffe 1990, chapter 4). Whether an agent strives for the (absolutely) complete end or acts according to categorical rationality, in neither case is he or she following natural ("physical") motive forces such as incentives, needs, or passions, but rather he or she transcends them and thus attains a metaphysical determining ground of action.

Since the term "metaphysics" often denotes something more ambitious and perhaps obsolete, one might want to do away with it – on pain of having "internalized" metaphysics "so conclusively" that one can neither "perceive it nor reflect on it" (Portmann 2000, 125). But one element is not dispensable, and it, too, Aristotle and Kant have in common: the fundamental importance of practical reason. Just as Kant opposes all three levels of practical reason to what is anterior to rationality or irrational, that is, to the feelings of what is agreeable and disagreeable (GMM IV 413), Aristotle opposes the level of practical logos, including the pragmatic ideas of what is expedient and inexpedient [*to sympheron kai to blaberon*] and the moral ideas of the just and the unjust [*to dikaion kai to adikon*], to the idea of pleasure and pain (*Politics* I 2, 1253a10ff.). And in the *Ethics*, he discredits the life of enjoyment, the *bios apolaustikos*, as slavish (EN 1095b19–22). One who lets him- or herself be guided by pleasure and pain is a slave to his or her own desires.

The actual difference between Kant and Aristotle first emerges from this shared basis. Kant does not diverge from Aristotle with his notion of practical reason and its gradation up to the highest absolute level of unlimited practical reason. They also do not differ because Kant rejects

Aristotle's supposed doctrine on the precedence of the good over the right and just. Aristotle actually considers justice to be a part of the good life and prior to the other obligations. But if one cannot qualify justice in the name of the good, one can hardly say that the good has precedence over the just. The difference between Kant and Aristotle also does not derive from their theoretical metaphysics, as Korsgaard (1996a, 246) assumes; for practical metaphysics is here more important and also in decisive respects identical for Aristotle and Kant. Their difference rather is due to the concepts of action to which they apply their common notion of the unsurpassable good. The point of disagreement thus does not concern the genuinely normative side of their theories, nor a questionable theoretical metaphysics, but the theory of action (this is not acknowledged by Engstrom and Whiting 1996 or Sherman 1997).

Aristotle understands human and animal action (*De motu animalium* 6–7) as a striving (*episthai* or *orexis*) toward an end. The superlative of an appropriately defined notion of happiness thus emerges as an end of which no greater end can be conceived. Kant changes the underlying theory of action in a radical way. He is concerned no longer with the end of action, but with its beginning.

For Kant, human actions typically occur in agreement with the representation of laws (GMM IV 412), not the (lawless) feelings of what is agreeable and disagreeable (IV 413). Which laws are meant is controversial among interpreters: Are they moral laws (Duncan 1957, 103), natural laws (Cramer 1972, 170–174), or both (Haegerstrohm 1902, 269; Vorländer 1965, xxf.), or are all of these options compatible with one another (Laberge 1999, 91)? The debate can be resolved if the sentences immediately following in the text are considered: Kant is concerned with objective principles (413, 9) that are "necessitating for a will" and that thus deserve the name "a command (of reason)." They consist in imperatives (413, 9–11). He is here referring to practical laws to the extent that they represent "a possible action as good and thus as necessary for a subject practically determinable by reason" (414, 18–20); these are "objective laws (of the good)" (414, ll. 1f.). Because what matters here is any will, not just the moral will, these laws include the pre-moral, technical, and pragmatic imperatives, or rather problematic and assertoric-practical principles (cf. 415, ll. 1f.), along with the moral, categorical imperatives or apodictic-practical principles. Kant clearly speaks of "volition in accordance with these three kinds of principles" (IV 416, l. 15).

In her Tanner lectures on *The Sources of Normativity* (1996b, 31), Korsgaard calls the Kantian laws of autonomy "positive laws," since moral laws exist only because we legislate them as laws. This interpretation is both strange and misleading. The reason for this is not only of a terminological nature, as it would be if we appealed only to the fact that Kant *calls* laws positive "that do not bind without actual external lawgiving (and so without it would not be laws)" (VI 224, ll. 31f.). Kant's text suggests that positive laws are contingent and chosen (VI 227, l. 14), but a theory of morals (of law and right), the so-called doctrine of right, "must supply the immutable principles for any giving of positive law" (DR, section A; see chapter 6). It is indeed correct that moral laws do not originate outside human beings. However, the human being, as a particular biological species or even as a finite being of reason, does not act as their legislator. The source of normativity is not the specific human faculty of choice, but general practical reason. The latter is not the foundation for moral laws alone, but for all laws, including technical and pragmatic laws. But this still leaves out the distinguishing feature of moral legislation: It is not subject to qualification.

Whereas the simple, otherwise undetermined will acts according to imperatives, whichever these may be, there is an intensification from the technical imperatives to pragmatic and categorical imperatives that culminates in the categorical imperatives. In technical imperatives, only the relationship between end and means is rational, whereas the assumed end does not fall under rational criteria: "Whether the end is rational and good is not at all the question here, but only what one must do in order to attain it" (GMM IV 415, ll. 14f.). The pragmatic imperatives induce an intensification of rationality that presupposes not discretionary ends, but that exceptional end that necessarily pertains to all finite rational beings: "happiness" (ll. 28–33). This assumption, however, is only a necessity of nature, not of reason, and is thus an alien element for reason. Because the categorical imperative distances itself from this assumption, it commands "conduct immediately" (IV 416, l. 9). Unbound by any external assumptions, it is unconditional and entirely commanded by reason, and therefore culminates in the superlative. The superlative of an ethics of the will lies in practical laws that repudiate all guidelines external to the will and thus, *e contrario*, are internal to the will. Kant consistently concludes that the will gives itself its own laws; the moral principle is called autonomy.

Because Aristotle and Kant share the superlative, but have disparate concepts of action, further queries should begin with their concepts of action. What is already decided by these concepts? Most significantly, the concept of action determines the moral principle. In the context of a concept of striving, the good without limitation is a given end-directed guideline and as such is not among the objects of human responsibility. We take morals to lie within our responsibility; thus, the concept of striving results in a limited moral concept. The limitation, however, is minimal; the guideline given is in fact minor and formal. It does not consist in concrete goods, nor in their leading concepts, general goods such as pleasure, wealth, or respect. What is given is solely the transcendental condition of happiness, according to which all common goods prove to be actually or only apparently good. Because only the final end of happiness is given, a wide range of demands is placed on human responsibility; but since something given remains, responsibility does not reach the highest degree that is humanly possible.

2.5. Does Aristotle Already Have a Concept of the Will?

Against the stark opposition between an ethics of striving and an ethics of the will, one might object that Aristotle actually is not unfamiliar with what we call the will. Even Hegel grants Aristotle the concept of the will (*Lectures on the History of Philosophy*, in *Werke* XIX, 221). Aristotle at most seems to lack a comprehensive concept that includes the various forms in which the will is present. This objection is of great relevance to the history of philosophy, for it concerns the question of whether the concept of will, which was so important to modernity, was first conceived in post-antiquity, foremost in Augustine, or whether it has an ancestor in Aristotle. And since the concept of the will is important to Kant's legal ethics – it in fact belongs to the concepts that pervade the entire *Metaphysics of Morals* (VI 226) – the question plays a role in the systematic investigation of the scope of Kant's legal ethics: Is the validity of his legal ethics restricted to a specific epoch due to one of its fundamental concepts?

A negative response is given by those who maintain that the good life, according to Aristotle, depends on only two factors: striving for the good and deliberation on the appropriate means (Gauthier and Jolif 1970, II 218; Dihle 1985; MacIntyre 1990, 111; and Horn 1996). It is also the response of previous authors such as Hume (*An Enquiry Concerning the Principles of Morals*, app. IV) and Kierkegaard (*The Sickness unto Death*, sec. 2, chap. 2), but with respect to classical antiquity or the Greeks in general. The positive response is older and more widespread.

It is already given by Aspasius (XIX, 27–32), the Greek commentator on Aristotle, and later by Thomas Aquinas, who translates Aristotle's *boulêsis* as "*voluntas*" (*Summa theologiae* I, q. 80 a.2; *De veritate*, q. 22 a. 3–4). Kenny (1979) and Irwin (1992) also ascribe a concept of the will to Aristotle.

In order to resolve the dispute, a precise definition of the concept of will is mandatory. The will could be understood in a wide sense as every urge from within as opposed to an external force. A person acts on his will if he acts voluntarily, or from a free impulse. Kant's narrower and also more ambitious concept in the *Groundwork* has two characteristic aspects: a volitional and a rational aspect. The will on the volitional side is present not in a "mere wish," but only in "the summoning of all means insofar as they are in our control" (GMM IV 394). Existential decisiveness thus belongs to willing: The will takes a wish seriously and makes us pursue it with all possible force. On the rational side, willing consists in the capacity "to act in accordance with the representation of laws, that is, in accordance with principles" (IV 412).

Later, in the "Introduction to the Metaphysics of Morals," Kant distinguishes between the will in a narrower sense and the faculty of choice (*Willkür*). Unlike a wish, the faculty of choice is bound to the consciousness of being able to bring about the object in question through action. Choice is the faculty of desire "in relation to action," whereas the will is "in relation to the ground determining choice to action." The will is "practical reason itself" (VI 213), but not necessarily pure practical reason. It is the legislative and, at the same time, objective moment from which the laws (VI 226) proceed. These include not merely the moral, but also the technical and pragmatic laws. The faculty of choice, by contrast, is an executive and subjective moment. Maxims proceed from choice (ibid.) and are defined as rules that the agent "makes his principle on subjective grounds" (VI 225). (On will and choice, see also Allison 1990, 129–135.)

Aristotle provides an inventory of the various theoretical alternatives in the domain of voluntary action and decision with a meticulousness that remains admirable today (EN III 1–7; cf. Rapp 1995). Aside from the two familiar modalities, willing (*hekôn*) or voluntary (*hekousion*) action and involuntary (*akousion*) action, he also discusses the third possibility of involuntary action (*oukh hekôn*) that arises from ignorance but is assented to *post factum*. Further, he acknowledges mixed forms of voluntariness and force; for example, a captain throws away some of his cargo in order to save his ship from a storm. Of inebriate or angry action, he says that it does not arise "from" but "in ignorance"; and he answers negatively to the question as to whether one could use temptation by desire as an excuse, since it is in one's own power not to give in to desire.

Voluntariness is primarily a volitional precondition of the will. Children and animals may also be imputed their actions; moreover, their voluntariness still allows for those nonrational motive forces, such as desire and anger, that are excluded by the will as a rational motive force. *Boulêsis*, a second volitional moment that is characteristic of human beings, does not, in my view, sufficiently define the will, contrary to the views of Thomas Aquinas and Irwin, or even Gigon (1991). *Boulêsis*, namely, is also directed at things that can be willed only through ignorance, such as what is unattainable or impossible. Even if it does have a rational component (*De anima* III 10, 433a22–25), it is something between a wish and a genuine will.

Aristotle's third volitional element, *prohairesis*, choice (of precedence) or decision, also is not shared by children or subhuman beings (EN III 1111b8). *Prohairesis* concerns only what is conducive to ends (EN III 1112b12). But since *prohairein* (prefer, choose) is mentioned in connection with the concept of life-forms (*bioi*), which are of decisive importance as an intermediate step to happiness, one must understand the domain of what is conducive to ends in a comprehensive sense. It encompasses the entire domain of the good life, including final ends, but excluding happiness as the final end at a higher level.

In one passage in the *Rhetoric* (I 10, 1368bff.), Aristotle comes very close to articulating the full-fledged concept of the will. Wrongdoing is there described as bad action arising not only voluntarily (*hekonta*), but also from reflected deliberation (*prohairounta*). What is bad is defined as what contradicts the law (*para ton nomon*), and the law expressly takes into account the human, but no doubt unwritten law that has kinship with the moral law. Aristotle is thus familiar with injustice that arises knowingly and willingly, or from deliberation. But he again does not acknowledge the consequence this has for moral theory: the qualification of the principle of happiness in light of the new principle of the autonomy of will.

A volitional component also belongs to the acquisition of virtues of character, which are necessary for happiness. Aristotle emphasizes that it is in our power to be good or bad (EN I 7). Finally, the volitional character of action appears in the treatise on *akrasia* or moral weakness (cf. Robinson 1995). Kierkegaard's diction about the "intellectual categorical imperative" of the Greeks (*The Sickness unto Death*, sec. 2, chap. 2) is true for Socrates, for whom it was coined, since he held that mankind would not violate what is good if it had greater knowledge (*Menon*, 77af.). Aristotle also interprets moral weakness as a deficiency of knowledge. But since he traces it back to the motive forces of desire or anger, which compete with the good, he is referring more to a volitional than to a cognitive deficiency.

The volitional side of the will thus cannot be denied in Aristotle. But what can be said about the second, rational moment? What Kant calls the "representation of laws" is hinted at by Aristotle in several forms of the practical syllogism. In the following inference, the major premise (1) articulates a practical law: (1) Smoking is noxious and (2) this here is an instrument for smoking. (3) Thus, it is noxious. Does it diminish the lacuna between the models of striving and of willing if Kant's second defining moment is incorporated in Aristotle's model? A positive answer would have consequences for the moral principle and would allow the disparity between the principles of happiness and freedom of the will to melt away.

At least one difference between the two models remains. Since the law contained in the example of the syllogism is pragmatic, and not of a moral nature, it submits the will to what is given and is concerned only with what is conducive to it, but not with what is conducive to the final end of happiness itself. Morals can, according to Kant, demand that one act contrary to happiness, even though happiness is a naturally necessary goal of all human beings (GMM IV 415, ll. 28ff.). It seems that this obligation would not even be conceivable for Aristotle, since all obligations rest on happiness. But the appearance is somewhat deceptive. Courage, for instance, requires the acceptance of one's own death in situations of commensurate danger. This gives honor to the courageous, but is not effortlessly compatible with the principle of happiness. Aristotle thus sees the possibility of a contradiction between virtues and their guiding principle of happiness. But he merely draws the epistemological conclusion that the statements concerned are only normally valid: that is, usually, but not always valid (*hôs epi to poly*: 1094b21 etc.; cf. Höffe 1996b, Part II, and 1995a, chap. 2.2, along with Reeve 1992 and Anagnostopoulos 1994). He does not ask, from a moral theoretical standpoint, whether this provides a reason to deny that happiness is the highest and most comprehensive principle.

Aristotle does not disregard cases in which happiness is not entirely in the hands of human beings, but in part granted to them by fate or by the gods. Nor does he deny the possible contradiction between courage and happiness or the possibility of becoming wretched at an older age (EN 1100a8 and 1101a8). Priam's lack of luck (1100a5–9) recalls Job's biblical experience: Even one who is upright in his pursuit of happiness is at the mercy of a superior power. Aristotle, as a secular thinker, understands this power not theologically but as the sum total of what contingently happens to us. The term *eudaimonia* thus rightly has overtones of what "is animated by a good spirit," or of blessing and salvation.

The fact that happiness is a fragile state and not entirely accessible to the human being does not lead Aristotle to draw the conclusion that a human agent is responsible only for his worthiness of happiness, not for happiness itself. This conclusion would overly restrict happiness, or even lead to the collapse of eudaimonic ethics. Instead, Aristotle maintains that constancy is nowhere greater than in virtuous activity (1100b12f.). His thesis, which qualifies without dismissing happiness, is as follows: Even if moral uprightness does not safeguard against wretchedness, every other path is more likely to lead to disaster.

Let us take provisional stock with regard to the question "Aristotle or Kant?" We have dismissed both the older view that Aristotle advocates a *via antiqua* and is completely superceded by Kant's *via moderna* and more recent attempts to rehabilitate Aristotle to the detriment of Kant. We have finally declared all attempts at mediation to be inadequate that do not uncover semantic similarities and differences in the theory of action. At least eight positive points have been established: (1) In the intention of his ethics as a practical philosophy, Kant is an Aristotelian. (2) The fundamental elements of his ethics show that Aristotle is a universalist and thus a precursor to Kant. (3) In the distinction between phenomenal and intelligible concepts of virtue, Kant acknowledges Aristotelian insights and at the same time transcends them toward a theory that is more adequate to the phenomena. (4) Aristotle and Kant both define the moral good as an unsurpassable good. (5) They differ in the fundamental concepts of their theories of action: In Aristotle, this concept is striving, and in Kant, the will. (6) Since the concept of the will radicalizes the notion of responsibility, a fundamental ethics cannot return to the Aristotelian concept of striving, nor to its corresponding principle of happiness. Kant's concept of the will and principle of freedom are in this respect superior. Kant's ethics is not more "universalistic" than Aristotle's, but more radical in its understanding of human responsibility and morality. (7) Some of Aristotle's reflections reach beyond his own theory of striving and his principle of happiness. (8) One further point emerges in anticipation of the next chapter: With respect to the power of judgment, where Aristotle's philosophy is supposedly superior to Kant's, the latter in fact not only integrates judgment, but even takes it further (see chapter 3). In sum, Kant's and Aristotle's ethics do not substantially diverge, as generally assumed. And where they do differ, Kant's view on morals turns out to be more radical. Thus, neo-Aristotelianism cannot lead us to expect an alternative that is superior to Kant.

3

UNIVERSALISTIC ETHICS AND
THE FACULTY OF JUDGMENT

The question of whether Kant's ethics of universal principles is open to the faculty of judgment, considered so portentous by his supposed adversary Aristotle, plays a vital role in determining the scope of his moral thinking. The question merges with his ethics of law and peace, since the evaluation of concrete cases requires competence in "application," which is precisely the faculty of judgment. Furthermore, since this question concerns universalistic ethics as a whole, it merits a fundamental investigation.

3.1 A Deflationary Theory of Judgment

According to a widespread reading among critics, Kant's ethics patently ignores the faculty of judgment. Evidence for this is both simple and persuasive: The faculty of judgment does not appear among the core concepts of Kantian ethics, nor even among its important subsidiary concepts. Because it is of central importance in the third *Critique*, attempts have been made to remedy the thematic deficiency from this standpoint. However, the relevant studies, such as those by Vollrath (1977, 146ff.) and Pleines (1983, 89ff.), come up against limiting factors: The leading tasks of the third *Critique*, the mediation between theoretical and practical philosophy and the theories of aesthetics and of the teleological faculty of judgment, do not make allowance for what is most central to ethics, namely, the mediation between moral principles and the singular case.

Inspired by H. Arendt's line of thought (1958; cf. 1982, esp. lectures 2 and 10), Vollrath correctly emphasizes that while common sense unquestionably plays a role in aesthetical judgments, it is also called for in political judgment. Kant takes it for granted that common sense pertains to every type of rule application (*Anthropology* VI 139). And tactfulness, the main concern for Pleines, is no doubt relevant to moral action. But it does not already account for the principal task of a practical or political power of judgment, that of applying moral principles. Moreover, the distinctive mark of modern politics, its commitment to universalistic principles such as basic and human rights, is missing in Vollrath's study. The rehabilitation of the faculty of judgment in Kant's ethics requires assigning it a place within universalistic morals; Kant develops the latter not in the *Critique of Judgment* but in moral philosophy. (On the faculty of judgment in the philosophy of right and law, cf. Wieland 1998; for a "faculty of judgment reading" of Kantian ethics, in lieu of a radical deontological reading, cf. Herman 1993, and more generally on the practical faculty of judgment, see Pieper 1991.)

In the second *Critique*, however, the faculty of judgment does not play a major or even minor role. This gives rise to the popular criticism that Kant ignores experience and succumbs to "political moralism," or in the words of Herman Lübbe's (1987) general apprehension, which is not specifically directed at Kant, that he assures the "triumph of disposition over the faculty of judgment." If the issue of judgment is neglected altogether, one could repeat Hegel's criticism of Kant and speak of a (gross) overestimation of the "ought," a hypertrophy of "ought," and with Odo Marquard (1986, 249) adjoin the reproach that a universalistic ethics is deaf to history and tradition. One might also, like Paul Ricoeur (1986, 249), lament the disruption ["*démantèlement*": dismantling] emerging from the transcendental method, or, with Oswald Schwemmer (1986, 154, 166) claim that Kant "excludes real problems of action facing agents," in particular through "abstraction from their respective individuality." Furthermore, one might entertain Nancy's fears (1983, 8): "*l'impératif supprime la liberté de l'initiative, et l'impératif catégorique supprime la liberté de la libération.*"

Increasingly influential is also Larmore's view (1995, 4), according to which Kantianism generally implies that "what is morally correct can be entirely specified by rules." This may go along with the wholesale rejection of universal principles, since instead of demanding uniform action in various singular cases they denote hollow forms that have no relevance to orientation. McDowell (1981) raises this objection in the footsteps of Wittgenstein. However, in the *Philosophical Investigations*, sections 185–241, the attack is hardly meant to be comprehensive. Wittgenstein rather takes aim only at the "Platonic" view that rules can, like algorithms, be applied mechanically to singular cases (see Baker and Hacker 1985; Kripke 1987; and Puhl 1998; cf. also O'Neill 1996, esp. secs. 3.4 and 6.7). This view in fact is not advocated in this manner by Plato, nor by Aristotle as the theorist of the faculty of judgment, nor even by Kant as the paradigmatic philosopher of universal principles. And because nonmechanical subsumption under rules belongs to daily routine, right as a domain of life in which the faculty of judgment plays an almost existential role has its own institution for the application of rules: the court. Jurisprudence as the discipline assigned this role has long rejected "algorithmic" interpretations of universal rules (cf. Wassermann 1985; Hassemer 1994; Schroth 1994; and Barbey 1996). Their fundamental flaw lies in equating incomplete determination with indeterminacy.

Even if Kant's ethics does not concede a conspicuous role to the faculty of judgment, the latter does appear; it even comes to the fore in the program of his ethics. In the "Preface" to the *Groundwork*, Kant says of moral laws that they "no doubt still require a judgment sharpened by experience" (IV 389, l.30). Kant thus does not deny the importance of the faculty of judgment; on the contrary, he takes it for granted. Already in the first *Critique*, he refers to examples in medical, judicial, and political practice (CPR B 171–174). Thus, what one believed to be missing in Kant's ethics he actually declares to be indispensable: experience in the practical sphere and recognition of its individuality. What Ricoeur longs for is, at least "in principle," invoked in the cited passage: conscious attention to the transitions that are required to mediate between the a priori and experience.

According to the "Preface," the faculty of judgment is needed "partly to distinguish in what cases" the moral laws "are applicable and partly to provide them with access to the will of the human being and efficacy for his fulfillment of them" (GMM IV 389, ll.30–33). The faculty of judgment here obtains both tasks articulated in Aristotle's doctrine of *prohairesis*: choice (of preference) or decision (EN III 4–7). In *prohairesis*, namely, two elements coalesce in a single unity: *bouleusis* (EN III 4–7), along with the intellectual virtue appropriate to it, *phronêsis* (VI 5 and VI 8–13), and the virtues of character (*aretai êthikai*). This duality incidentally opposes an overestimation of *phronêsis*, since *phronêsis* is responsible for only one of the tasks of judgment mentioned by Kant. One can best translate *phronêsis* as "prudence," not "moral insight." Aristotle also considers animals to be prudent, insofar as they possess the ability to plan ahead (EV VI 7, 1141a27f.) and gather provisions, as do ants and bees (*Historia animalium*, Book I, cf. *Meta-physics* I 1, 980b22), or to take precautionary measures, as do cranes in the advent of a storm (*Historia animalium* IX 10, 614b18f.).

Kant's faculty of judgment on the one hand performs a primarily theoretical or cognitive task, comparable to reflection and prudence. It mediates the general – in Aristotle, a moral attitude, and in Kant, a moral law – with the single case (cf. GMM IV 403f.). On the other hand, it takes on the practical task of contributing to the real acknowledgment of principles, which for Aristotle is performed not by the faculty of judgment itself but by the virtue of character, a moral attitude that precedes judgment thematically, but is also bound to it. Since both aspects of Aristotelian *prohairesis* can be reencountered in Kant, this again evinces an elementary agreement instead of two disparate positions.

If the second aspect of Aristotle's theory is fulfilled, actions follow according to rule, and precisely those customs and habits arise for which Marquard (1986) provided an apology. But a significant difference still exists between the neo-Aristotelian Marquard and Aristotle himself. Marquard, namely, sets aside the *aretê* in Aristotle's two-part concept of *aretê êthikê* and contents himself with the other part, the *ethos* (habit) or *hexis* (disposition, *Haltung*). This move has many consequences. Because Aristotle's moral components are missing in the concept of mere convention, Marquard supports only half of Aristotle, bereft of all morals. Kant, who commits the faculty of judgment to a moral guideline, here proves to be the more faithful Aristotelian. This also confirms the observation noted in chapter 2 that rehabilitating Aristotle relies on defending him against neo-Aristotelianism. Kant no doubt mentions the link between the faculty of judgment and experience, along with its twofold task, in a subordinate clause. As a result of this, he at least seems to underestimate the importance of the faculty of judgment. But he does stress the importance of its volitional side, because the human will, "though capable of the idea of a practical pure reason, . . . is not so easily able to make it effective *in concreto* in the conduct of his life" (GMM IV 389, ll.33–35).

Despite its terseness, the "Preface" already treats the faculty of judgment extensively, thus rendering it even more surprising that judgment receives no mention in the *Groundwork* or later in the *Metaphysics of Morals*. If it plays a role in the program of ethics, why is it absent from its realization? One reason lies in Kant's precise delineation and narrowing down of the relevant subject matter. This no doubt leads to a methodological advancement: the strict division between nonempirical and empirical considerations. One who ignores this distinction and seeks in a *pure* moral philosophy a central locus for a faculty of judgment that is interwoven with *experience* falls victim to an error analogous to a "category mistake": the confusion of separate philosophical disciplines. To search for an empirical object in an emphatically nonempirical ethics would confound a metaphysics of morals and its groundwork with its counterpart, a practical anthropology.

Narrowing down the subject matter, however, is only prefatory to the decisive argument. Kant surely acknowledges that concrete moral action arises from the interaction of non-empirical and empirical elements. But because the genuinely moral component lies not in the interaction but exclusively in the single element of the determination of the will independently of all experience, he is forced to strip the other element, experience, of its supremacy. This also has implications for the faculty of judgment that is "sharpened by experience." But it does not entail a devaluation of individuality or a "triumph of disposition over the faculty of judgment." In ancient Rome, "triumph" meant the ceremonious reception that is granted to a victorious commander along with his army. The expression is justified where a dangerous opponent has been vanquished, and precisely because the opponent is dangerous, the victor senses satisfaction and deserves a celebration or triumph from those who have been saved. In Rome, the victor had to be particularly successful; if a commander did not leave at least 5,000 enemy soldiers on the battleground, he had to content himself with a "minor triumph," the ovation. If "disposition" merits not only an ovation but a triumph, then the faculty of judgment must be a particularly insidious adversary and the victory over it must turn out to be remarkably unequivocal.

The faculty of judgment assuredly does not play the part of a dangerous and finally vanquished opponent in Kant's ethics. Experience is indeed to be overcome, but not that experience that mediates the singular case with the rule – rather, only experience that determines the rule or, more precisely, the subjective ground of action, the maxim, and also lays claim to a moral standing. Experience is not overcome as an element relevant to concrete action, but rather only insofar as it determines the underlying will. Put in Kantian terms: With respect to morals, duty vanquishes inclination.

3.2. A New Faculty of Judgment

The faculty of judgment is not absolutely overcome even in the case of the moral will; it merely excludes the form of judgment that is dependent on experience. Kant presses the faculty of judgment into service for his moral criterion, the universalization experiment, albeit not in the *Groundwork*, but later in the second *Critique* (V 67ff.). (This is not even discussed by Sherman 1997, 311ff., in the section on "Kantian 'reflective' deliberation," although her study is otherwise insightful.) Kant thus underplays the faculty of judgment that is dependent on experience in his search of a form independent of all experience: "the judgment of pure practical reason", which, abbreviated, is called "pure practical judgment" (CPrR V 67f.).

For the sake of the latter, Kant asserts what Larmore considers disturbing (1995, 2f.), namely, that one "could [not] give worse advice to morality than by wanting to derive it from examples" (GMM IV 408). Kant does not disapprove of "the use of examples in moral considerations." On the contrary, he portrays noteworthy ideas in the *Groundwork*, such as action from duty (IV 397) or the test-procedure of the categorical imperative (421f.) in its various forms (423f.), through "experiences" (429). The examples do not, however, have what Larmore's term "derivation" lays claim to, namely, the power of justification.

The crucial points become more perspicuous in their appropriate context. As already in the "Preface," Kant pleads for a "completely isolated metaphysics of morals, mixed with no anthropology" (410), and decisively rejects "a mixed doctrine of morals" (411). Examples have no justified relevance for the "grounding" of morals (409). "For every example . . . must itself first be appraised in accordance with principles of morality, as to whether it is also worthy to serve as an original example, that is, as a model" (408). Pure practical judgment is needed for the appraisal of "principles of morality," whereas judgment sharpened by experience is needed for application. Here, examples perform the same task that was already noted in the *Critique of Pure Reason*: They "sharpen the faculty of judgment" (B 173) or, as in the *Groundwork*, make the practical rules "intuitive" (IV 409). Furthermore, they serve for "encouragement" (ibid.) and thus belong to what is posterior to the "grounds," although they perform the "very commendable" task of "[providing] access" to the doctrine of morals (409/20–24).

Now Kant does not generally have much esteem for examples. One who has the "talent of judgment" in the theoretical sphere or so-called "mother-wit" hardly needs them, especially since they "only seldom adequately fulfill the condition of the rule" (CPR B 172f.). Examples are the "leading-strings of the power of judgment" that are only of indispensable utility to one who "is lacking in natural power of judgment"

(B 173f.). With respect to morals, one must add that for genuine morality, action from duty, "no certain example can be cited" (GMM IV 406). What is commanded by duty may be stated with certainty, but "it is always doubtful whether it is really done from duty and therefore has moral worth" (ibid.).

Since only pure practical judgment decides about the genuine morality of an action, it alone can be considered a "moral faculty of judgment." But Kant introduces this expression relatively late and only in passing. He apparently gains clarity about the significance of moral judgment in successive stages: Ever since the *Groundwork*, he maintains the fundamental insight that decision for what is genuinely moral is a performance of a nonempirical nature. The *Groundwork* suggests that this, too, lies within the competence of judgment, since it addresses the "principle of moral cognition of common human reason" as a "norm for its appraisals" in distinguishing "what is good and what is evil, what is in conformity with duty or contrary to duty," and as a "practical faculty of appraising" (IV 403f.). The concept of this faculty of judgment is first introduced in the second *Critique*, in the "Typic of Pure Practical Judgment." And perhaps it goes without saying that the nonempirical faculty of judgment alone has a genuine moral character only after the appearance of the *Critique of Judgment*, namely, in Kant's work on religion (Book 2, §4: VI 186).

An ethics that downgrades experience, it is feared, would give preponderance to the universal over the individual, to the point where it becomes impossible to perform adequate concrete action. One might contend that the universal should play either no role at all or only a disruptive role in morals; more important, or perhaps even exclusively decisive, is the sensitive perception of the singular case. Several criticisms of Kant covertly uphold this view, but it is clearly announced by Schwemmer; it is advocated explicitly and independently of discussions on Kant by Dancy (1993). The latter calls the position "particularism" – or more precisely, moral particularism – and opposes it to an ethic of principles (similar to McNaughton 1988, chap. 13, and, within a discussion inspired by Kant, McDowell 1998). However, particularism overlooks a structural characteristic that already applies to the descriptive form of perception and remains valid for the practical form. This characteristic pertains to the theory of action, and thus to a pre-ethical ground, and speaks against skepticism of the universal. To perceive something means to apprehend it *as* something and to consider the singular as an instantiation of the universal. Let us take a look at an example from the *Groundwork*, the injunction to help others, concentrating not on Kant's solution, but only on its "moral logic."

In order to apprehend the relevant situation as a moral demand, it is to be treated as an individual instantiation of that type of situation that occasions the possibility of help in general: the state of distress. An economical theory of action would distinguish between two moments; in both, the as-structure is invoked, that is, the apprehension of the individual *as* the universal, and both moments require judgment sharpened by experience. The theoretical or descriptive side of perception and judgment identifies the situation as one of distress. The practical or normative side at the same time perceives in this descriptive perception an appeal to the observer to take a stand on the distress, not theoretically, but practically: as a being capable of action.

Judgment sharpened by experience is also needed for the second step, that of weighing alternative options. In order to make the individual action amenable to moral evaluation, it must be apprehended as the instantiation of a maxim and thus, again, of the universal. In the example given, there is the alternative between either opening oneself up to the situation and attempting to help, or closing one's mind to the plight and remaining indifferent to those in search of help.

Whereas empirical judgment with reference to both rules and instantiations is indispensable for the initial two steps, it is no longer justified in the third step, the question as to which of the maxims deserves the moral status. But even in this case, judgment is not overcome as an opponent. It is not up to judgment to provide an answer; it is thus rendered altogether unemployed. But this is only momentary, since one who resolves to help for reasons that are valid prior to empirical evidence must still reflect on how he or she can help. For this, he or she requires practical experience and specialized competence concerning the distress in question, both of which are exterior to decisions about one's reasons for action.

Because judgment that depends on experience itself refers to the universal, the dethronement of experience cannot imply the precedence of the universal over the individual. There are, rather, two concepts of the individual and likewise two concepts of the universal, along with a reason to reject one of the two in favor of the other. Both the situation and the response to the situation are individual; the moral response, moreover, is no less individual than the nonmoral response. Conversely, the rule guiding one's interpretation of the situation is universal, as is the rule according to which the response follows. Both moral and nonmoral rules have a universal character. Therefore, pure practical judgment bestows priority not on universality over individuality, but rather on moral over nonmoral universality. Because moral action is an instantiation of a moral rule, individual cases can be distinguished in the same way.

Kant's theory thus does not endanger the individuation of action. Kant supports a theory of action – no doubt only in its formative stages – according to which concrete actions or omissions are examined on three levels. The subtraction of all experience is required exclusively on the third level. Whereas the mediation of the individual with the universal occurs on the first two, experience-laden levels, what matters on the third level is only the type of universality. The operation of judgment independently of experience on this level implies only the priority of moral over nonmoral universality, not the sacrifice of the individual to the universal.

Kant does not fall victim to a thematic deficiency; on the contrary, he extends the scope of judgment. The ability to appraise an individual situation in light of a rule, which often receives the oversimplified description "application" or "subsumption" but in truth is a creative performance, is not the only ability that belongs to moral action. An additional requirement emerging from a moral perspective is the prior ability to assess the rules themselves. Since Aristotle is not familiar with this ability, "his" theme, the faculty of judgment, has been fundamentally extended by his supposed antipode, Kant. Whereas Aristotle's *phronesis* is moral only on the condition that the ends of action are moral, Kant's pure practical judgment contains a moral character directly.

The appearance of "conditions" in Aristotle of course does not mean that his *phronesis* is only conditionally good in Kant's sense. Unlike Kant, Aristotle views prudence not as a morally neutral competence, and even less as veering toward the amoral prudence of the snake or the slyness of the fox. Clearly aware of the relevant nuances, Aristotle draws a tripartite distinction among types of competence. Whereas morally indifferent judgment or cleverness (*deinotes*) is limited to an instrumental, or at best pragmatic competence, judgment veering toward amoralism, shrewdness, or villainy (*panourgia*; EN VI 13, 1144a24–27) bypasses morals without compunction in cases where this is demanded by self-interest. *Phronesis* is directed at what is good and useful to the person in question, but is not thereby committed to moral guidelines. Aristotle emphatically asserts that it is impossible to be prudent (*phronimos*) without being good, here in the sense of virtuous (EN VI 13, 1144a36f. and a30).

Prudence, determined as a mean between cunning and simplicity (*eueteia: Eudamian Ethics* II 3, 1221a12; EN VI 5, 1140a24f.), merely governs the choice of means and instruments, in view of not discretionary ends but an end in the singular and with a definite article, consisting in the good life in general (EN 13, 1145a6, and VI 5, 1140a27f.); it denotes a comprehensive, worldly prudence. Whereas virtues of character assure the agent's fundamental orientation toward happiness, the intellectual virtue of prudence governs the concretization of virtue appropriate to relevant contexts. Whoever has prudence is capable of reflection that is committed to happiness as an end for one's entire life. Prudence is of a practical, not only theoretical nature, since it not only passes judgments of understanding (*synesis*) and good understanding (*eusynesis*), but also commands execution. In saying what ought to be done or not done (EN VI 11, 1143a8ff.), prudence develops one's power to determine action. However, it is not capable of putting the passions in their place as forces that obscure one's view of the correct end, and for this very reason prudence depends on cooperation with virtues of character. For instance, the virtue of character assures that a courageous person will not react to dangers in a cowardly or rash manner, but intrepidly, whereas prudence is needed for reflection on what particular action to take. Thus, one can speak neither of a genuinely moral power of judgment, nor of morally indifferent judgment. *Phronesis* is no more and no less than a moral-practical faculty of judgment.

Aristotle's antithesis of *phronesis* and *panourgia* also has a counterpart in Kant. In the "Appendix" to the treatise *Toward Perpetual Peace*, Kant speaks of "sophistry" (VIII 376) and of the "twistings and turnings" of "an immoral doctrine of prudence" (VIII 375), thus of amoral judgment that in politics is frequently labeled Machiavellianism. Kant rather speaks of a "political moralist" and contrasts it with an equivalent of Aristotle's *phronesis*, a "moral politician" (VIII 372 and 377). Whereas the political moralist "frames a morals to suit the statesman's advantage," the moral politician takes the principles of political prudence "in such a way that they can coexist with morals" (372).

The criterion of pure practical judgment, as is well known, is given by the test of universalizability. The disputed question as to whether this test can be executed independently of experience cannot be answered definitively here. One might easily be under the impression that Kant proposed the thought-experiment in order to support the livelihood of generations of doctoral and postdoctoral students. It suffices to point out a distinction that could help to articulate the core of the debate more precisely (cf. Höffe 1990, chap. 7).

According to a widespread view, universalization is free from experience if it does away with all reflections on consequences, and, by contrast, is dependent on experience if it requires such reflection. In fact, Kant makes allowance for reflection on consequences. They come into play not in the choice of maxims, but rather in two cases: in answering the question of how to follow through with one's choice of a maxim *in concreto* and in deciding which maxims are appropriate to a given situation. In both cases, reflections on consequences belong to what the *Groundwork* calls "the concept of the action in itself" (IV 402, ll. 33f.). One can call them "reflections on consequences internal to action" and contrast them with reflections external to action that, for Kant, are not permissible.

Consequences are external to action when they have nothing to do with the concept of the action itself, although they can codetermine a decision about the reasons for action. Someone who allows himself to be led by reflections external to his actions qualifies his doings and omissions as the means to something else, that is, he justifies them through an external reason, which proves to be the true determining ground of his action. In the case of the injunction to help others, the consequence external to his action could lie in the expectation of an ideal or material award ("gratitude" or "money," respectively). The consequence internal to action would consist in actually redressing a need at the end of a possibly complicated chain of actions. One cannot, however, attain certainty about how to bring about consequences external to one's actions. Hence, Kant's ethics of the categorical imperative does not attempt to emancipate human beings from all uncertainties concerning a moral conduct of their life, as some would have hoped and others feared.

3.3. An "Esprit Moral"

The traditional form of judgment as sharpened by experience is overshadowed by Kant's innovative form of judgment. But the former is still vindicated by the subsidiary role it plays in morality. This evidently presupposes a fundamental condition. If Kant's ethics does not devalue individuality or overlook experience – if it in fact has affinities with experience and is sensitive to the faculty of judgment – it must accept a moral guideline for concrete action that offers more than what an

ethics of principles is supposed to be limited to: mere empty formu-
las without relevance to situatedness. Moreover, this guideline cannot
be exhaustive without becoming "loose, vague, and indeterminate,"
as Adam Smith asserts for all rules of virtue excluding those of justice (*Theory of Moral Sentiments*, sec. IV). The principles must rather set
aside everything that does not lie in their domain to ensure that their
universality does not finally amount to the uniformity of their application: They thus abstract from everything individual about persons
and situations and from everything particular about groups, subcul-
tures, and cultures. Without renouncing the importance of situatedness, the principles must enable us to have a good command of the
art of abstraction and expose its expediency. An "ethical asceticism" is
needed that emphasizes the essential universal character of principles
and yet remains open to individuality and particularity. The fundamental requisite condition thus consists in the convergence of the determinacy of the moral guideline with openness regarding concrete practical
activity.

This convergence is apparent in Kant. It allows us to counter objections that are frequently understood as the limiting factor of all deontological ethics. The extension and correction of the latter through a
utilitarian or, more generally, "consequentialist" ethics are made redundant by Kant's solution. The bond holding together moral determinacy
and practical indeterminacy is manifest in the twofold shape of judgment. Pure practical judgment concerns not action itself, but only the
most essential component of action: the will as the determining ground
that accounts for morality. The moral guideline shows that the will is
already defined. The openness complementary to it lies in the fact that
only the will is determined, but not the means toward its realization.
The determination of these means requires in addition the faculty of
judgment sharpened by experience.

How far does this openness reach? To what extent does an ethics
that is supposed to be cleansed of experience with respect to moral
rules (or, more precisely, moral principles) leave room for experience,
individual digression, and reflection on consequences, but also and
most important for borderline cases in which the need to make a decision is inescapable? Surprisingly plentiful, and even structurally diverse
openings can be found. They complement one another materially with
different grades of complexity. An enthusiast about classification could
speak of various levels within judgment sharpened by experience. Characteristic problems of the present day fit onto these levels. The theory of

a complex faculty of judgment presented in the following thus extends far beyond the resolution of the alternative "Aristotle or Kant"; its parallel concern is a diagnosis of our times.

Whether one contemplates environmental protection, new "techniques" in biomedicine, the age of nuclear power, military politics, or multidimensional globalization, societies are confronted with new kinds of problems that can be interpreted as new thrusts toward modernization (cf. Höffe 2000b; 2002a). Their characteristic difficulties, I claim, can be justly diagnosed by philosophy only if the alternative "Aristotle or Kant" is overcome.

The catchword "legitimation crisis" stems from Habermas (1973, sec. II.6); Lübbe (1980, 36) contrasts it with an orientation crisis; Wieland (1989) speaks of "the *aporias* of practical reason," albeit without relegating them to a historical epoch (for a more recent account, see Wieland 1998); Larmore (1985, 323) maintains the heterogeneity of practical reason; and Tugendhat (1990) laments "the helplessness of philosophy in face of the moral challenges of our time." Following the catchphrase of "the tasks of judgment," I here propose an alternative for a wide range of contemporary problems. My diagnosis is more clearly moral than Lübbe's, is morally homogenous in contrast with Larmore, is more morally sober-minded in comparison with Habermas and Wieland, and finally is less pessimistic than Tugendhat's.

Kant does not put forward a theory of practical judgment. Because he fully develops only very few elements, we are confined to the task of selecting possible building blocks for the theory still outstanding and using them to compose a provisional outline. We will not consider Kant's repeated remark that judgment is "a special talent that cannot be taught but only practiced" (CPR B 172; cf. *Anthropology* VII 199), which is why mere knowledge of the rules or principles and understanding in general are not sufficient, brilliance notwithstanding. We will also exclude reference to Kant's own faculty of judgment, although it is remarkable. The judgments he passes concerning questions as difficult as the moral status of the French Revolution are finely nuanced and guided by principles. Further, the *sensus communis* will be left out of our discussion. The *sensus communis* governs judgments (of taste) and denotes a commonly shared, not common (ordinary) sense (CJ §40; cf. *Anthropology* VII 139). Finally, we will not address the fact that the reference point of the categorical imperative, the maxims, are often the result of intense experience and thus are evidence for a successful capacity of judgment. Only the following elements are considered.

(1) The quoted passage from the Preface to the *Groundwork* might give the impression that the openness toward individual differences does not stretch very far. If "judgment sharpened by experience" is needed only to "distinguish in what cases" moral laws "are applicable," then only morally trivial tasks seem to remain, namely, virtually mechanical subsumptions of the kind: Here someone is suffering from the weariness of life, a case for the prohibition of suicide. One sees someone in distress, therefore help is required. And if information is queried, then honesty is called for.

In fact, the first structural problem of application consists in the identification of a moral task. This is accomplished by the aforementioned perception, in which theoretical competence is combined with moral sensitivity. Due to this cooperation, the task of identifying moral obligations proves to be twofold. Contemporary examples verify that this is not a trivial matter. The first example concerns primarily the theoretical side, whereas the second is a matter of moral sensitivity. Both confirm: *Nostra res agitur.*

In the face of new possibilities in biomedicine, the perpetually provocative question arises as to when life begins that merits legal protection and when it ends. The command to protect human life is not subject to compromise, and is also taken for granted; but judgment has to determine independently of experience what precisely this command consists in. The other example is provided by animal protection. Moral sensitivity is called for in cases of such new phenomena as animal experiments, large-scale animal husbandry, and the transportation of animals, in which truly traditional commands should not be disregarded nor the ability of animals to suffer pain "forgotten" in the light of scientific or economic advantages (cf. Höffe 2000b, chap. 15).

(2) Once the moral task has been identified, its concrete fulfillment remains. In the case of imperfect duties, openness (or even multiple openness) in this respect is implied by their very concept. First, there is the question of how to realize moral willingness, such as the willingness to help in singular cases. The numerous errors committed by developmental aid verify the relevance of this task today. Furthermore, there is the question of degree. This is alluded to in the *Doctrine of Virtue* (§31) when Kant asks how far one should expend one's resources in practicing beneficence, and then answers: "surely not to the extent that he himself would finally come to need the beneficence of others." The *Doctrine of Virtue* generally contains clear examples of application in the "Casuistical Questions."

Moreover, questions of priority arise: In which order of precedence is the injunction to help others called for, and with respect to which groups of persons? There is an established rule of precedence in the Christian-Aristotelian tradition, according to which beneficence or *caritas* is due first to one's spouse, then to offspring and parents, and further – in the following order – to siblings, relatives, and friends, and finally to one's benefactors (Thomas Aquinas, *Summa theologiae* II-II, *quaest.* 26, 6–13).

Such rules of precedence are only generally, not universally valid; they depend on the ceteris paribus clause. In cases where this condition does not hold, conflicts over addressees may result (on a fourth component level). They occasionally intensify in a veritable dilemma, as for example in the one expressed by Sartre (1946, 40) about whether one should care for one's invalid and widowed mother or commit oneself to the *résistance*. The conflict does not, however, concern competing principles, as it is often interpreted. Here, a theory of judgment is sobering: What is in fact an existential dilemma in practical life often emerges as a particular conflict of application or as a conflict over addressees in the theory of judgment.

One cannot expect a single objectively valid solution to such conflicts, no more than for other tasks. Nevertheless, the faculty of judgment does not operate arbitrarily or merely according to subjective feeling. It rather discloses a certain degree of objectivity in conflicts over addressees by determining several parameters of judgment: the extent of one's need, one's own capacity to help, and the substitutability of help. The third parameter – "For which of the tasks might a surrogate task be found?" – shows that judgment requires far more than the hedonistic calculation provided by utilitarianism, since this calculation already presupposes certain given possible actions from which one can choose the relatively best. In many cases, however, the actual task is the exploration of new possibilities, and this demands a great deal of creative imagination.

The estimation of consequences plays a role in questions about how and to what extent to realize given rules, what priorities to set, and how to settle conflicts over addressees. It thus plays a role in all questions that arise on the four component levels of the second level of application. According to the customary interpretation, Kant does not make allowance for these considerations; but in view of the difference between the determinacy of the will and the openness of action, they are in fact admissible. Reflection on consequences is permitted only

after what one wills has been determined, for instance, one's willingness to help. Reflection on consequences is not permitted if it is involved
in the determination of the will itself or qualifies one's willingness to
help in favor of other ends. This distinction exactly corresponds to and
reinforces the aforementioned difference between reflections on consequences that are internal to action and those that are external to
action.

Although these questions are self-evident for imperfect duties, they
are problematic for perfect duties: Do the latter leave little room for
judgment sharpened by experience, as Kant suggests (DV VI 411)? Is
his favorite example of a legal command, namely, the command to
return a deposit (e.g., CPrR §4 Remark), even valid "if the deposit is
a kind of weapon demanded by a proprietor who has lost his senses?"
Wieland (1989, 17) elucidates a difficulty with the aid of this inquiry
that he refers to as an aporia of application: "Even if every distinguishing feature considered by the norm corresponds to the regulating concrete situation, one cannot ever ascertain whether the application of
the norm is permitted." Wieland's proposed solution – that the norm
should not be applied in borderline cases – seems to carry conviction
from a moral point of view, but not from that of moral philosophy. Not
applying the norm, namely, signals an exceptional case that contradicts
the concept of this norm. For, as a duty of right, the norm belongs to
perfect duties that *per definitionem* do not allow for exceptions. Have we
reached the first limits of Kant's ethics, since it places a ban on questions of evaluation that according to moral common sense should be
permitted?

Before drawing this conclusion, one might attempt an alternative
interpretation. In the situation described by Wieland, the return of
the deposit is not absolutely irrational, but irrational only as long as the
description of the case remains true. One who patiently waits for the
proprietor of the weapon to regain his senses and become legally competent before returning the deposit is not thereby exempt from duty,
nor is he guilty of its irrational application. Rather, he recognizes that
perfect duties cannot be applied mechanically, but require reflections
on the relevant situation that nevertheless remain internal to the action.

Once again, it has been shown that judgment allows for a more
structurally perspicuous interpretation of moral problems. Wieland's
example illustrates not the limits of a norm, but rather its openness with respect to practical activity. Even perfect duties are incomplete in the sense that they do not in addition define the means of

fulfillment. Concrete action in the case of perfect duties also occurs only under conditions that Aristotle summarizes in the concept of individual circumstances: *kath' hekasta.* Aristotle puts forward the following catalogue of headings for these conditions: "who he is, what he is doing, what or whom he is acting on, and sometimes also what (e.g., what instrument) he is doing it with, and to what end (e.g., for safety), and how he is doing it (e.g., whether gently or violently)" (EN III 1, 1111a2–6). Whoever refrains from creative appraisal in his actions, who disregards the *kairos* and returns the weapon at an inopportune time, acts not morally but foolishly. Whoever does this despite his ability to reflect even lacks a good will, namely, "the summoning of all means insofar as they are in our control" (GMM IV 394). Not only does he act foolishly – his action is only partially moral.

The efficacy of moral principles may be compared to that of the grammatical and semantic rules of a language. Whoever disregards grammar and semantics will speak incorrectly, and whoever regards them but can do nothing other than apply them mechanically is a mere pedant who maps out his life in arid fashion. The faculty of judgment is had only by those who in actual life know how to speak the language of moral principles in a sensitive, creative, and flexible manner – in short, intelligently. For this, more than subsumption is needed, but also more than mere contextualization. Universalistic principles are not some finished screenplay, but rather just a fundamental idea on the basis of which one writes the screenplay during the filming, and that means throughout one's entire life.

Whoever acknowledges the openness inherent in every moral duty possesses an "*esprit d'un principe moral*," in short, "*esprit moral.*" As O'Neill (1996, sec. 3.4, 115) rightly contends against McDowell (1981), "rules and principles enter our lives not because they dominate us, but because we dominate them" (84). In the case of the deposit, the "*esprit moral*" would consist in the ability to guard against fraud and theft while also postponing the return of the deposit. In other situations, waiting can indeed become "immoral." If one who takes charge of insured letters speculates on them while protracting their return in order to avoid unpleasant costs or losses, he is not entitled to an "*esprit moral.*"

Kant's own "*esprit moral*" is evidenced by the "Casuistical Questions" in the *Doctrine of Right.* However, if one looks for something like concrete orientation in that work, one will be disappointed. Kant does not discover unambiguous instructions for action in the face of the complicated cases that are portrayed. While Kant otherwise passes clear judgment and has a predilection for strict rigidity in the case of morals, he proceeds here with caution. He remains open to competing points of view and is often indecisive in his final appraisal. In the "Introduction to the Doctrine of Virtue," he announces the reason for this: the "Casuistry" is not a "doctrine about how *to find* something [but] rather a practice in how *to seek* truth" (VI 411). He understands it as the task of cultivating a cautious and circumspect search for truth by portraying the great complexity of the matter.

For instance, Kant asks, "Can an untruth from mere politeness (e.g., the 'your obedient servant' at the end of a letter) be considered a lie?" The answer is left open, but the following direction is suggested. Because the end of the letter is a mere complimentary close and those involved know this – "no one is deceived by it" – it can hardly be considered a lie (DV VI 431). With regard to another issue Kant rejects simplified moralizing appraisal. He answers the question as to whether one can "justify . . . a use of wine bordering on intoxication" – this itself is a reprehensible vice according to §8 – rather affirmatively with the observation that the use of wine "enlivens the company's conversation." And the "banquet," defined as "a formal invitation to excess in both food and drink," has "something in it that aims at a moral end . . . : it brings a number of people together for a long time to converse with one another." But if the company is so large that one can converse only with few neighbors, "the arrangement is at variance with that end" and becomes a mere "temptation to something immoral, namely intemperance" (DV VI 428).

3.4. Conflicts of Principles

On the first two levels of problems, Kant's ethics leaves surprisingly ample room for individuality and experience. But does this also hold for the third task of weighing various duties against one another? Here, the conflict internal to duty or *intra*principle opposition is complementary to *inter*principle opposition. The latter collision of duties is a structurally new problem that arises not only in Kantian ethics.

It is a common assumption that many collisions of duties are so basic that they cannot be resolved by a single foundational norm. Larmore (1985) vindicates the heterogeneity of practical reason based on three equally plausible basic norms: "partiality," "consequentialism," and the notion of inviolable duties ("deontology"). This view grafts the ideal of the modern development of states onto ethics. Where rivalry is unceasing – as among religious denominations in the development of states and among duties in ethics – validity is granted to both sides, although, by the same token, both are equally invalidated: The modern state becomes neutral toward religions.

Although this account of heterogeneous norms may capture truths about politics, it is not an appropriate view with respect to normative ethics. Strictly speaking, it is not accurate about politics, either. The modern state is not radically pluralistic; it rather acknowledges religious truth as a secondary theme, but readily consigns it to the private sphere for the benefit of the primary political task of promoting social peace. In the case of normative ethics, the search for a foundational norm is not of secondary concern, but rather the very core task itself. Normative ethics cannot shirk away from the question of how to determine the real foundational norm in the face of competing foundational norms; for three conflicting guides are as good as none at all (cf. Spaemann 1989, 10).

There certainly are "tragic choices" that have to be made, such as those to which Larmore points. However, Sartre's dilemma between caring for an invalid mother and joining the Resistance shows that a "tragic choice" – which is here much less tragic than the choices made in Greek drama – does not entail the heterogeneity of practical reason, since tragic choices may arise for single duties. Moreover, one of Larmore's foundational norms is not of a moral nature; partiality corresponds to Kant's concept of inclination. Consequentialism, by contrast, can be integrated in a deontological ethics, as has already been suggested. For this reason, one might easily suspect that in a genuine collision of duties the duties rather follow the same, more formal foundational norm of universalization, and yet still collide. In order to resolve this kind of collision, an upgraded competence of judgment is no doubt needed, since the abilities already called for – sensibility, flexibility, and creativity – are demanded in a more complex manner.

Traditional discussions concerning the collision of duties often appeal to the conflict between the prohibition against lying and the injunction to help others. Here, Kant supports a clear rule of priority; the prohibition against lying prevails without exception. This might lead to honesty toward a murderer ("Supposed Right" VIII 425), which is at odds with well-reflected moral convictions. Now, the prohibition against lying has priority because it is a perfect duty, whereas the injunction to help others is the description of an imperfect duty. (Leaving aside, for the moment, the argument in the *Doctrine of Virtue*, §9, that by a lie "a human being throws away and, as it were, annihilates his dignity as a human being.") Kant thus invokes not external, but rather moral grounds for his contention, implying that his rigorism and uncompromising prohibition against lying are not the contingent faults of a "Prussian puritan," but rather follow from the very approach of his moral philosophy. This would lead to the unwelcome consequence of a counterintuitive moral philosophy or of a moralizing approach that "systematically" denies priority conflicts.

In order to actually elucidate Kant's approach, we would be well advised to set aside his dispute with Constant and instead consider the *Groundwork* (cf. Höffe 1990, sec. 7.3). The latter also treats the prohibition against lying as occasioned by a state of need; however, it is not a third party that is in the state of need, but rather the agent himself or his family. Kant thus does not discuss a conflict of priorities, but remains true to the theme of the *Groundwork*, the rivalry between duty and inclination. The rigorism countenanced here merely opposes exceptions for the sake of self-love; it prohibits lying for one's own benefit. This prohibition goes hand in hand with the rigorism of disposition [*Gesinnung*]. As a genuine moral rigorism, it differs from that legalistic rigorism that not only prohibits exceptions, but also forbids exceptional cases that would have benefited other moral duties.

The moral question as to whether a lie is justifiable under certain conditions can be set aside. Only two points are relevant to an investigation of judgment: For one thing, Kant's theory of the determination of will independently of all experience leads only to a relative prohibition against lying (explicitly in the *Common Saying* VIII 286ff., and in the "Idea," VIII 19f.); a lie employed for the fulfillment of other duties such as saving a life is not *eo ipso* immoral. Second, because moral rigorism does not imply a tendency toward legalistic rigorism, Kant is in need of a theorem that is independent of the approach in the *Groundwork* in order to vindicate the absolute prohibition against lying. This he takes from traditional debates: the theorem of the precedence of perfect over imperfect duties.

This theorem is not implausible. Because perfect duties toward others carry the weight of duties of right and contain the addressee's legal rights, they cannot be qualified for the sake of imperfect duties. Herman's (1993, 79ff.) attempt to resolve conflicts of duty by concentrating disproportionately on judgment would thus be more convincing if the moral precedence of perfect over imperfect duties were taken into account. Both a collision of duties only among the perfect duties and a collision among the imperfect duties are far easier to deal with morally. Positive law and philosophy have long been aware that a duty of right can be depreciated by another such duty or by a state of need. Where commitments of a higher rank exist within the same group of duties, this is due to the higher rank of a rule or of the situation in which it is applied. In these cases, the moral esprit copes relatively well with dilemmas that may arise. However, the question remains difficult even for a moral esprit's sensitive and creative power of judgment as to how an owed duty of virtue can be qualified by a duty of virtue that is only merited.

Does Kant's ethics leave us with more than the merely negative result that legalistic rigorism is not implied in its overall approach? Does Kant also provide theoretical tools, if not to resolve a collision of duties, then at least to broach a rational discussion of them? An important tool lies in the distinction just mentioned between an owed duty of right and a merited duty of virtue, along with the priority of owed duty. Further, Kant incorporates the traditional doctrine of the lesser evil and acknowledges – although only in the cautious form of a question – a "permissive law of morally practical reason." Accordingly, something can be "permitted that is in itself not permitted (indulgently, as it were), in order to prevent a still greater violation" (DR VI 426, ll.12–24). This is illustrated by the situation of need or distress. A "theory" of the choice among conflicting preferences would certainly have more to say on this point.

In the supplement "indulgently, as it were," Kant alludes to one of the limitations that could be worked out with more precision in a theory of the choice among conflicting preferences. Because the permission is valid only "indulgently," the agent would have to remain conscious of violating a command, and this speaks against moral self-righteousness. To say that the means justify the end is an overly facile moral excuse. Furthermore, in order to prevent the agent from paying mere "lip service" to awareness of a violation, one might require that he make an effort to ameliorate the situation. This would eventually invalidate those conditions under which a permissive law is valid. Finally, a theory of the choice among conflicting preferences would have to settle the question as to whether there are actions that are absolutely immoral; these might include torture and especially manslaughter.

A third tool for deciding between conflicting preferences is provided by the concept of "the right of necessity" [*Notrecht*], according to which certain actions that violate the rights of others are not inculpable, yet are to be considered unpunishable (DR VI 235f.). Fourth, Kant distinguishes between obligation and the grounds of obligation and declares that in the case of conflict, the stronger grounds of obligation take precedence over the stronger obligation (DR VI 224).

Legal morals contain multiple principles that are equally called for in singular cases, but from the standpoint of their moral content, they suggest different guidelines for action. Today, structurally difficult moral problems are often precisely of this kind. In reproductive medicine, for example, a woman's right to self-determination might permit methods that could be detrimental to the future child. The advancement of a theory or at least of theoretical tools for dealing with these collisions of principle belongs to the currently urgent tasks of a truly practical philosophy.

Often enough, one is not even conscious of a collision of principles. This deficiency has practical ramifications; it nurtures a precarious alternative. Whoever is willing to act morally will fixate on one of the relevant principles and is in danger of falling prey to legalistic rigorism. But one who lacks moral motivation may effortlessly find apologetic grounds to veil his or her shortcomings. A deficiency in awareness of the problems thus fosters precisely that two-dimensional alternative that unleashes rhetorical potential on both sides, but also hampers a substantively convincing solution: that is, the currently popular alternative between "moralism and the release from morality."

The tools proposed by Kant for coping with collisions of duty are no doubt helpful, but one cannot seriously claim that they are sufficient. (On the interpretation of the Kantian position, see also Herman 1990b.) Is the reintroduction of Aristotelian elements in ethical theory therefore imperative? Skepticism is warranted for two reasons: First, our community is determined by universalistic principles such as human rights; in the face of the corresponding conflicts, an ethics of tradition and custom or an ethics of the ethos leaves us in the lurch. This might induce one to try to apply the theoretical tools advanced by Aristotle and his successors to the new tasks at hand. What are today called conflicts of principles would have been conflicts over ends or collisions of various duties for Aristotle. However, theoretical tools for solving these conflicts – herein lies the *second* reason for skepticism – cannot be found in the *Nicomachean Ethics*. The tools would have had no utility anyway, since a collision of virtues is foreign to Aristotle.

The doctrine of *bouleusis* or *phronesis* is concerned solely with means, and with ends only if they have an intermediate character. The doctrine of "circumstances" (*kath' hekasta* or *circumstantiae*) is likewise only relevant to "contextualization"; the same holds for the priority of *epikiê* over justice (EN V 14). The aforementioned rule of priority (spouse, then children and parents, etc.) does not help to resolve conflicts between diverse yet equally moral ends. The only expedient rule of priority here is the precedence of justice over compassion, the rule that became prominent in the medieval Aristotelian tradition. The priority of duties of right over duties of love, however, does not exceed the tools already provided by Kant. For it is a correlate to the precedence bestowed on perfect over imperfect duties among duties toward others.

One might still see reason to appeal to a metatheoretical thesis in the *Nicomachean Ethics* (I 1, 1094b 16–22), according to which ethics is restricted to propositions that are mostly, but not always true: "*hôs epi to poly*" (cf. Höffe 1996b, Part II). Thomas Aquinas translates "*in pluribus*" (*Summa theologiae* I–II, *quaest.* 94, 4): The propositions are valid under restrictions and with exceptions, that is, generally but not universally. The concept of mere general validity makes allowance for exceptions on grounds of self-love, which are excluded in appraisals according to purely moral principles. More specific tools are thus needed for the choice among conflicting preferences. In the conflict between duty and self-love, duty should appear as uncompromisingly valid; in the conflict between two duties, on the other hand, a balance is acceptable, albeit only under rigid restrictions.

This indication is sufficient to conclude our – admittedly provisional – inventory. Theoretical tools that go beyond what Kant has provided have not been found. Hence, no reintroduction of Aristotelian influences is needed, but rather a theory for which the building blocks have been gathered: a theory of principles that are of a universalistic nature and yet still remain open to the faculty of judgment. (On the "Cultivation of Timeliness," see Höffe 2000b, Chap. 16.)

4

ON EVIL

Evil appears to many as a metaphysical or theological concept that cannot be easily accommodated by a secular ethics. Kant, however, introduces the concept both in his general ethics (CPrR V 58ff.; *Religion*, Book 1) and in his cosmopolitical ethics of peace (*Peace* VIII 344, 355, 366, 375f., 379 and 381; cf. also DR VI 321f. and *Religion* VI 34): Is he thus in danger of weighing down his theory with an obsolete metaphysics or with theological assumptions that merely win subjective credence?

A metaphysical concept of evil is undeniable: This is the *malum metaphysicum* or sum total of the world's imperfections as it appears in Leibniz and previously in Plotinus (*Enneade* I 8, 51; cf. O'Brien 1971; 1992) and Plato (*Republic* II 379bf., *Phaedrus* 256b, *Theaetetus* 176, and *Laws* X 896dff.). Evil is also a subject in the philosophy of religion and is a characteristic theme of monotheistic religions that cannot escape the problem of theodicy, or vindication of God in the face of ills and above all of existent evil. The concept of evil does have a genuinely moral significance that may be considered apart from its other meanings. It is linked to an obviously secular theme: the pathology of the good. Consequentially, it plays an unproblematic role in secular works such as Aristotle's *Nicomachean Ethics*, where it appears as what we should call "bad, simply" (*haplos kakon*, VII 6, 1148b8).

In accordance with his general maxim of setting the phenomena before us (*tithenai ta phainomena*: VI 1, 1145b2–7), Aristotle is concerned with different levels of the morally bad: "softness" (*malakia*: VII 2 1145b9), "incontinence" (*akrasia*: VII 1–11), and self-indulgence (*akolasia*: VII 2, 1145b16 and VII 4, 1146b19f.). He concludes with a discussion of harmful and wicked acts contrary to law, a level of depravity that at least comes close to the concept of moral evil (cf. *Rhetoric*

I 10, 1368b12–14). In addition there is "brutishness" [*thêroitês*], which does not pervert what is good, but also does not have anything good to begin with (EN VII 7, 1150a1ff.; cf. VII 1, 1145a17, and VII 6, 1149a1). In Plato, too, the concept of evil is free of metaphysical or theological implications; it is personified in the tyrant (*Republic* IX 571a–576b).

The concept of evil has oddly vanished from the philosophy of the last century, although plenty of occasions would have warranted its consideration. Secular components are not foreign to the history of the idea, as already suggested. Around the turn of the century, the phenomenologist Max Scheler was still attentive to the concept of evil (*Formalism in Ethics*, 1916, 186ff. etc.; later Hartmann 1926, e.g., 39ff.). But subsequent studies of evil seem to appear only in histories of philosophy (e.g., Welte 1959; Pieper 1985; Schulte 1988; see also Holzhey and Leyvraz 1993). Besides the significant contributions by Jaspers (1973, 170ff.) and notably by Ricoeur (1969), the "insignia" of a larger philosophical debate are missing: the nuanced elucidation of the concept (evil is taken to be conceptually indeterminable; cf. Schulz 1972, 219, and Schmidt-Biggemann 1993, 7), proposals of theses and antitheses, the sketch of a "theory" and skeptical responses, and finally the attentiveness toward this debate among individual sciences and among the public it addresses.

In order to tackle the question of whether the concept of evil in Kant's ethics of peace brings along metaphysical or theological baggage, or is instead a sign of his sensitivity toward a great range of issues, one must first regain the concept for philosophy in general. At least three tasks contribute to this end that fortunately may be considered from the standpoint of Kant's own reflections on evil. One must establish a clear concept of evil (section 4.1), examine whether it does justice to the phenomena ("Does it have a correlate in experience?" section 4.2), and finally consider its universal relevance: What is the importance of evil to the *conditio humana* (section 4.3)? Kant gives answers to all three questions; unlike most alternative responses, they remain relevant up to the present day. In particular, they do not unnecessarily encumber his ethics of peace.

4.1. The Concept

In colloquial German, the expression "*böse*" (evil) has various surface meanings. Right from the start, Kant leaves them aside in his determination of the concept: He thus excludes a person's state of mind who is angry, furious, or raging (to be in "evil spirits") and the designation of a spoiled child (*"böse"* in the sense of a bad child), along with the denotation of an infected body part (a bad eye or bad finger) and *"böse"* in other adverbial (badly taken) or adjectival senses (a "bad dream," a "bad hunch," a "bad end," etc.).

In a further common figure of speech: "I was badly duped," it remains open whether one is the victim of evil or of bad fortune, that is, whether this is a case of *malum morale* or a *malum physicum.* Leibniz (*Theodicy* I 26) regards the existence of physical evil as the consequence of a moral evil. But if suffering is punishment for the evil that entered the world with mankind, this urges a question, often suppressed by philosophers and theologians, as to why beings must also suffer who are not free and thus cannot be evil. Why must the innocent, including children and animals, also be punished? Whoever sees cats play with the mortal fear of mice knows that animals are able to inflict pain on others of their kind and are not themselves completely guiltless. But because we would not ascribe knowing and voluntary action to them, they can hardly be held responsible for the infliction of pain.

In Kant, evil is invariably related to the will; as a minimal condition, evil can be attributed only to someone responsible ("imputable") for his or her actions. An uncontroversial element belongs to the more accurate concept of evil: the negation of moral good. Controversy exists only over what kind of negation this implies. The less harmful type of negation, the *privatio boni,* or omission of good acts, is not a serious option for Kant. He first sees evil in purposeful opposition to what is good. The difference between the two levels of moral good, legality or the mere external conformity with the moral law and morality or inner consent, has an analogous counterpart in the levels of opposition to what is good. But they are mentioned only *en passant* in the treatise on religion.

In calling evil those "unlawful" actions that contradict the *moral* law (*Religion* VI 20; similarly, GMM IV 404, l. 3), Kant assigns them to the simple level or "first grade" of evil as mere unlawfulness or counter-legality. In the case of evil in the full sense, evil as the "property" of a person, the "objective" side is not intensified to culminate in a particularly heinous unlawfulness or "bestiality" (cf. DR VI 363). Rather, only the subjective side is intensified: an unlawful action as such is willed. A good will or good disposition is replaced by an evil will or evil disposition, amorality in the sense of countermorality. Whereas the complete moral good consists in an unsurpassable positive respect for the law, complete moral evil consists in unsurpassable negative unlawfulness that has become an incentive. Here, the view of the good is not only tarnished but knowingly and voluntarily contravened. This holds both for single actions or crimes and for basic attitudes or vices, since vice relates to moral evil in the same way that virtue relates to the moral good.

Within the ambit of conscious "transgression of the law," the *Doctrine of Right* distinguishes between a criminal that commits his misdeed on a maxim he has taken as an objective rule and one who commits it only as an exception to the rule (VI 321f.). Whereas in the latter, weaker case the criminal opposes the law "by way of default only," the criminal opposes law in the former case "by rejecting it (*contrarie*) or, as we put it, his maxim is diametrically opposed to the law (hostile to it, so to speak)." This intensified misdeed of a formally "wholly pointless" evil nature is, "as far as we can see," impossible for a human being. Kant does not support this with a direct argument. However, in qualifying the intensified evil as "pointless," he is referring to self-love as the ground of human evil. He thus releases our sensuous nature from responsibility for evil and rehabilitates human sensibility for the tradition of moral philosophy. Evil has its source not in sensibility but in the deliberate subordination of morals under self-love.

From this it surely follows that no motive can explain evil that is "pointless" or that does not promote self-love. Nevertheless, this does not entitle us to exclude the possibility of extreme *hubris*, that moral arrogance by which a human being purposively follows maxims that are inherently evil because they contradict the moral law. The possibility of *hubris* is accounted for by the concept of freedom. There are thus three levels or gradations of evil: (1) mere counterlegality, (2) the lower level of countermorality, occasional "single cases" of evil, and (3) the worse level of evil "as a rule." Whereas incontinence or weakness of will appears on the second level of evil, which comprises cases of giving in to a temptation, a strong, but evil will is characteristic of the third level.

Ever since writing the *Groundwork*, Kant was primarily concerned not with the preliminary stage of morals or legality but with morality as the peak stage of morals. In the same vein, Kant mentions negative legality or evil actions only in passing in his work on radical evil, and only as a means to determining evil in the full sense. Full-fledged evil designates the constitution of an agent or of an agent's maxim. The title of Kant's work is thus misleading, for it suggests that it is no more than a treatise on the philosophy of religion. In fact, Kant continues to develop the theory of moral subjectivity that he introduced in the *Groundwork* and worked out further in the second *Critique*. This deflates objections that accuse his theory of evil of commitment to theological assumptions. In the treatise on religion, Kant maneuvers "within the boundaries of mere reason." Further, he does not make any borrowings from metaphysics, at least none that overrides his general philosophy of morals. Therefore, Kant's ethics of peace is not weighed down by additional metaphysical or theological baggage from the concept of evil. Problems rather arise around its commitment to subjectivity, such as the question: To what extent can nations be considered moral subjects?

The fact that moral philosophers seldom show interest in the positive side of moral subjectivity could account for their lack of interest in evil. Apel and Habermas cannot be included among the exceptions to this rule (see Krings's justified criticism, 1979, 370), but Rawls can (1971, §66: "The Definition of Good Applied to Persons"). Because Rawls, like Kant, distinguishes three levels of increasing negativity: unjust, bad, and evil people, he may be inspired by Kant on this point, as in his "interpretation of justice as fairness" (§40).

Like Rawls, Kant first considers the lower forms of moral depravation. Unlawful action that merely contradicts the moral law is comparatively innocuous, but conscious transgression of law is worse; and the worst form is reached when unlawfulness provides the ultimate determining ground and the will itself becomes evil. Because this third level cannot be intensified any further, it has the status of a superlative. Analogously to the opening sentence of the *Groundwork*, one could say that it is impossible to think of anything at all in the world, or indeed even beyond it, that could be considered evil without limitation except an *evil will*. This will is manifest when the ultimate subjective determining ground, the supreme maxim, is itself unlawful.

The full extent of freedom, the free recognition of the moral law, is possible only when there is the alternative of freely opposing this recognition. Therefore, evil does not necessarily belong to freedom as a reality, but surely is a possibility of freedom, and as such even belongs indispensably to the core of freedom. Any theory of freedom that does not take evil into account must be considered incomplete. The second *Critique* rightly contends that reason "does not at all raise" the human being "in worth above mere animality if it is to serve him only for the sake of what instinct accomplishes for animals"; rather, the human being has reason "for a higher purpose: namely, . . . also to distinguish the good from the bad" (V 61f.).

A further attractive feature of Kant's theory is his account of various levels of the nonrecognition of the moral law (*Religion* VI 29f.). The "evil heart" appears in three gradations of "the will's (*Willkür*) incapacity to adopt the moral law in its maxims." At the first, perhaps even prefatory stage, that of the frailty (*fragilitas*) of human nature, the moral law is not recognized to its full extent. In line with the "complaint of an Apostle: 'What I would, that I do not!'" the moral law is the weaker incentive in comparison with inclination. This is the same weakness of will that was examined by Aristotle. In contrast to Aristotle, however, the criterion for ascertaining weakness of will is not the principle of happiness, but the moral law; it is clearly a *moral* weakness of will. At the second stage of the evil heart, impurity or insincerity [*impuritas*], "actions conforming to duty are not done purely from duty," but rather "often (and perhaps always) need still other incentives." Adherence to the moral law occurs only under the proviso of an auspicious convergence of duty and inclination.

Only at the third stage of depravity [*vitiositas, pravitas*] or of the corruption [*corruptio*] of the human heart is the recognition of the moral law purposively refused; for the power of choice [*Willkür*] has the propensity to adopt maxims "that subordinate the incentives of the moral law to others (not moral ones)." Kant also speaks of the *perversity* [*perversitas*] of the human heart, "for it reverses the ethical order as regards the incentives of a *free* power of choice." With this reversal "there can still be legally good [*legale*] actions," but the "mind's attitude is thereby corrupted at its root (so far as the moral disposition is concerned), and hence the human being is designated as evil" (*Religion* VI 30). One calls a human being evil "not because he performs actions that are evil (contrary to law), but because these are so constituted that they allow the inference of evil maxims in him" (VI 20).

It is significant that the last stage of the depravation of moral subjectivity or morality in Kant's theory of evil does not coincide with the highest degree of depravation of moral "objectivity" or superlative counterlegality. On the contrary, (subjective) depravity may preside even where public actions conform with the moral law. This means that the topic of evil is dispensable in a legal ethical theory, since legal ethics concerns merely (juridical) legality. Surprisingly, the willingness of nations to engage in war against each other appears both as a fundamental problem for the right of nations and as one of Kant's examples of the corrupt propensity in the human being. This example cannot easily be put aside as ill-considered, for it appears in three works: in the work on religion (VI 34), on peace (here repeatedly), and finally in the *Doctrine of Right* (VI 321 f.).

4.2. Does Moral Evil Exist?

Kant's concept of evil as unlawfulness that has been taken up in one's maxim seems to a large extent "well-constructed" in comparison with that of moral subjectivity. But the question still looms large as to whether the concept of evil also corresponds to reality. Does evil thus defined actually occur in the world?

After the conception of his first critical work on ethics, Kant relentlessly stresses that there are no secure examples of morality (GMM IV 408, cf. CPrR V 27; DR VI 221 and 226). This is true for the same reason that holds for the negative side of morals. One cannot observe in one's own or in others' concrete action whether lawfulness as such is willed. At best, one can only infer the ultimate determining ground or maxim of action (*Religion* VI 20).

Although phenomena that can only be inferred warrant caution, Kant refers to a "multitude of woeful examples" (VI 32ff.) of evil with astounding conviction. These examples come from two groups, civilized societies and primitive peoples. Kant includes both viewpoints from "civilization" and the "state of nature" in a third group, which is characteristic of an international perspective or of the state of "a people in its external relations" (VI 34). With respect to the first group, Kant speaks of the "vices of culture and civilization," citing as examples "secret falsity even in the most intimate friendship" and the propensity to "hate him to whom we are indebted, to which a benefactor must always heed." Examples from the second group are meant to oppose "an optimistic presupposition on the part of the moralists, from Seneca to Rousseau," namely, the belief in the natural good of man (VI 20). As a counterexample, Kant mentions "the scenes of unprovoked cruelty in the ritual murders" among some primitive peoples (VI 33). In the *Theodicy*, Leibniz had called persons evil who "find pleasure in causing suffering and destruction" and cited as examples Caligula and Nero, since they both wreaked more destruction than an earthquake.

Kant takes the third example from the right of nations as evidence for a condition "where civilized peoples stand vis-à-vis one another in the relation of raw nature (the state of constant war) and have also firmly taken it into their heads not to get out of it" (*Religion* VI 34). According to the treatise on peace (*Peace* VIII 355), "the malevolence of human nature" is in no way hidden, but can be seen "unconcealed" in this state of "free relations of nations." Kant is referring to the willingness of states to settle conflicts with other states not by right and law, such as by trial in an international tribunal, but rather by force and war.

Under closer scrutiny of the example of the Dog Rib Indians in particular, knowledge of ethnology is indispensable to determining whether the primitive people Kant discusses are actually guilty of unprovoked cruelty. Kant's informant on this point is "Captain Hearne" (VI 33), probably the same Samuel Hearne (1745–1792) who was famous at the time as a British furrier, explorer of Northern Canada, and author of a *Traveler's Diary*, although the latter was posthumously published in 1795, following Kant's treatise on religion. Our question is whether an evil maxim can be inferred from Hearne's observations. Kant does not immediately appeal to blatant and conscious, yet "simple opposition to duty," such as knowing and voluntary manslaughter that does not involve self-defense. He rather considers three increasingly intensified conditions under which manslaughter is performed: cases of murder, killings from a reprehensible disposition, and further acts of "cruelty." The perpetrator wills more than simply annihilating the life of another. And because this third intensification is "unprovoked," it cannot be excused as an action brought about affectively. This knowing and voluntary cruelty or "free sadism" is the first instance in which Kant infers an evil inclination.

There is no denying that there are humans who murder out of cruelty or that this can be intensified in unprovoked cruelty. Thus, the second condition for a promising rehabilitation of the topic of evil can be considered fulfilled: Kant's "theory" of evil does justice to the phenomena and is confirmed by experience. Whoever ascribes unprovoked cruelty to another person is in each isolated case saddled with a weighty burden of proof. However, it is no doubt overly optimistic to assume that such proof is never provided. This is similarly true for the first example of "secret falsity even in the most intimate friendship," whereas the third example is to be tested below, in the ethics of peace (see section 11.4).

4.3. Evil by Nature?

Kant does not rest content with forming a concept of evil that is confirmed by experience. He reprises Augustine's query "*Unde malum?*" ("Where does evil come from?" *Confessions* VII 7 and 11) and famously replies that evil belongs to human nature itself. This view makes no exceptions for individuals, groups, or cultures and thus may seem pessimistic. It opposes optimism according to which evil can be completely stamped out at some place or time in history, either among primitive peoples, the supposed "*bons sauvages*" (good savages), or in the future when civilized peoples are even more civilized. However, it also counters strong pessimism that imputes a predisposition to evil to the human being. Rather a predisposition exists only to do good; moreover, the predisposition to good acts is indelible and unremitting. Anthropological optimism and pessimism, each in their strongest form, are transcended by Kant's more sober position asserting a mere propensity to evil.

The predisposition to good does not mean that the human being has a good character by nature. Due to his capacity of practical reason, the human being possesses only a well-determined "susceptibility" to respect for the moral law as a single sufficient incentive for the power of choice (*Religion* VI 27). Real respect or a good character are by no means innate but must be acquired through commensurate action. As long as the human being can be attributed responsibility for his actions (imputability), however, one cannot deny his susceptibility to develop respect for the moral law. Consequently, evil cannot have the same status as the good in human beings, yet it retains anthropological significance. Because the good at first exists only as susceptibility to develop respect for the moral law, every human being has a "propensity" that consists in the "subjective ground of the possibility of an inclination" (VI 28) to divert from the maxim of morality despite one's consciousness of it. In emergencies, one might sacrifice the moral law to self-interest and then voluntarily and knowingly oppose the moral law.

Before Kant, two other options held sway that were not easily compatible with the "essence of moral evil." The available alternatives were: Humankind is by nature either good (seen optimistically) or evil (seen pessimistically). If human beings are good by nature, one would have to put the blame for evil on society, thereby acquitting individuals of responsibility and denying evil in the full-fledged moral sense as voluntary disregard of the moral law. If the second option were tenable, evil, because it is already given by human nature, would be removed from the sphere of human decision. This again runs counter to the freedom involved in evil.

Since both options supersede the moral concept, Kant's third, intermediate solution, which is neither optimistic nor pessimistic in the strong sense of these terms, becomes even more pressing. Kant's solution does not amount to the coexistence of good and evil in human nature, which he likewise repudiates. The reality of evil is rather perceived when evil is "more than not present as a natural constitution," when it accompanies human nature as such, but also exists "less than as a predisposition [*Anlage*]." Since the concept of propensity [*Hang*] denotes precisely what is less than a predisposition and more than absence and signifies "actually only the predisposition to desire an enjoyment" (*Religion* VI 28), Holzhey's thesis (1993, 24) is not tenable that the very assumptions of Kantian ethics undermine all access to evil. On the contrary, discarding Kant's concept of evil would undermine fundamental assumptions of his theory, since the primary moral task of Kant's philosophy of freedom, that of accounting for decisions between good and evil, would be impossible without it. If evil were more than a propensity, if it were instead a predisposition, overcoming evil would be too difficult a task to be expected of human beings.

What then does recognition of the concept of evil afford and what does its denial entail? There are two forms of denial. One might either contest the very existence of evil or accept its existence but reject that it has anything to do with human nature. If the former view is convincing on empirical grounds, there is still a blind spot in its optimistic outlook on the world. Moreover, this blind spot would appear as cynicism to a victim of "unprovoked cruelty." The second form of denial touches on one's self-image as a human being. If a person is good by nature, he or she cannot be responsible for "unprovoked cruelty." Blame would rather fall on his or her parents and instructors, milieu, and society – thus acquitting him even of severe immoral action. The following dual strategy is more convincing. The question of whether a particular person is evil should be met with an attitude of strictest restraint. Contrary to the tendency constantly to subsume reprehensible action under the concept of aberrant behavior, which both minimizes guilt and levels out differences among singular cases, qualitative differences must be acknowledged. Two types of hyperbolization should be acknowledged: the radicalization of *action* from simple to grave to extreme aberrant behavior, and the radicalization of *motivation* from negligent to premeditated aberrant behavior to aberrant action that is willed as such.

A further difference deserves mentioning: Whoever forfeits the concept of evil tacitly sustains the danger of overestimating oneself, of human arrogance. Whoever believes that evil can be stamped out forever must confront Kant's accusation of zealotry [*Schwärmerei*]. Perhaps this zealotry already underlies the definition of evil as "unsurmounted inhumanity" (Oelmüller 1973), for it implies that evil might be completely surmounted in the future. This expectation, or even mere hope, is weakened by the possibility that lies in freedom itself of recognizing moral commands and still purposefully acting against them. The human being can develop moral action into a distinctive mark of character, virtue; however, he never achieves that holiness in an ontological sense that would make him an unwavering moral agent.

If human beings were aware of their natural propensity to evil, they would reckon with the possibility of its sudden appearance and thus would take precautionary measures against it. The initially moral-philosophical discourse about evil would, as a consequence, be supplemented by a pedagogical and legal-political discourse. Both national and international spheres fall within the purview of the legal-political dimension. Moreover, an extension of this sort would reach as far as Kant's criticism of Plato's principle of philosopher-kings (see section 8.2).

PART II

RIGHT AND MORALS

Ever since Antigone's resistance to Creon's prohibition against performing the rites of burial for her brother, and ever since the controversy over the essence of right and justice among Sophists and Platonists, that is, from the very outset of Occidental legal thought, philosophers have asked whether positive law is committed to general moral principles. These principles of legal morality have been articulated in theories of natural law or justice. The domain they belong to is taken to be "right and justice" or "right and morality." Kant above all relates justice to the judiciary: "The moral person that administers justice is a *court* (*forum*)" (VI 297, ll. 6f.; cf. 306, ll. 11–16). But he also suggests that justice is to be equated with the moral concept of right, or the opposite of what is wrong according to laws, in Latin "*iustus.*" He thus translates "*iniustus*" not only as "wrong" [*Unrecht*], but also as "injustice" [*Ungerechtigkeit*] (VI 229, l. 26 and 312, l. 23). Moreover, he develops the notion of natural law.

Morals not only designate the sum total of obligations actually in force among a group of persons, that is, positive morals, even if they are of legal relevance to stipulations such as "fidelity and faith" or "good morals." At issue here is rather the general and moral concept of morals. The question of how this concept relates to right and law may be divided into a vast array of partial and secondary questions that also refer to facets in the sphere of "right and (general) morals." Kant is one of the few philosophers who gives serious thought to virtually the entire spectrum of problems.

As a preliminary to the ethics of peace, this section does not elucidate the entire set of issues that remain relevant today. However, the scope of these issues is extended by Kant's theory (chapter 5) and they are considered in exemplary fashion by focusing on two perennial topics (chapters 6 and 7). Difficult questions thereby arise both for interpretations of Kant and with respect to independent substantial issues. For instance, how does the primarily thematic distinction between right and virtue or ethics relate to the primarily motivational difference between legality and morality (chapter 5)? Does Kant actually develop a moral concept of right, or is he committed to viewing right as the domain of laws of pure practical reason that are independent of moral law (chapter 6)? Finally, the question looms large as to whether right rests on foundations that, as inner duties of right, contradict the "essence" of right as external lawgiving for others: Can right at all be justified by factors immanent to right?

5

KANT'S MORE NUANCED APPROACH

5.1. Morality and Political Justice

Before turning to the relation between right and morals in the *Doctrine of Right*, Kant first devotes his attention to the pivotal preliminary quest for a *groundwork* of morals. Within the ambit of his famous assertion that only a good will can be considered good without limitation, he implicitly defines the moral good as the good without limitation. He then shows that the inquiry into what it means to be good is only completely and radically thought out by the notion of the good will. This radical inquiry is not per se limited to specific domains such as the personal sphere of individual decisions and actions or the maxims and attitudes that underlie them. It extends to the institutional and public sphere, namely, to law and government.

The terms "moral" or "morality" may be taken to mean the absolute good in general, without limitation to the personal or the institutional sphere (*Sittlichkeit*: Morals 1). "Moral" or "morality" may also refer to personal action in particular (Morals 2.1), whereas "politically (just)" or "political justice" (Morals 2.2) are attributed to a legal or state order. For the sake of comprehensiveness, conventional or positive morals are the sum total of norms actually in force (Morals 3).

The *Groundwork* extracts only one concept from this list for consideration, the personal sphere of morals or morality as action from duty. There is no separate investigation of institutional morality or of political justice. The moral will is the sole candidate under consideration that is justified as good without limitation; and as possible rivals, only (natural) personal characteristics are discussed, such as (1) natural gifts or intellectual and emotional capacities, including (1.1) mental talents, for instance, understanding, wit, and the power of judgment, (1.2) qualities

81

of temperament, such as courage, determination, and constancy;
(2) bestowments of fortune, for instance, power, wealth, honor, health,
and even happiness; and finally (3) qualities of character, such as temperance, self-control, and calm reflection. To the extent that this challenge to the absolute good is itself based on personal action, whichever
side prevails must belong to the domain of personal action.

This limited application of the meta-ethical criterion "absolute good"
is confirmed by further elements in the *Groundwork*. For instance, Kant
puts forward obligations only of persons, not of institutions, as examples
of morality. And they are discussed under the heading of the antithesis
between "in conformity with duty" and "from duty," which has a bearing
only for persons. (We shall have to examine whether this antithesis is
also meaningful for institutions, in particular for states: see section 9.3.)
Also related to persons are the notion of the maxim as the "subjective
principle of volition" (GMM IV 400) and the categorical imperative,
to the extent that it relates to maxims. Thus Kant's first main work
on ethics at least immediately lays the grounds not for all of practical
philosophy, but only for personal action, whereas law and government
are ignored.

The same thematic limitation can be ascertained in the *Critique of
Practical Reason*, since it seeks to find practical laws from the first paragraph onward and determines these laws not only as maxims but as
principles of a natural subject endowed with a will. Here, too, Kant is
concerned solely with the morality of a person and not also of a community.

Kant does not, however, attempt to justify this limited application
of morality. On the contrary, he extends its scope in the first section
of the *Metaphysics of Morals* to include the domain of right, namely,
its foundational concept and the principal areas of private and public
right. In sharp contrast to strict legal positivism, according to which the
content of law is arbitrary (e.g., Kelsen 1953, 153f.; and versions of "legal
positivism" in Hart 1961, chap. 5, and Luhmann 1993; for discussion,
see Höffe 1994, chaps. 5–6), Kant commits positive law to obligations
that he in some places describes as laws of freedom, in others as moral
laws (DR VI 214, ll. 13f.), laws of morality (216, ll. 7ff.), and "laws of pure
practical reason" (216, ll. 26f.). Right and politics are also grounded on
the moral law in the treatise on peace (VIII 372, ll. 1ff.), and – as we shall
see (chapter 6) – Kant brings to the fore three dimensions of "political
justice" that have been comprehensively discussed only by a miniscule
number of political philosophers today.

Kant considers the first dimension of political justice *en passant*, in comparing a merely "empirical doctrine of right" to the wooden head in Phaedrus's fable (DR VI 230, ll. 5f.). The ironic comment – "a head that may be beautiful but unfortunately it has no brain" – is directed against attempts to define right without any reference to moral legal principles. Put positively, it claims that morals or justice *define* rights. Kant is dealing with the foremost targets of the debate over "legal positivism or natural law," which later gained popularity and is still discussed by Hart (1961), Böckle and Böckenförde (1973), Finnis (1982) and Mayer-Maly and Simons (1983), whereas it is ignored in Rawls (1971) and Nozick (1974).

Kant subsequently turns to the second dimension of political justice, morals or justice that *legitimize* right. He shows that a positive legal order, in particular, its authorization to use coercion, must have a moral underpinning. The debate over philosophical anarchism serves as a backdrop to this argument, whereas it is ignored in recent political philosophy (including Rawls 1971 and Habermas 1994). Wolff (1970) and Taylor (1982) still challenge the legitimacy of all control over human beings, whereas Kant attempts to defend it.

Kant discusses the third dimension of a normative criterion in a similar fashion. Rawls famously determines this criterion with reference to Kant, whereas it is ignored by influential legal theorists, such as Niklas Luhmann (1981, 1987, and 1993). Here, with respect to morals or justice as a *norm* for right, moral principles are sought in order to provide a guideline for a legitimate positive legal order.

A fourth question concerning the continuation of justice as a norm for right and law deals with the more precise arrangement of a legal order. Contrary to contemporary theories of law and justice, Kant does not limit normative justice to the topic of human rights. He also legitimizes the institution of property, discusses marriage and family, and elucidates criminal punishment as the institution of most far-reaching public authorized enforcement.

As a fifth and final point, Kant raises questions concerning legal obedience, civil disobedience, and the right of resistance, which have been regained in discussions after a long period of silence (cf. Bedau 1969; Isensee 1969; Kleger 1993; and Zancarini 1999; also Höffe 1981). Is there a moral obligation to obey the regulations and prohibitions of a positive legal order? Can the disobedience of individual legal norms or resistance to the entire legal order in exceptional cases be morally permitted or even become a moral duty?

5.2. Morality as an Improvement on Legality

Kant's distinction between legality and morality is of particular significance to the debate on right and morals. Four aspects should be brought
to the attention of contemporary systematic ethical theory.

First, the meta-ethical criterion of the absolute good and its relation
to the agent through the good will are not comprehensive. An anthropological element enters Kant's theory with the intermediate concept
of duty: The good will, subject to competing impulses from natural
inclinations, acts "under certain subjective limitations and hindrances"
(GMM IV 397). This is not the case with pure intellects such as God
(cf. CPrR V 72 and 82), but applies only to rational *natural* beings
(DV VI 379), such as human beings. Whenever the *Groundwork* operates with the concept of duty, it pursues the aim of grasping the human
being as a moral being and for this purpose assumes the basic anthropological fact that human desires are not necessarily good. This might
seem to contradict the "Preface," which disregards practical anthropology altogether as an empirical section of ethics (IV 387f.). But the
anthropological fact does not impinge on the "grounds of an obligation"; it merely accounts for the mode of morals specific to the human
being namely, their normative character. It does not concern the particularities of one biological species, but rather refers to features of every
kind of impure being of reason.

An anthropological element also enters the moral concept of law (see
section 6.3). Finally, Kant's criticism of Plato's principle of philosopher-
kings contains an anthropological argument (see section 8.2), but it
again is not taken from empirical anthropology, which is dismissed as
irrelevant to ethics.

Second, mere conformity with duty, referred to as "legality" from the
second *Critique* onward (V 71f., 81, 118, and 151), has gradations of
intensity. Hence it does not fulfill the criterion of the good without
limitation, as does action "from duty." Unlike action that conforms with
duty but arises from "selfish intentions," moral action comprehensively
attains a full-fledged moral dimension.

With reference to Kant, McDowell considers action purely from duty
absurd (1998, 77ff.). The notion of duty is not suitable for explaining
action and a fortiori cannot sufficiently explain it. Action results not
from a general ought, but only from a specific, situational reflection that
is *supported* but not constituted by "overall moral verdicts." McDowell's
assumption, if correct, not only jeopardizes Kant's conception of moral

reason as a pure practical reason but calls into doubt the very idea of practical reason. Practical reason, namely, is the faculty of setting aside agreeable and disagreeable feelings and instead acting according to principles, which include not only moral, but also technical and pragmatic laws (GMM IV 412f.; see section 2.4). According to Kant, all rationality applies to principles, but these are second-order rules that combine a normative determination with an openness toward reflection on particular relevant situations (see chapter 3). Even if good reasons speak against the assumption that rules are constitutive elements of rationality, this cannot be used to criticize Kant's thinking on morality. It is not the difference between the "situational" and the "general," but rather that between empirically conditioned reasons and those that are universal independently of experience that is relevant to his theory (see section 3.2). One's own needs and interests are decisive in the former case, whereas they are set aside as grounds for decision in the latter case. Situational reflections may also yield to universal reasons.

Third, Kant's distinction between legality and morality brings to light a neglected aspect from the general problem of "right and morals": There are not only two groups of moral obligations, the legal morals (owed to one another) discussed in the *Doctrine of Right* and the merited obligations from the *Doctrine of Virtue*. One must also differentiate two kinds of internal relations with respect to one and the same obligation, whereby the moral relation in a full sense or morality cannot be gleaned from the action alone. All ethical theories that attempt to conceive morality in terms of duties, norms, and values, or in line with recent theories, as rules for solving conflicts of preference, thus present not only a fragmentary moral philosophy, but rather, according to Kant's rigid concept, no *moral* philosophy at all. They do not offer any theory of the absolute good in relation to the agent. Whether one considers the more dated ethics of value in Max Scheler (1916) and Nicolai Hartmann (1926), the different versions of utilitarianism or the Erlangen model of future conflict management (Lorenzen and Schwemmer 1973), the contemporary principle of universalization (e.g., Habermas 1983), or behaviorist and sociological theories (e.g., Durkheim 1967; Bischof 1978; and Luhmann 1978) – all are at most theories of the conformity of action with duty: theories of legal, but not also of moral practical activity. This may also be true of recent constructivism in John Rawls (1993) and his independent followers Herman (1990a and 1993), Korsgaard (1996a), and 1996b, and O'Neill (1996; see Kain 1999).

Fourth, criticism of this sort is countered by the view that Kant's theory of morality, as a mere ethics of conviction, promotes a world of passive introspection. This implies a turn to the private individual that is dangerous for two reasons: First, subjective conscience lacks any objective standard of measure. Second, there would be no reason to express one's individual moral conscience in the real world. However, this objection rests on a twofold misunderstanding:

On the one hand, according to Kant, willing consists not in a mere wish, but in the summoning of all means insofar as they are in our control (GMM IV 394). The will is thus not above and beyond reality, but rather the ultimate determining cause of action. To be sure, the expression of the will in action may nevertheless fall short of what is willed due to physical, psychological, intellectual, and economic deficiencies. For instance, help may be too little or come too late despite supreme efforts. But finite beings of reason can never escape this danger. Their doings and omissions occur in contexts that depend on natural and social conditions. The agent's will does not alone determine this context and cannot even grasp the context in its entirety. Because personal morality relates only to the sphere of an agent's responsibility and to what lies in his or her power, observable success, as the bare result of an action, cannot serve as a rule of measurement. Any alternative to a "mere ethics of conviction" that takes actual success to be the criterion for morality is thus fundamentally inhumane. Misjudging the *conditio humana*, it makes people responsible for conditions they cannot completely determine.

On the other hand, legality is not an alternative to morality but instead its necessary precondition. Contrary to the conventional interpretation supported by Max Weber's division between an ethics of conviction and an ethics of responsibility (1971, 551–559), Kant's distinction between morality and legality does not separate two mutually exclusive ethical stances. Morality does not compete with legality but instead has more strict demands. An action *from* duty is *first* an action in conformity with duty and *second* makes the fulfillment of this duty a determining ground for the action. Morality is not a rival of legality but instead radicalizes and surpasses legality; *mere* legality is for Kant no more than a contrastive concept that highlights the essence of actual morals or morality. Moreover, Kant proposes an objective criterion for morality, the universalizability of rules, which, as maxims, must constitute the necessary determining ground of action.

5.3. Juridical and Ethical Legality

The Kantian concepts of legality and morality do not correspond to the customary understanding of the antithesis between right and morals if these are taken to designate different groups of obligations. They would then denote two different objective laws and would differ referentially or objectively. Kant, on the contrary, is concerned with two ways of subjectively relating to law, in some cases even to the same law; that is, he is concerned with a motivational or subjective difference. His awareness of both objective and subjective distinctions once again demonstrates his sensitivity to a vast range of issues. However, difficult problems of interpretation arise with regard to the relation between them. These have led Willaschek (1997) to call them two conflicting perspectives, an "official" and an "alternative perspective," and to conclude that the *Doctrine of Right* does not belong within the *Metaphysics of Morals* (226). Can cutting the Gordian knot in this way resolve the difficulties?

In the "Division of a Metaphysics of Morals," Kant distinguishes between lawgiving that is juridical or "rightful" [*rechtlich*] and lawgiving that is ethical. The *Metaphysic of Morals* thus comprises two parts, the *Doctrine of Right* and the *Doctrine of Virtue*. Kant also discusses duties in accordance with juridical lawgiving, in short, duties of right, along with duties in accordance with ethical lawgiving or duties of virtue. Whereas "in ancient times" ethics signified the entire doctrine of morals and thus comprised all duties, it seems better to reserve the name for one part of moral philosophy and to identify "ethics" with the "doctrine of virtue" (DV VI 379).

A relatively simple complication lies in the fact that duties of right constitute a component area of ethical duties, despite the opposition between juridical and ethical lawgiving. On the one hand, namely, "duties in accordance with rightful lawgiving can be only external duties, since this lawgiving does not require that the idea of this duty, which is internal, itself be the determining ground of the agent's choice; and since it still needs an incentive suited to the law, it can connect only external incentives with it" (DR VI 219). On the other hand, all juridical duties also belong to the domain of ethical duties, which is why one must distinguish those ethical duties that are *solely* of an ethical nature from those that are *also* duties of right. The former "straightforwardly ethical" duties correspond to duties of virtue, whereas the latter duties of right are only "indirectly ethical" duties (VI 221).

Astonishingly, Willaschek views the motivational difference between legality and morality as an alternative to the thematic difference between duties of right and duties of virtue, although it would appear that both pairs should be combined, yielding four possibilities: (1) duties of right may be fulfilled in conformity with duty (juridical legality) or (2) "from duty" (juridical morality); likewise (3) duties of virtue may be fulfilled in conformity with duty (ethical legality) or (4) "from duty" (ethical morality). Kant does not explicitly present these possibilities anywhere. However, they are already implicitly present in the *Groundwork*. Examples there anticipate the systematic division in the *Metaphysics of Morals*: A duty of right is exemplified by the prohibition against false promises (cf. DR VI 220). Three classes of duties of virtue are illustrated by other examples: A perfect duty toward oneself is manifested by the duty to stay alive, an imperfect duty toward others by the duty of beneficence, and an imperfect duty toward oneself by the duty to cultivate one's talents or by the indirect duty of securing one's happiness. In all four cases, the elucidation of the examples proceeds foremost along the lines of the alternative "in conformity with duty" (for legality) and "from duty" (for morality: GMM IV 397–399).

Since the *Critique of Practical Reason* bestows less importance on examples, its supporting arguments are less prominent. The chapter "On the Incentives of Pure Practical Reason," which is a central passage on the antithesis of morality and legality, is concerned primarily with morality, whereas its central concept, respect for the moral law, is developed separately. Nevertheless, Kant emphatically ("it is of the greatest importance") demands respect for the law "in all moral appraisals" (CPrR V 81; cf. on the CPrR as a whole, Höffe 2002b). Thus it is self-evident that the morality-legality antithesis is valid for all duties, for both those of right and those of virtue. This is at least attested for duties of virtue by Kant's casual glance at the third example from the *Groundwork* – "to be beneficent" (GMM IV 398) or, here, "benevolence" (CPrR V 82). Kant here reflects on action in conformity with duty but resulting only from inclination – doing "good to human beings from love for them and from sympathetic benevolence" – and emphatically opposes it to "the genuine moral maxim," the "respect for this law." He thus, in effect, distinguishes ethical legality from ethical morality; and in his reflection no. 6,764, he explicitly says: "[L]egality is either juridical or ethical" (XIX 154).

This interpretation, however, is put to the test by the following remark in the "Introduction to the Metaphysics of Morals": Ethics that accounts for the duties of benevolence is a lawgiving that "can be only internal" (DR VI 220). Accordingly, benevolence and all other duties of virtue are not conceivable as purely external constraints. The legal order, as an authority of external coercion, can in fact enforce actions for the welfare of other human beings. But this concerns taxes or other dues, that is, rightful duties or even duties of (positive) law, and precisely not what is meant by benevolence: a voluntary and supplementary performance.

On the other hand, it cannot be denied that morality is to be equated with what is "only internal." It follows that Kant apparently acknowledges only the morality of benevolence and of other duties that belong to ethics, while excluding the possibility of mere legality in conformity with them. However, this is called into question, at least for substantial reasons, by the possibility presented in the *Groundwork* of beneficence from grounds other than duty, such as from the "inclination to honor" (IV 398). One's will to refrain from suicide, even when adversity and hopeless grief "have quite taken away the taste for life" (GMM IV 398), likewise does not need to arise from respect for the moral law. It can also be motivated by fear, such as the prospect of punishment in the hereafter or of defamation in this life. Finally, the "development and increase of one's natural perfection" or even the "increase of one's moral perfection" may result from nonmoral motives, such as the prospect of furthering one's career, obtaining respect, or aggrandizing oneself. According to Kant, it cannot ever be inferred "with certainty that no covert impulse of self-love . . . was not actually the real determining cause of the will" (GMM IV 407).

This skepticism about the availability of unquestionable examples of morality is reaffirmed in several passages (CPrR V 84; *Religion* VI 36; DV VI 392). There is thus no reason to suppose that Kant abandons his position on the four possibilities between the *Groundwork* and the *Metaphysics of Morals*. He nevertheless calls lawgiving "ethical" that "makes an action a duty and also makes this duty the incentive" (VI 219). Since Kant "also" includes morality here, he seems to contradict both his reflection no. 6,764 and the real moral experience of beneficence that follows from motives merely in conformity with duty and not invariably from duty. Does he thus acknowledge only ethical morality and not ethical legality in the "Division of a Metaphysics of Morals"?

Before ascribing such a grave contradiction to Kant, it would be better to reconsider our interpretation. First, we have so far left out a distinction that should be made explicit: Bene*ficence* is not the same as bene*volence*. Acts of bene*ficence* can result not merely from duty, but

also from other motives. Bene*volence*, on the contrary, is a quality of volition and occurs only when one does not merely conform to the duty of
doing good for other human beings, but also performs the good deed
from the act of willing their well-being: "[B]enevolence is satisfaction
in the happiness (well-being) of others" (DV §29: VI 452). If volition
and pleasure coincide, actions are performed *eo ipso* "from duty." Kant
analogously defines gratitude not by the actions ensuing from it, since
these may have motives other than duty. One might want to prevent
losing one's benefactor in the future or act from fear of defamation, or
one might be too proud to accept one's benefactor's good deeds without offering gratitude in return. Kant's definition, by way of contrast,
refers to the underlying will and determines it *eo ipso* as a good will. Gratitude consists not in "love toward a benefactor on the part of someone
he has put under obligation," but rather in *"respect* for him" (DR §35:
VI 458).

Apparently, ethical lawgiving is not already satisfied by action in conformity with duty such as beneficence and the expression of gratitude.
It extends to the underlying will itself, to benevolence or gratitude
defined as respect. On this assumption, however, there can only be ethical morality. But if one regards the actions alone, one may also ascertain
ethical legality. In the "Introduction to the Metaphysics of Morals," Kant
omits this perspective and for this reason alone does not entertain the
possibility of ethical legality. Interpretive problems thus arise not from
a contradiction between an "official" and an "alternative reading" but
from the nonappearance of an option that is nevertheless congruent
with the concepts introduced. Kant thus does not rule out the fulfillment of duties of virtue that is merely in conformity with duty, which
may be called "ethical legality."

An additional problem is raised by the duties toward oneself in the
first part of the doctrine of the elements of ethics, for they share essential features inherent in the concept of duties of right. The actions considered – "killing oneself," "defiling oneself by lust," and "stupefying
oneself," along with lying – are prohibited without exception, and thus
are narrow and perfect duties. Moreover, these are external, not internal actions. The only element that is indispensable to right but missing
in duties toward oneself is the social perspective on mutual relations
with others. They thus present a special class of duties, "mixed duties,"
as it were. They are both duties of right, since they are perfect duties
with regard to external actions, and duties of virtue, since they concern
one's relation to oneself. Seen from the standpoint of the ultimate

end of promoting one's own perfection, however, the duties lose their mixed character, and the same then holds for them as for benevolence: One's own perfection as a whole depends on inner, not external actions. Moreover, self-perfection is an imperfect duty, for there are gradations of its fulfillment. Whereas single predispositions may be developed to greater perfection, this is not the case in the collective: In their entirety, they cannot all reach the distributive perfection attained by single dispositions. Finally, due to the human being's enduring propensity to evil (see above chapter 4), the "cultivation of his *will* up to the purest virtuous disposition" (DR VI 387) is a command, but only for perpetual progress. Virtue itself is an ideal and unattainable (VI 409). Finally, one's own perfection is an end, but "I can never be constrained by others to *have* [it]" (VI 381).

5.4. Against an Ethics of Private Conviction and Moralizing

The first group of duties of virtue leads to a further, henceforth systematic difficulty: The conception of duties toward oneself is in conflict with our understanding of morals today. Ever since utilitarianism, up to Baier's rehabilitation of the moral standpoint (1965, 106ff.), and from Rawls (1971) through Apel (1973) and Habermas (1983) to Tugendhat (1984), morals have been defined exclusively as a social obligation. Kant also does not take duties toward oneself for granted, but asks whether the concept involves a contradiction, since the person imposing obligation [*auctor obligationis*] could always release the one put under obligation [*subiectum obligationis*] from the obligation [*terminus obligationis*] (DV VI 417f.). Kant resolves the apparent contradiction by distinguishing between the human being as a rational natural being, a *homo phaenomenos*, and as a being endowed with inner freedom, a *homo noumenos* (418; here, a two-world theory emerges that today is considered obsolete).

With regard to the relation between morals and right, it can be left open whether the contemporary rejection of duties toward oneself is more convincing than Kant's recognition of these duties. Of decisive importance is rather the assignment of these duties – if they indeed exist – to the sphere of morals in a narrow sense, not to the broader sphere including (moral) right. Because a duty to one's own perfection is a moral, not a legal task, a legal order cannot enforce the self-perfection of its citizens. Whoever violates the moral duty to one's own perfection may not be prosecuted.

On the one hand, with respect to the human being as an animal, Kant includes the prohibitions against killing oneself, defiling oneself by lust, and stupefying oneself among the duties toward oneself. On the other hand, with respect to the human being as a moral being, duties toward oneself comprise the prohibition of lying in the sense of deliberate untruthfulness even when the rights of others are not violated, the prohibition of avarice (here in the sense not of greed or niggardliness but of "restricting one's own enjoyment of the means to good living so narrowly as to leave one's own true needs unsatisfied": DR VI 432), and the prohibition of servility (understood here as "waiving any claim to moral worth in oneself," not as humility, i.e., the "feeling of the insignificance of one's moral worth in comparison with the law": VI 435). Kant also includes here the command of moral self-knowledge and that of developing one's (intellectual, emotional, and physical) talents.

In accordance with Kant's criticism of an unacceptable moralizing of right, these commands and prohibitions are all excluded from the sphere of right. For this reason he criticized contemporary jurists who wanted to make the preservation of one's own body a duty of right (cf. *A Lecture on Ethics*, 196). In opposition to the prosecution of suicide attempts, which was prevalent in Great Britain even up to the Second World War, suicide or suicide attempts, including excessive consumption of alcohol, nicotine, or drugs, are morally reprehensible, yet not unjust and thus not admissible as a matter for penal law. This is analogously true for duties of virtue toward others and thus for duties of love, which comprise the duties of beneficence, gratitude, and sympathy (sympathetic joy and sadness), along with the respective prohibitions against envy, ingratitude, and malice. The duty to respect other human beings or the prohibitions of arrogance, defamation (not slander, which is already legally prohibited), and ridicule likewise may not be prosecuted.

Let us take stock of our findings in both legal theory and legal politics. Since a legal state order can exist only to the extent that and for the very reason that morality does not everywhere rule mankind, the legal order is at once separated from morality and yet is a moral extension of an order determined by morality. Since the extension is by all means moral in nature (see chapter 6), that version of legal positivism is untenable that, ever since Austin (1832), defines right solely in terms of positive law, state authority, and empirical reality. On the other hand, due to its severance from morality, the extension of a legal order has to do not with the structure of the subjective faculty of desire, but only with the free power of choice from a social perspective. Contrary to an inadmissible ethical usurpation of the philosophy of law and an equally inadmissible moralizing of positive law, the legal order may not by any means assume a moral perspective from which to determine personal morality and its principle, the autonomy of the will. Since an order of relations between agents' powers of choice that fulfils the criterion of morals or universal lawfulness [*Gesetzlichkeit*] is, as it were, posited by the general or communal will [*volonté générale*], one may also speak of autonomy in the sphere of right. Autonomy in this sense does not qualify a subjective faculty of desire, but rather the objective order of relations among powers of choice – in other words, it qualifies the general, not the individual will.

6

THE MORAL CONCEPT OF RIGHT
AND LAW

In the "Introduction to the Doctrine of Right," Kant unfolds a multi-layered program that is in all of its components both compelling and irritating. He (1) mentions the subject of investigation, the natural doctrine of right, and (2) determines its status in right and in legal theory (section A). He (3) develops the moral concept of right (section B), presents its criterion, a general principle of right (section C), (4) justifies the objectionable authorization to use coercion (sections D–E), and (5) opposes the strict meaning of right to two equivocal concepts of right, equity and the right of necessity (*Notrecht*; both in the "Appendix").

The moral concept of right is compelling from the perspective of a natural doctrine of right, but its identification with invariant natural law is irritating (section 6.1). The priority of the moral concept over the positive concept of right is likewise compelling, but it is even more irritating that merely the moral concept or natural law has a scientific character (section 6.2). It is convincing that Kant subsumes the entire domain of right under a single principle, a categorical imperative (of right), but problematic that he denies any reference to maxims, although they are constitutive elements of the "familiar" categorical imperative. And the metaphysical claim made in the title of the entire work is virtually obsolete (sections 6.3 and 6.5; section 6.4 digresses in an "Excursus: The Welfare State"). Kant's endeavor to legitimize the authorization to use coercion is compelling, but his understanding of this task as an analytic one is problematic (section 6.6). With respect to equity and the right of necessity, it is interesting that they are investigated at all, but problematic that they are banned from the domain of right in a strict sense (section 6.7).

Under these circumstances, the question becomes pressing as to whether the irritating aspects of the theory can be extracted or whether they are inseparably bound to its compelling features. Can we rehabilitate Kant's vindication of right by reducing it to those components that are still advocated today, or must we reject the "whole package" altogether?

6.1. A Rehabilitation of Natural Law

We may easily get rid of the irritation arising from identifying the moral concept of right with natural law (see section 1.2). Kant sharply opposes positive law to natural law, as was customary at his time, and deals only with the latter. But he leaves aside three conceptions of natural law that are dubious, and rightly so: the justification of right by a given world order ("cosmological natural law"), by divine command ("theological natural law"), and by the essence of the human being ("anthropological natural law"). Because the natural component of natural law does not correspond to "nature" in the familiar dualism "nature or freedom," Kant avoids the is/ought fallacy. Grounded in "mere reason" (*Religion* VI 230) and knowable "a priori through reason" (VI 224, l. 30; cf. 247, ll. 15f.), natural law is not a contrastive concept to freedom, but rather one of its very aspects; it corresponds to pure (rightful: [*rechtlich*]) practical reason.

As a law of reason, natural law does not answer the *quaestio facti*, the positive question about the scope of law, but rather solely the *quaestio iuris*, the moral question of justification: the question of right and wrong in the sense of basic justice and injustice. For Kant, the expression of "natural law" that is obsolete today is equivalent to the task of a legal ethics that is still relevant. It is also unproblematic that Kant begins with the most general criterion by which "one could recognize right as well as wrong [*iustum et iniustum*]" (VI 229, ll. 25f.). Kant later reduces the scope of inquiry to more general principles, is reticent about middle principles, and does not even consider individual determinations. He thereby allays fears that a detailed account of a legal order might be derivable from natural law. Instead, Kant acknowledges differences in individual determinations of right that are national ("what the laws in some country [prescribe]"), geographic ("at a certain place"), and historical ("at a certain time") (VI 229, ll. 20–24).

Furthermore, no problem is posed by the contrast Kant draws between his theory, on the one hand, and both "dogmatic" theories of natural law and their adversary, "dogmatic" legal positivism, on the other hand. He does not concede exclusivity to either the positive or suprapositive notions of right. However, he questions their comparative status and answers with a clear rule of priority. At first glance, this would even provoke the positive jurist: Kant asserts that positive lawgiving should comply with natural lawgiving, and not vice versa, for, "like the wooden head in Phaedrus's fable, a merely empirical doctrine of right is a head that may be beautiful but unfortunately it has no brain" (VI 230).

The criticism implied by this image is exceptionally severe. A head without a brain is only a head in an equivocal sense, but in a literal sense not a head at all. Kant fully denies an empirical doctrine of right the status of a doctrine of right. He does not dispute that "there can be an external lawgiving" that contains "only positive laws"; "but then a natural law would still have to precede it, which would establish the authority of the lawgiver (i.e., his authorization to bind others by his mere *choice*)" (224, ll. 33ff.). Otherwise, the rule of law would only be apparent, as in the case of Phaedrus's head, but in truth all would be ruled by brute force. This speaks against Habermas's thesis (1994, 153) that Kant's "subordination of right under morals" (not morality!) is "incompatible with the autonomy realized in the medium of right itself." Kant's subordination is in fact a minimal condition placed on all right, namely, the prohibition of naked force. It also demonstrates the first instance of justice that *defines* right: Without a minimal element of justice, right cannot be defined *as* right.

Ever since early modernity, Kant's expression "empirical doctrine of right" has been interpreted with a view to positive juridical science. It has been a common assumption that Kant renders the empirical doctrine "blatantly" brainless and harshly criticizes positive juridical science ("Rezension von Kants Rechtslehre" 1797, 306). This reading rests on a misunderstanding. The expression "doctrine of right" designates not the (scientific) investigation of right, but its subject matter, right itself, insofar as it is embedded in a system. "Doctrine" [*Doktrin*], namely, also means the "entire content of a lesson, that which is coherently taught in a specific branch of knowledge" (Grimm 1854/1984, vol. 12, p. 554). As reinforced by the Latin appendage "*ius*" (line 6), the "doctrine of right" is for Kant the sum of specific laws (VI 229, l. 5). Likewise, the doctrine of natural law is not called the science of natural law, *doctrina iuris naturae*, but is natural law itself, *ius naturae* (line 13f.). And an "empirical doctrine of right" designates (merely) positive laws.

Kant is here taking aim at any system of positive law that repudiates moral principles, that is, not at partial, but thoroughly amoral right. He claims that this is not 'right' in a proper sense. It is comparable to "right without right"; as a *ius* without *iustum*, it is an obligation that lacks the minimal component of (juridical or political) justice, a constitutive moral requirement of right. Kant thereby reminds jurists that they are committed to laws that change according to the precepts of a lawgiver. The lawgiver, in turn, must submit his laws to moral principles of right.

Of merely secondary concern to Kant are legal *theories* that detach positive law from all moral commitments. These include overtly positivistic legal theories such as those proposed by Kelsen (1960) or even Lundstedt (1947), and covertly positivistic theories such as the one implied by Luhmann's claim that law is self-regulating (e.g., 1993, chap. 2). A legal system that neglects all queries about what is right and wrong due to its fixation on proceedings and the power governing them is, for Kant, "brainless." The definition of right articulated by the predecessor to sociological jurisprudence, Rudolf von Jhering, may be positivistic – though perhaps *à contre-coeur*: "[R]ight is the sum of all norms of coercion in force in a state" (1877/1893, I 320; for a systematic discussion of legal positivism, see Höffe 1994, Part I).

6.2. Is Natural Law Alone Scientific?

Kant's theory of natural law is the source of a further irritation related no longer to the legitimation of right but to the theory of scientific knowledge. He first introduces an instructive distinction among four kinds of increasing legal competence that have to do with an increase not in material resources but in self-moderated legal conduct. At the first two stages, legal competence consists in merely technical knowledge, that is, a juristic familiarity with means and ends. (1) Whoever is aware only of (invariably external) laws, is a jurist [*iurisconsultus*]; (2) if he also knows how to apply them to cases, he is experienced in the law [*iurisperitus*]. (3) The ascent ("also knows them ... ") to legal prudence or expertise [*iurisprudentia*] concerns well-being, since according to the *Groundwork* (IV 416f.) it is incumbent on prudence to give advice about the choice of means to well-being as a given end. One who has legal expertise is capable of employing legal knowledge in the service of well-being, whether it be one's own well-being or that of those who seek legal advice.

It is problematic, let alone curious, that Kant identifies the highest epistemic level, (4) juridical science [*iurisscientia*], with the "systematic knowledge of the doctrine of natural law" or natural law itself (DR VI 229, l. 13), despite its serious epistemic deficit of a lack in legal experience and prudence ("without both together"). The addendum "mere" juridical science does indicate that it is in some way connected to legal experience and prudence, but the connection is contingent.

The doctrine of right is divided as follows according to section A:

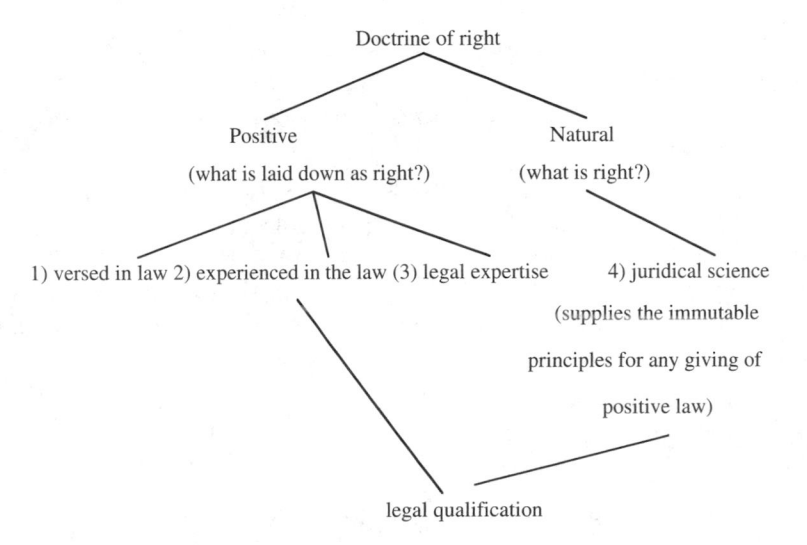

This division is not solely intended as a systematic order of right, but also contains three claims that elucidate the title of the entire work and its characteristic epistemic claim.

For one thing, Kant raises the status of philosophy by granting it alone the honorific title of a science; it investigates prepositive and general natural laws. One might detect in this claim a typical philosophical prejudice that has long since been overridden by the history of science. Positive right has been established as an unquestionably scientific domain, but the scientific status of natural law is considered dubious. Kant does not jeopardize what is today called juridical science. But he does have a demanding definition of science as systematic knowledge from principles (cf. DR VI 229, ll. 13 and 15; see also CPR B 86off.; and Höffe 1998), which no doubt exceeds the notion implied by a common juridical science. The *General Doctrine of Right* may be thought to be a science, but it is ruled out due to Kant's rigid concept of principles. If "principles" were understood merely in the broad and comparative sense as "universal propositions in general," even a positive juridical science could fulfill Kant's scientific ideal. According to the rigid definition of "principles absolutely," however, principles are "synthetic cognitions from concepts," which "understanding" – or in this case, legal understanding – "cannot yield" (CPR B 357f.).

The *Critique* (B 359) continues with the following statement: "It is an ancient wish – who knows how long it will take until perhaps it is fulfilled – that in place of the endless manifold of civil laws (in the sense of public right, O.H.), their principles may be sought out; for in this alone can consist the secret, as one says, of simplifying legislation." Kant's philosophy of law exemplifies conceptual simplification in this philosophical sense. Two fundamentally different reflections thus lead him to infer the superlative status of natural law in the domain of right. Supreme knowledge as it is presented in section A in a normative sense, that is, knowledge of the immutable precepts for all positive law-giving, coincides with supreme knowledge according to the *Critique,* or synthetic cognition from concepts.

According to the second claim implied by Kant's division of the doctrine of right, one could also understand the purpose of juridical science as a descriptive one. It would then extrapolate the principles of right in general, in the same way this is done by Hans Kelsen in the *Pure Theory of Law* (1960). Although Kelsen is a neo-Kantian, his principles are not "immutable" in the Kantian sense. For they lack the (synthetic) a priori quality that in turn distinguishes metaphysics. In substance, then, section A elucidates the provocative title of Kant's work. As a theory of moral commitments of right or as a legal ethics, juridical science is a metaphysics of right.

Whereas Kant raises his stakes with these first two claims, the third thesis in section A is a plea for modesty: Juridical science in a strict sense lacks both legal experience and prudence. Because they cannot be expected of philosophy, however, this indication suggests that Kant does not consider knowledge an end in itself in the domain of right. A genuine practical philosophy in Aristotle's sense (see above section 2.1) would put natural or moral right in the service of "cases that come up in experience" and finally of well-being, as implied by legal expertise or prudence. But it must remain committed to principles of natural law. As a mere science of principles, strict juridical science is thus not receptive to the supreme purpose of a philosophy of law, that is, the application of its insights to reality. Whereas the application of justice to cases here and now falls under the competence of public powers or the administration of justice and alone legitimizes identifying justice with the judicial system, the philosopher is only partly responsible for the public use of reason (cf. "What is enlightenment?" VIII 379, and *Peace*, Second Supplement and Appendix).

Two fundamentally different ways to apply law must still be distinguished, although they are not elaborated in Kant's highly condensed remarks. Whereas the jurist (lawyer or judge) applies given laws of positive right to concrete cases, the lawgiver should apply the "immutable principles" of natural law in such a way that morally legitimate positive laws emerge. Application in both cases is remote from a mechanical subsumption and evidently requires a creative, methodically complex process of appraisal (see sections 3.3 and 3.4).

6.3. An a Priori Construction

According to the second immodest claim, already stated in the title of Kant's work, the moral concept of right as a criterion of right and wrong must be of a metaphysical nature. As a foundational principle of science, it must be synthetic and a priori. The criterion is composed of two methodically different elements, "obligation" and the matter of obligation (VI 230, l. 8), whereby the criterion for applying obligation is to be understood as a legal task. Must both elements be of a metaphysical nature?

A positive answer seems obvious for the former element, at least on Kantian premises: Obligation, defined as "the necessity of a free action under a categorical imperative of reason" (VI 222, ll. 3f.), is a moral concept. Since it is not mingled with empirical motives, it belongs to a practical metaphysics. It commands for everyone "without taking account of his inclinations" (216, ll. 7f.). Because this is already familiar from the *Groundwork* and from the second *Critique*, and taken up again in the "Preliminary Concepts," Kant turns to the other, descriptive legal task in the second relevant paragraph of section B. But instead of arguing that it, too, is metaphysical, he simply states what the legal task is. Later, the method it rests on is determined as construction (section E), although not in the sense of contemporary constructivism in ethics.

According to the broad concept of construction in Rawls's *Theory of Justice* (e.g., sec. 7), construction is understood as any procedure that, unlike intuitionism, permits the resolution of concrete moral problems. Rawls famously specifies this general, but vague method as distinctive of his own version of contract theory. But after dismissing contractualism in later articles and in his second major work, *Political Liberalism* (esp. lecture 3), he begins to use the word "constructive" to mean any procedural interpretation of Kant's analysis of justice that discards transcendental idealism. Constructivism in ethics thus should do without Kant's metaphysics of the two-world theory, but also should not, like empiricism, search for principles in the (natural) world.

O'Neill (1996, chap. 2, cf. chap. 6 and 1989, chap. 11) endorses Rawls's project. Although she criticizes his execution of it as overly ambitious and forgoes his idealizations of the agent and of the conditions of action, she holds on to constructivism as a procedural interpretation.

Kant, by way of contrast, ever since the *Critique* adheres to a methodically more demanding concept of construction, but it is more limited in scope. He calls all rational cognition that arises "from concepts" philosophical, and cognition "from the construction of concepts" mathematical (B 865, cf. B 741). To construct a concept means for Kant "to exhibit a priori the intuition corresponding to it" (B 741). Thus philosophy is a "discursive use of reason," whereas mathematical construction is "intuitive" (B 747; cf. B 750 and MFS IV 469). Since morality is a genuinely philosophical topic for Kant, it cannot result from construction. He nevertheless speaks of "construction" with regard to the moral concept of right and thus seems to contravene his own concept of philosophy. In the "Introduction to the Doctrine of Right," construction refers not to the moral concept of right as a whole, but only to a part, namely, the legal task not of a moral but of a descriptive nature. Mathematics or, more specifically, Newton's theoretical mechanics as a mathematical physics, and not geometry, serves as a model exclusively for this legal task.

For Kant, the legal task arises from the concept of right as the "sum of those laws for which an external lawgiving is possible" (DR VI 229, ll. 5f.). The concept thus seems to analytically contain an answer to which necessary and sufficient conditions enable external lawgiving. In fact, this is precisely the question answered by the legal task. However, fulfilling the legal task depends on creative reflection, and this is "as it were, the construction" of a concept, namely, "the presentation of it in pure intuition a priori" (section E: VI 232, ll. 32f.). This kind of construction – or more precisely, due to the "as it were," quasi-construction – is for Kant not an analytical but a synthetic performance. Moreover, since it is performed independently of all experience, it turns out to be synthetic a priori and a component of a quasi-mathematical theoretical metaphysics. The concept of right is thus composed of

two different, yet equally metaphysical parts: a genuine practical metaphysics or moral obligation and an a priori construction that extends
to the domain of theoretical metaphysics.

Since the construction of external lawgiving concerns human beings,
it belongs to anthropology and extends the anthropological portion of
Kant's moral philosophy (see section 5.2). The anthropology of right
at issue here is different from that "moral" or didactic anthropology
that "deal[s] only with the subjective conditions in human nature that
hinder people or help them in fulfilling the laws," along with other
"similar teachings and precepts based on experience" (VI 217, ll. 10–
16), which Kant adamantly ousted from moral philosophy. It likewise
differs from anthropology from a physiological point of view, or "the
investigation of what Nature makes of man," and from anthropology from a practical point of view, which aims at what man "makes,
can, or should make of himself as a freely acting being" (*Anthropology*
VII 119).

The anthropology practiced in the *Doctrine of Right*, like the anthropological assumptions of the concept of duty, designate a fourth version of
anthropology that is often ignored, since it is not among Kant's explicit
concepts of anthropology. In the foundational anthropology of right,
the question of why right is at all needed, given the *conditio humana,*
is answered not by a list of distinctive species properties, but rather by
characteristics that pertain to several species. These shared characteristics are as follows: Right is needed among (1) persons held responsible
for their actions (imputable persons) who (2) share the same world, (3)
mutually influence each other, and thereby are (4) rational, contrary
to subhuman beings, but, unlike pure rational beings, are not necessarily determined by reason. If such beings exist in another world,
they are equally subject to Kant's conditions of the application of right,
even if they are not themselves members of the biological species *Homo
sapiens.*

The anthropology of right follows a procedure that, as Kant explains
(VI 205, ll. 5f.), is a counterpart to the method familiar from the *Metaphysical First Principles of Natural Science.* Its "Preface" distinguishes three
kinds of metaphysics. The transcendental or general part in the metaphysics of nature, which does not relate "to any determinate object of
experience" (MFS IV 469), is opposed to two disciplines of special metaphysics, "in which the above transcendental principles are applied to the
two species of objects of our senses." These special disciplines require
fundamental, underivable concepts, which are nevertheless empirical.

Kant surprisingly uses the term metaphysics to describe them, despite their empirical character. (Metaphysical) physics relies on the empirical concept of matter and (metaphysical) psychology on that of a thinking being (IV 470) in order to arrive at further concepts in their development. Kant's distinction between general and special metaphysics may be illustrated using an example from "mechanics" in the third section. Its third proposition, the Second Law of Mechanics, which Kant calls the "law of inertia" (IV 544), states that "every change in matter has an external cause" (IV 543; the more familiar first Newtonian law is put in parentheses). By way of proof, Kant adduces the proposition "that every change has a *cause*" (IV 543, l. 21; cf. the "Second Analogy" in the first *Critique*, B232). Whereas this proposition stems from "general metaphysics" or from the "transcendental part of metaphysics," the additional notion of an "external" cause transforms it into a special metaphysics: (metaphysical) mechanics. Since the metaphysics of morals is "a counterpart of the metaphysical first principles of natural science, already published," as stated in the "Preface" to the *Doctrine of Right* (VI 205, ll. 5f.), it has the status of a special metaphysics. But it pertains to freedom, not to nature. It applies the principles of transcendental and general metaphysics of freedom either to external lawgiving, as in the (metaphysical) doctrine of right, or to inner lawgiving, as in the (metaphysical) doctrine of virtue. The former concerns the morals of living together or social morals, whereas the latter examines the morals of the inner attitude or personal morals.

From an epistemological viewpoint, at issue here is a synthetic, but impure a priori, in which the pure synthetic a priori, the moral concept, is applied to an elementary empirical situation. In the case of the doctrine of right, this situation is the coexistence of finite rational beings in limited space, a noninferential fact given in intuition. Due to the spatial limitations of the planet, a moment of scarcity, one has no choice other than to live in community with others of one's own kind. This is the very basic situation that is the topic of the "construction" mentioned in section E.

There are thus at least four kinds of anthropology to be distinguished in Kant:

Anthropology

Moral or didactic   physiological   pragmatic   *conditio humana*: synthetic impure a priori

As is well known, Hume also takes scarcity to be a necessary condition for the application of moral right, which he calls justice (*A Treatise of Human Nature*, 1739, Book 3, Part 2, Section 2; *An Enquiry Concerning the Principles of Morals*, 1751, Section 3, Part I). Rawls (1971, §1) likewise adheres to this Humean tenet. In comparison, Kant's theory is remarkably simple. His construction of a concept of right proves to be relatively indifferent to the fact that, as Hume says, human beings have similar physical and mental powers and, moreover, that goods are relatively scarce. Two more modest assumptions are sufficient for the construction of the concept of right: Finite rational beings must share limited living space with each other. Within this space, rational beings exhibit forces that inevitably affect each other, which is why the metaphysical doctrine of right corresponds to metaphysical physics. The moral concept of right "only" designates the conditions under which the reciprocity among these beings is of a moral or rational standing: This is the case when reciprocity follows a rigid universal law and action and reaction are always equal to one another, just as in the third Newtonian law, the principle of reaction [*Reaktionsprinzip*] (see section 6.5).

Since the aforementioned situation is given in experience, despite its high degree of generality, one might question the nonempirical nature of the moral concept of right. However, the concept is not derived from the empirical situation, but instead emerges from the interplay of empirical and pre-empirical elements. The given character of unavoidable social relations is empirical, but the (moral) principle according to which these relations are formed is non-empirical.

Like Kant's metaphysical physics, his metaphysical doctrine of right hinges on further, again relatively general, but empirical conditions: Finite rational beings have a body and live, and they can be hurt in these respects; there are objects in space that one can be entitled to own; one cannot live without these objects as a vital corporal being; contracts are concluded and money is used; there are men, women, and children, and so on. But these elements, too, only specify the range of application of right and do not impair its moral configuration. Kant only later announces the decisive point for the construction of the legal task, the inevitability of living side by side with all others (§42: VI 307, ll. 9f.). But he already substantially develops the issue in paragraph B of the *Doctrine of Right* in three steps.

(1) The first tripartite step (VI 230, ll. 9–11) begins (1.1) with a legally imprecise assumption that is nevertheless valid throughout the

metaphysics of morals. Not natural forces, but persons – for Kant, imputable subjects (VI 223, ll. 24f.) – are agents. (1.2) This becomes legally specific when more persons reciprocally influence each other by their deeds – or for Kant, imputable actions (227, ll. 21–23). Even if one can suffer internal conflicts, several persons are needed for external, juridical lawgiving (1.2.1: Plurality). They must stand to one another in a relationship (1.2.2: Intersubjectivity) that is not exclusively aesthetical or theoretical but, rather, practical (1.2.3: Intersubjectivity in Reciprocity; cf. 256, l. 4). (1.3) This is due to two general empirical conditions. Since the "earth's surface is not unlimited but closed" (§43: 311, ll. 23f.; cf. §62 and previously §13), the persons share the same spatially limited world. And persons are not pure intelligences; they have bodies that because of their extension already claim a part of the common world. In addition, they have needs and interests, for the satisfaction of which they require goods. Kant clearly highlights the decisive point by means of these three component elements, thus rendering the discussion of additional questions superfluous. In this way, his theory becomes more convincing and philosophically elegant. In particular, he undermines the charge, familiar since Hobbes, that modern theories of law and of the state rely on the economic and social conditions of a competitive civil society.

(2) The second condition of application is an elaboration on the first. Kant rightly excludes "the relation of one's choice to the mere wish" from the domain of right (VI 230, l. 12). Since *mere* wishes take no account of bringing about the "the object he wants" (ll. 14–19), they remain internal. Different inner worlds, no matter how heterogenous, can exist beside one another without problems. Mere wishes thus do not call for any *external* lawgiving. It is choice that first exhorts action in the external world and creates unavoidable social relations.

(3) According to a further specification of the first condition of application, reciprocal relations of choice concern not the matter of choice but its form (VI 230, ll. 16f.). The "formalism" this signals is illustrated by Kant's example: It is irrelevant whether someone who buys goods will gain from the transaction or not. Here, the choice lies in the transaction of goods and money; the matter of the partners' intentions remains internal and thus is not of legal relevance. The form of the reciprocal relation consists in free (VI 230, l. 21) transaction, that is, remote from coercion and fraud. And precisely because one is (in a negative sense) free in one's transaction, no account must be taken of the intentions of the partners, insofar as they do not influence the kind

of action taken. Moreover, since both partners have a right to transact (without coercion or fraud), it would not even be justifiable to maintain that their intentions are of legal relevance.

6.4. Excursus: The Welfare State

Among the wishes that Kant sets aside in the second condition of the application of right (VI 230, ll. 12f.), Kant includes needs [*Bedürfnisse*] and thereby also their fulfillment, happiness. He explicitly sets "actions of beneficence or callousness" outside the sphere of right (ll. 13f.). Only in the *Doctrine of Virtue* is "the happiness of others" an end, and in relation to others it is even the only end that is also a duty (VI 385ff.). Kant opposes utilitarian theories of right that are advocated not only in Anglophone philosophy, but also by Samuel Pufendorf (*De iure naturae et gentium*, 1672, I, 1) and Christian Wolff (*Institutiones*, 1750, I, 2, §43). In incorporating the duties of humanity [*officia humanitatis*], they blur the distinction between duties of right and of virtue. Furthermore, Kant rejects the welfare state of enlightened absolutism, since it entails a paternalism that legally incapacitates the citizens. A sovereign who wants to make the people happy "in accordance with his concepts" treats his citizens as immature children and himself becomes a despot (*Common Saying* VIII 302; cf. *Religion* VI 96).

With these claims, Kant seems to be taking a position in contemporary debates that divide political liberalists over the welfare state. Whereas the "Kantian" John Rawls spearheads supporters of the welfare state with the difference principle (1971, §13), the "Lockean" philosopher Robert Nozick (1974) vehemently disparages the welfare state. Kant seems to speak out against the Kantian and for his opponent. In truth, he does not reject all taxation "by way of coercion" (VI 326, l. 21) for the sake of the social and welfare state. And it is not necessary to fall back on the duty of virtue foreign to law, as A. Rosen does (1993, chap. 5), in order to promote the well-being of others. In the sphere of public right, particularly in the "General Remark, Section C" (cf. Appendix 8), Kant supports organizations that provide for the poor, which include "widow's homes, hospitals," and foundling homes. (On the state's obligation to "organize" universities, see *Conflict* VII 21f.) He even mentions the "needs of the people" (VI 326, l. 17), despite having eschewed the concept of need in paragraph B (230, l. 13). Does section C thus contradict the concept of right from the "Introduction to the Doctrine of Right"?

The argument that draws from the concept of need in section C, the welfare state argument, is missing not only in the "Introduction to the Doctrine of Right," but also in the decisive argument for the rule of law in general, the "state argument." According to the latter, the state is merely "a union of a multitude of human beings under laws of right" (DR §45). Its task of ensuring that previously provisional right becomes peremptory (§§41–45) indicates that the state is the rule of law in an emphatic sense, but not that it is a welfare state. The welfare state also seems to be prohibited on moral-legal grounds according to paragraphs B to E, since all coercion that transcends the universal compatibility of individual freedom contradicts this freedom. The state argument thus rules out a genuine welfare state. A welfare state can be legitimate only if it is conducive to the rule of law while also guaranteeing the freedom of its subjects, that is, only if it is a "freedom-functional welfare state" (Höffe 1981, 255; cf. Höffe 2002a, sec. 3.4).

In the "General Remark, C," Kant justifies the welfare state by means of a novel idea: the "argument from perpetual stability." It asserts that the "general will of the people has united itself into a society which is to maintain itself perpetually." If the society to be maintained is a civil society, or in Kant's terms, a society under the rule of law [*Rechtsstaat*], the argument opens up the path to a welfare state that guarantees the freedom of its citizens. If the foundational claim of moral right is correct, that is, if the peremptory form of moral law or the rule of law is itself morally imperative, then a welfare state that is indispensable to the rule of law is morally imperative. In order to make peremptory right actually durable ("perpetual," VI 326, l. 5), poverty must be combatted, since it endangers stability.

This legitimation strategy is apparently modest both in its purpose of maintaining a collective and in the scarce means it requires for achieving stability. A functional legitimation, however, could be extended in two directions. On the one hand, one could argue for the functional role of the welfare state with respect to *private* right, in this case to what is both internally and externally mine or yours. Partly social, partly economical and pedagogical conditions must be fulfilled to actualize what is internally mine or yours, that is, innate right, and to actually become one's own master (cf. VI 238, l. 1). Moreover, they are required for the permission not only to possess something external as one's own, but also actually to have it, in short: to be a real, not merely possible legal subject in both dimensions of private right. These conditions may be considered imperative on grounds of their functional role in securing freedom and justice. On the other hand, *public* right may also be conducive to freedom and justice if Kant's offensive position is rejected according to which a large portion of legal subjects should be only passive, not active citizens of a state: "[A]n apprentice in the service of a merchant or artisan; a domestic servant . . . ; all women and, in general anyone whose preservation in existence (his being fed and protected) depends not on his management of his own business but on arrangements made by another. . . . All these people lack civil personality" (314).

In section C, Kant does not undertake either of these extensions. He does not attempt to respond to the social question of early capitalism, nor to fraternity as the third principle of the French Revolution. The legitimation of the welfare state appeals to its functional role in securing freedom and justice only if one understands the "society" that "is to maintain itself perpetually" in a public-legal sense as a "civil society." Since the title of the "General Remark" contains the concept of a "civil union" (VI 318, ll. 15–17), this reading seems straightforward, making it seem that the point at issue is "the abiding existence of a state of law" (Ludwig 1993, 231). But the expression in the relevant passage refers to a people before the introduction of law. It is required not of the state of law [*Rechtszustand*] that it "maintain itself perpetually," but rather of the society into which a people unites itself before the establishment of the state. And since all persons (cf. "the members of the society," VI 326, l. 6) deserve care who cannot procure sufficient means "for even their most necessary natural needs" (326, ll. 8–10), the guarantee of collective stability coincides with a guarantee of individual subsistence. The duty to provide a guarantee thus becomes more urgent. For as cynical as it sounds, the collective will survive even when several of its poorest citizens starve, a possibility that the guarantee of individual subsistence excludes. According to section C, the state has a duty to care for its subjects not only when poverty jeopardizes its existence as a whole (Ludwig 1993, 238), but even when poverty endangers individual survival. This reflects a social human right or a social civil right. For Kant, every member of the society has a genuine social right, a right to the means for one's own subsistence.

An argument is still missing to support a convincing legitimation of the welfare state: On what grounds should a society be "perpetually" maintained in a distributive sense before it is subjected to law? According to the *Doctrine of Virtue* (§30), there is the duty "of beneficence toward those in need . . . because they are to be considered fellow human beings, that is, rational beings with needs, united by nature in one dwelling place so that they can help one another" (VI 453, ll. 12ff.). But this is an ethical, not juridical duty, and it is a "general" duty (l. 13), which means that it is applicable to any human being whatsoever. The guarantee of perpetual stability in the "General Remark," however, refers only to the members of one's own society. The missing argument may be gleaned from the first paragraph of parental right (paragraph 28). It asserts that parents have the duty to preserve and care for their children and that children even have an "original innate" and moreover freedom-promoting right "to the care of their parents until they are able to look after themselves" (VI 280, ll. 18–20). If this right is taken from the immediate family and applied to the extended family, to clans, and finally to an entire people, a universal duty to care for others emerges in the sphere of private right. The state is obliged in this way because it should make private right peremptory. But an argument of this kind does not appear in the *Doctrine of Right.*

Setting aside the argument still outstanding, section C points out the direction toward a legitimate welfare state that supports the individual over the collective. The path to be taken, however, is not conducive to individual freedom, since the individual is not considered a "private" or "public" legal subject. The individual is rather the member of a people or of a society prior to law and thus is granted the right to survival as a natural human being. This right evidently does not denote a right to survival absolutely, and thus does not forbid death by accident, by sickness, or by enfeeblement from old age. Kant restricts the guarantee of perpetual stability to the provision of means for the "care of the poor" (cf. 326, l. 22). He also attaches importance to preventing the abuse of this welfare: "Poverty" should not become "a means of acquisition for the lazy," for this would be no less than "an unjust burdening of the people by government" (ll. 31f.).

Which argument does Kant thus use to justify imposed taxes for the sake of those in need? According to section C, the "supreme commander" or "government" takes on the responsibility that emerges from the duty of the people, since the people subject themselves to the executive power only under the proviso ("for this end") that they are preserved "perpetually." But because this means that every member of society should be protected, the eternal survival of the collective and thus of the society as a whole is actually not at issue, but only the survival of the individuals. Since individuals submit themselves to a government only "under provisions," the government is committed to fulfilling the moral duties or the provisions by a sort of tacit contract. One might even call it a double moral duty. In addition to the duty of the state to commit itself to the contract, there is the task of administering compensatory justice that undergirds the contract itself. The government must take on the task of subsistence that the members of the society originally guaranteed each other, since, as an executive power, the government influences the scope of action taken by society. Kant thus endorses not welfare state that supports freedom, but one that compensates for the loss of power of the society prior to the introduction of law within a social state. (On the argument for compensatory justice, cf. Höffe 1996c, chap. 9; on the question of a Kantian welfare state, see also Kersting 1993, 58–67, and Merle 1999.)

6.5. The Moral Concept of Right

Let us return after this excursus to the conditions for the application of right. They are of a methodically descriptive nature and thus alone do not yield a moral concept of right. For this reason, their treatment in the second paragraph of section B is guided by the moral perspective of the first paragraph; the third paragraph then develops the concept of right by combining the first two. Because this concept is related to an obligation (VI 230, ll. 7f.) and denotes "the necessity of a free action under a categorical imperative of reason" (222, l. 3), it corresponds to the categorical imperative of right in the singular, that is, to the concept and criterion of morally mandated right. Both main sections of the *Doctrine of Right*, by way of contrast, develop the categorical imperative of right in the dual: the categorical imperative of private right and that of public right. Insofar as categorical imperatives also appear within these two domains – explicitly only in state right, where penal law is to be considered a categorical imperative – the categorical imperative of right also appears, on a third plane, in the plural.

   If the coexistence of persons who are accountable for their actions is evaluated according to Kant's moral criterion of universal lawfulness, the following well-known formula emerges: "Right is therefore the sum of the conditions under which the choice of one can be united with the choice of another in accordance with a universal law of freedom" (VI 230, ll. 24–26). Kant derives right from morals, but not from its personal principle of inner freedom or the autonomy of the will. Right is rather inferred from pure practical reason and its criterion of universal lawfulness. Pure practical reason is indifferent to the difference between personal and social ("rightful") morals. The supplement "universal" is not to be read explicatively. It is self-evident that every law formulated without proper names contains a certain degree of universality; hence, it need not be mentioned twice (VI 230, ll. 22 and 25). Kant instead recurs to his general criterion of morality and thus incorporates right into his program of a universal moral philosophy, but "universalization" in another sense is reserved for personal morals.

The degree of clarity achieved by Kant's theory becomes apparent when it is compared with the model work on jurisprudence at the time, the *Universal Prussian Law of the Land* (1794). The decisive paragraph 83 therein deals with "natural freedom" and determines it as freedom "to seek and to further one's own well-being without infringing on the rights of another." According to Kant, by way of contrast, the important thing is one's "legally determined freedom," and this, unlike any form of paternalism, allows for occasions in which one "rushes headlong into disaster."

Because Kant's philosophy of law needs to assume no more than the legal accountability or imputability of persons, we may dismiss Isaiah Berlin's objection (1969, 37ff.) that Kant is not a liberal thinker because he is adverse toward the negative concept of freedom. In truth, this concept is even decisive in Kant's legal ethics, which concerns the right to doings and omissions that are externally free from being constrained by another's choice. Internal or moral freedom, the independence of the will from drives, needs, and passions, is exclusively reserved for the domain of ethics or the doctrine of virtue. Political liberalism is also manifest in Kant's allowance for a great degree of pluralism on national and global levels: All persons and groups have an entitlement to their particularities, or even to unflagging conviction, under the proviso that they commit themselves to strict universal principles.

This general compatibility of Kant's theory with the freedom of action demanded by moral right first has a negative aspect: The freedom of action is limited. The reason for this is self-evident and thus not made explicit by Kant. When a multitude of persons share the same external world, no one of them can claim a living space for him- or herself, not even that space occupied by his or her body, without limiting the possible living space of all others. The second, positive aspect of Kant's concept of right is more striking: If the unavoidable limitation of freedom adheres to universal law, it entails a guarantee of freedom. And since individual freedom is protected only when all individuals limit their freedom, the cohabitation of imputable subjects must be of a legal nature if it is to be moral.

The requirement at issue is a requirement of the type of justice that no longer merely *defines* right, but also *legitimates* it. Lawful coexistence is, for Kant, morally obligatory. This of course does not mean that every positive legal proceeding is permitted or even demanded. On the contrary, Kant puts forward a criterion – a third type of justice that provides a *norm* for right – that assesses all positive laws according to their legitimacy. It has the primary task of procuring three foundational principles: an innate human right ("Introduction to the Doctrine of Right"), the right to what is externally mine or yours ("Part I"), and the right to a public order bound by law ("Part II").

The third type of justice is the juridical counterpart to the categorical imperative in personal morals. The moral concept of right and the categorical imperative of right subjugate communal external freedom to universal lawfulness, just as the categorical imperative of personal morals obliges the personal will. Legal ethics announces a more significant task, because it must not only provide a norm for right, but also constitute right by molding the coexistence of persons according to law. Due to its requirement that all human coexistence be subjected to a legal form, it must achieve more than a partial social ethics; it can only be a fundamentally social discipline and social theory.

To round off the moral concept of right, Kant again supplements it with the moral *principle* of right (section C). The moral principle of right articulates the same matter discussed already but from the perspective of subjective right, no longer from that of objective right. The principle of right is the sum of all subjective claims to which one is entitled according to objective right (VI 230, ll. 29–31). These are prepositive and general rights, that is, innate or human rights. Kant does not provide a catalogue of human rights, but only a uniform criterion. This criterion is, on his view, the only innate right: "Freedom (independence from being constrained by another's choice), insofar as it can coexist with the freedom of every other in accordance with a universal law, is the only original right belonging to every man by virtue of his humanity" (VI 237, ll. 29–32).

One may agree with Kant that all actions are permitted that are in conformity with the universal principle of right and that any additional demand is illicit, especially the desire "that this principle of all maxims be itself in turn my maxim" (231, ll. 3f.). Whether "in my heart" I acknowledge the freedom of another or am "indifferent" to it, or even would like "to infringe upon it," is unimportant as long as I do not "impair his freedom" by my external action (ll. 6–8). Kant does not recognize, however, that the unitary criterion is sufficient to account for a multitude of human rights, beginning with the right to what is externally mine or yours and the right to a public order bound by law. An open catalogue of human rights is therefore not out of the question (see sections 1.3.2 and 10.1).

Kant rules out all disposition-based concepts of law and probing for convictions by his remark that the principle of all maxims must not "be itself in turn my maxim" (see above, section 5.4). But they are traded in for another difficulty: Ever since the *Groundwork* and the second *Critique*, he defines morals and their criterion, the categorical imperative, not by any arbitrary form of universalizability but by the universalizability of *maxims*. But since the universalizability of *action* is a sufficient criterion for adherence to laws in the sphere of right, there is room for skepticism about the moral nature of right. It is true that the *Groundwork* and second *Critique* deal mainly with personal morals (see above section 5.1), whereas the *Metaphysics of Morals* revokes this unjustified limitation of scope by defining the concepts of obligation and the categorical imperative shared by both parts from the standpoint of action, not from that of maxims (VI 222). Only a few pages later, however, this is followed by the "classical" formula that makes reference to *maxims*: "[A]ct upon a maxim that can also hold as a universal law" (225, ll. 6f.). A discrepancy thus becomes manifest that is difficult to resolve: Since the conformity of "the maxim of action with a law" (here in the sense of the principle of duty, l. 32) is "morality" (ll. 31–34), the categorical imperative seems to be confined to morality. Since the categorical imperative is also valid for the *Doctrine of Right*, Kant thus binds right to morality in a way that he emphatically rejected in paragraph 9. However, the third perspective on legal morals in the "Universal Principle of Right" begins with the words: "act externally so that" (231, l. 10). Thus, with regard to legal morals neither must one limit one's own freedom (ll. 13–15) nor "represent that law of right as itself the incentive to action" (l. 20; cf. *Opus postumum* XXII 462: "The rule: 'Act according to laws of right' belongs to ethics").

6.6. The Authorization to Use Coercion

Ever since the Enlightenment thinker Thomasius (*Fundamenta juris naturae et gentium* 1718, *Prooemium*, also §23), the connection between right and the authorization to use coercion has been virtually taken for granted in legal philosophy. But Kant is the first to succeed in providing its justification, and thus also provides the theoretical solution

to a question that has remained relevant up to the present day, though
it is often ignored in legal theory: Why are human beings authorized
to exercise coercion over other human beings?

One might arrive at a response by playing out the antinomy (in right
and law) between strict anarchism and strict legal positivism. According
to the anarchistic thesis, all coercion would be reprehensible; according to the positivistic antithesis, the legal order would have *carte blanche*.
The resolution of the antinomy would consist in the legitimation of
coercion that would limit its scope: in legitimation plus limitation. This
strategy corresponds to the thought experiment in which one imagines
a primary state of nature that brings out the internal inconsistency of
this state and thus proves the necessity of overcoming it (cf. Höffe 1994,
esp. chap. 10). Kant himself does not carry through the thought experiment, however, and thus does not entirely exhaust the possibilities
of legal ethics. But in substantial respects all elements of the thought
experiment are to be found in his work.

Kant's vindication of the authorization to use coercion is prepared
in section C (section 2), elaborated in section D, and put to the test in
section E. The formal argument is as simple as it is convincing. Kant
refutes strict anarchism with the argument that all instances of coercion
are morally legitimate when they constitute a response to an illegitimate
instance, that is, to an injustice. But coercion is legitimate only under
two restrictive conditions that oppose the positivistic antithesis: To begin
with, coercion is permitted only where it already exists, where someone
infringes on the sphere of another person's legitimate freedom. Legitimate coercion is not aggressive but protective in nature; it does not
attack but defends. And reactive force that is neither vengeance nor
self-defense is legitimate only insofar as it is directed against injustice.
Without this second restriction, a thief who tried to prevent his victim
from regaining his property would be morally in the right. Legitimate
defense against injustice can take one of two forms: It is preventive
when one tries to foil a robbery, and restitutive when one retrieves
stolen property. Whoever deliberately injures the thief or takes back
more than was stolen, however, commits an injustice.

Kant's more detailed justification of reactive force is derived from two
practical negations. Because the simple negation of morally legitimate
action, "the hindering of an effect," is an example of moral injustice
(cf. VI 230, ll. 32–34), the negation of this negation, "resistance that
opposes the hindrance" (cf. 231, ll. 24f.), regains an affirmative position. When an injustice is resisted, whether preventively or restitutively,

the injustice is superceded and rightfulness is once again recognized (cf. 231, ll. 28–32). This argument is analytic (cf. "there is connected with right by the principle of contradiction . . . ," ll. 32–34) insofar as it operates solely with the concepts of right and wrong and with double negation. The authorization to use coercion is thus contained in the concept of right: A first-order permission of right includes the second-order permission of its enforcement. A subjective right is not made up of "two elements," of "obligation in accordance with a law" and the authorization to use coercion (232, ll. 6–9), but rather "right and authorization to use coercion therefore mean one and the same thing" (l. 29).

Kant compares the test in paragraph E to the procedure used in mathematics: the construction of a concept "in pure intuition a priori." However, as already mentioned (section 6.3), he draws not from geometry, but from an axiom of theoretical mathematics, the third Newtonian axiom. If it is assumed that beings interact, as in the axiom of the equality of action and reaction, then a society constructed from them is conceivable only by "a fully reciprocal and equal coercion." Without coercion, however, the community is not even possible.

The domain of right is comparable to mathematics also because the sum of laws, that is, the doctrine of right, determines what belongs to persons or what they are rightfully entitled to "with mathematical exactitude." This "cannot be expected in the doctrine of virtue" (ll. 19–21). This difference between the doctrine of right and that of virtue is reminiscent of Aristotle's definition of justice (see section 2.3) as the mathematically determined mean [*meson pragmatos*], in contrast with all other virtues defined as means relatively to us (*meson pros hêmas*, EN II 5, 1106a29–31 and V 9, 1133b32f.; cf. Höffe 1999a, chap. 14).

6.7. Appendix: Two Partially Legal Phenomena

In order to underscore the stringency of his concept of right, Kant discusses two distinctive phenomena in the "Appendix to the Introduction to the Doctrine of Right." Both do not belong to right proper, but are of a partial legal nature. Equity is "a right without coercion" and the right of necessity is "coercion without a right" (VI 234, l. 4).

The idea of equity has a famously long history reaching back into classical antiquity. Since justice that proceeds according to rules (laws) is unjust in borderline cases, Aristotle introduces equity as a corrective (EN V 14; cf. *Rhetoric* I 13, 1374a26ff.). However, it is not up to the judge to demonstrate equity [*dikastês*], but up to either of the opposing parties who are ready to waive their rights even when they have the law on their side (EN V 14, 1137b34–1138a3), or to an independent institution, the arbitrator (*diatêtês*: *Politics* II 8, 1268b4ff.; *Rhetoric* I 13, 1374b19–22).

Equity played a role in positive law not only in classical Athens. It was also present in Roman law, although relatively late in its history. Under Christian influence, it took on the wider meaning of restraint, mildness, or even mercy. Furthermore, a division began to appear that recalls the difference between judge and arbitrator in Athens: It became common to oppose strict right ["*ius strictum*"] to equity right ["*ius aequum*"], the latter of which is more responsive to concrete situations. In Great Britain, this gave rise to a two-track jurisdiction from the fourteenth century onward, and equity jurisdiction prompted the establishment of the separate legal institute of trust (cf. Helmholz 1998; Jones 1998).

Kant's theory of the authorization to enforce right does not follow in the footsteps of these traditions. He has good reasons for claiming that strict right forbids the enforcement of personal waivers in court: A partner in an association ("a trading company") who has "[done] more" cannot demand more than an equal share of the profit, just as a domestic servant cannot demand compensation for the depreciation of his wages ("when he gets the same amount of money but it is of unequal value"). According to Kant's first "pragmatic" argument, "definite particulars (data)" are lacking (234, l. 22; cf. ll. 31f.) to enable a decision on what is owed the petitioner. This shortage of mathematical exactitude is not, on its own, sufficient to justify the exclusion of personal waivers. But Kant has a second argument that is overlooked by his critic Dahlstrom (1998). It is only hinted at, but is more fundamental: One would encroach on rights already laid down by contract, since another person would have to waive his rights (DR VI 234, l. 34) even though he could insist on retaining them "hard-heartedly." Equity can be taken into consideration only by a judge (not as a natural person but as a representative of the crown or of the state) who is prepared to incur the damages incumbent on him.

Now, one might think it is advisable to have a separate court of equity as in Athens and Great Britain. But for Kant this involves a contradiction (234, ll. 33f.). He agrees with the "motto [*dictum*] of equity" familiar from Cicero (*De officiis* I §33): "[T]he strictest right is the greatest wrong," but he sees that "this ill cannot be remedied by way of what is laid down as right." The demand for equity applies not to the mundane court [*forum soli*], but only to a court of conscience [*forum poli*]. It is tantamount to a right that is only moral (235, ll. 6–11), and thus belongs to the doctrine of virtue, although it is not discussed there. A related problem appears only in *Toward Perpetual Peace*. Kant here understands the sentence "*fiat iustitia, pereat mundus*" as an articulation of the strict rule of right – "let justice reign even if all of the rogues in the world perish because of it" – and not as a permission that opposes every consideration of equity, "a permission to make use of one's own right with utmost rigor." This permission stands in conflict not with the concept of right itself, but only with "ethical duty" (VIII 379).

Kant explicitly contrasts the second distinctive phenomenon, the right of necessity, with self-defense. If I forestall "a wrongful assailant upon my life," I am guiltless from the perspective of right. The right of necessity [*Notrecht*], by way of contrast, is only the "alleged right [. . .] to take the life of another who is doing nothing to harm me" (DR VI 235). Whereas self-defense refers to an attack against the law, the right of necessity concerns the (legitimate) right of a third party.

The problem is again familiar from classical antiquity. Although it was much discussed at the time, Kant does not take up the familiar example of theft from need due to hunger that does harm to an uninvolved third party. He rather puts forward the classical example that stems from the Greek philosopher Carneades (214–129 B.C.): "[S]omeone in a shipwreck, in order to save his own life, shoves another, whose life is equally in danger, off a plank on which he had saved himself" (ibid.; cf. Hruschka 1991).

This differs from the situation in which two people in a shipwreck swim to an unoccupied plank and fight for sole ownership of it with the expectation that it will support only one of them. In this case, no one is killed, and thus no offense is committed – at most, one might approvingly accept the death of the other. The action of both persons is selfish, to be sure, but does not violate a moral command of right.

In the case discussed by Kant, on the contrary, a person is made guilty of homicide by purposeful killing – for example, according to German penal law (§§212–213 StGB), or the *Universal Prussian Law of the Land* in force at the time (Part II, Title XX, §§106ff.). Kant rightly asserts that he who commits an offense of homicide is not guiltless in an objective sense [*inculpabile*]. But he may be pardoned "subjectively," meaning here "before a court" (DR VI 235, l. 25).

Surprisingly, Kant appeals not to an apologetic or even justificatory state of emergency but to the notion of prevention, even though the

validity he grants this notion in the theory of penal law is at best derivative (cf. Höffe 1990, chap. 8). The penal law does "not have the effect
intended" and an action is unpunishable [*impunibile*] only because "the
punishment threatened by the law could not be greater" than what otherwise threatens the person in shipwreck with certainty, "the loss of
his own life" (VI 235, ll. 31f.). With reference to the motto "necessity has no law" (236, l. 5) and in agreement with natural law as it
has been passed down from Thomas Aquinas (*Summa theologiae*, II, II,
q. 64, art. 7), Hobbes (*Leviathan*, chap. 14), Wolff (*Ius naturae*, 1740,
§1070), and Achenwall (*Elementa Iuris Naturae*, §§203–207; cf. §232),
self-preservation is here promoted to a supreme right, but again not
in the sense of the strict concept of right. Kant rather defines his own
view in contrast with divergent positions: ". . . and by a strange confusion
jurists take this subjective impunity to be objective impunity (conformity with law)" (VI 236, ll. 2–4).

7

CATEGORICAL IMPERATIVES OF RIGHT ACCORDING TO ULPIAN

Great works of philosophy set new standards even in small passages. Despite its achievements, a particular passage in Kant's "General Division of Duties of Right" in the *Doctrine of Right* is even overlooked by those familiar with Kant's oeuvre. The passage is seldom mentioned, despite the new standards it sets for legal philosophy in three respects.

First, it contains an entire legal ethics in considerably condensed form and compresses it into a single page, which is half the length of Gustav Radbruch's later *Five Minute Legal Philosophy* (1945/1990).

Second, and more important, it presents a novel interpretation of the well-known principles of Occidental legal thought. If one follows the customary understanding, the three formulae put forward by (Pseudo-)Ulpian essentially say the same thing: The duty to "be an honorable human being (*honeste vive*)" demands uprightness that, according to its negative determination, does not "wrong anyone (*neminem laede*)" and, put positively, gives to each what he is entitled to, "what is his" (*suum cuique tribue*). Kant rejects this reading, perhaps already due to its reduction of the three rules to homogeneity, but most certainly because of the absurdity it entails in the third formula (VI 237, ll. 4f.). He instead works out the significance of each formula separately, thereby often criticizing his own, albeit precritical, position. In the lecture from the summer semester of 1777, "Practical Philosophy" (lecture notes by Powalski), he had designated the second and third Ulpian formulae as "almost the same" (XXVII/I, 144). In his new interpretation, each formula corresponds to a distinctive duty of right, which itself acquires the status of a categorical imperative of right. For Kant, duty is the "matter of obligation" (VI 222, ll. 31f.), and obligation in turn is "the necessity of a free action under a categorical imperative" (ll. 3f.).

Kant introduces a new kind of original honor to the content of the first formula; it carries the weight of a categorically mandated preliminary achievement (section 7.1). The other two formulae apparently amount to the categorical imperative of private right and that of public right, respectively (section 7.2). Kant's curt explanations are assertoric, in part even cryptic. But it is not quite unjustified to say that they hint at a pattern of argument, since the issues are more extensively discussed in other passages. Only the first formula contains an idea that is not discussed elsewhere and is somewhat disturbing. Kant sets a new standard with this idea. He demonstrates that legal morals are based on an element that is foreign to right and even anomalous or in conflict with the system. Whereas the other duties of right are external and are directed at others, the first formula implies an internal duty toward oneself (section 7.3).

7.1. A Categorical Preliminary Achievement

In order to "apply" the moral concept of right, the universal compatibility of freedom, Kant must first establish whose freedom counts. Who is both the subject and object of coexistence? Apparently, the answer may not be found arbitrarily, but must bow to the demands of the issue at hand, (legal) morals. For what can remedy the pathos of a universally valid morals if its range of application cannot be established as universal?

The answer is only nonarbitrary if it begins with the moral concept of right itself and particularly with the first condition of its application, without which right is made redundant: the "practical relation of one person to another" (VI 230, ll. 9f.; see section 6.3). The person, in turn, is to be defined by the requirement of legal ability. This is imputability, the ability of being the author of actions that are legally relevant (223, ll. 20ff.). According to this criterion, every subject with a legal ability is granted a second-order right, the right to be reckoned with in his legal capacity and to integration in the community of persons living in a legal form. Every person with a legal ability has the (moral) right to legal community with all other persons of a legal ability. This basic "right to right" may also be justified by way of an argument *e contrario*. If only a selected few had legal ability, the question arises as to how one should relate to those excluded from the legal community. But the only morally acceptable answer – that one should relate to them "in a legal form" – negates selectivity and integrates those initially excluded.

Kant's explanation of Ulpian's first principle seems to contradict this conclusion of a universal right to right. For it presents not a subjective claim, but rather a duty to rightful honor that can be gained only by one's own doing (*honestas iuridica*). Usually, this is understood as uprightness in the sense of a doubly clean record: One has violated neither a prohibition of right ("*neminem laede*") nor a command of right ("*suum cuique tribue*"). One is rightfully honorable if one has not acted contrary to right. Kant, by way of contrast, draws attention to a new and also more profound dimension: initial or original rightful honor. Not content with the omission of violations of right, it requires more than mere conformity with right and law. As a supplementary achievement, Kant's moral philosophy recognizes the intensification of legality in morality. But this is not at issue here. The third necessary element escapes the attention of interpreters (including Kersting 1993, with an exception in chap. A, V, albeit only in formative stages), since they are not otherwise acquainted with it in Kant or in other moral philosophies. Rousseau is the only exception, insofar as he forbids self-enslavement (*Social Contract*, Book I, chap. 4).

In a remarkably provocative fashion, Kant declares that one has rightful honor in an original sense only if one asserts oneself as a legal equal. It is well known that the principle of self-assertion plays an overwhelming role in early modernity. As a rule, it is determined in an empirical-pragmatic manner: In content, it is taken to be the assertion of oneself as a corporal and living being that is physically self-preserving, and it is determined *modaliter* as a premoral right with respect to the kind of claim made (e.g., Hobbes, *Leviathan*, chap. 14: Pufendorf 1672, §7). Kant alters the meaning in both respects. In content, he is concerned not with physical but with legal-moral self-assertion, which *modaliter* consists not in a premoral authorization, but in a legal-moral duty. It requires that one assert "one's worth as a human being in relation to others," which is tantamount to the following duty: "Do not make yourself a mere means for others but be at the same time an end for them" (DR VI 236/25–28). One has honor in a fundamental sense, that is, in a sense that constitutes right, only when one refuses legal debasement.

In the passage at hand, debasement is understood as legal reification: One should not allow oneself to be degraded to a mere means, a thing liable to the discretionary disposal of others. The "Division of the Metaphysics of Morals as a Whole" speaks of "beings that have only duties but no rights" and takes these to be "human beings without personality," namely, "serfs, slaves" (VI 241). It may be tempting to subsume them under the notion of a thing. But because they have duties, even if "nothing but duties," it would be more apt to contrast them with mere things and to call them "quasi-persons." The legal defamation this implies should, as a deprivation of rights, be distinguished from the other form of legal defamation, legal "reification."

The duty to legal-moral self-assertion that Kant introduces demands not only a verbal, but also a truly active objection to both reification and the deprivation of rights. Since the basic right to right in this way depends on one's own achievement and is not granted by others, Kant opposes fundamental legal paternalism. In the *Opus postumum*, he aptly discusses this achievement as an "innate duty," but of course without addressing it as a duty of right (XXIII 462). In the same context, Kant implies that a previously potential legal capacity is actualized by this duty: One establishes oneself or asserts oneself as an actual legal subject.

Kant attains this insight into fundamental rightful honor relatively late in his work. In the "Preparatory Work on a Doctrine of Virtue" (XXIII 386), and even in the "Lectures on the Metaphysics of Morals" from the winter semester of 1793/1794, lecture notes by Vigilantius, and thus almost an entire decade after the *Groundwork* and only three years before the publication of the *Doctrine of Right*, he ascribes the maxim "*honeste vive*" to the counterpart of right. He declares it to be the "principle of ethics," containing "the entire complex of ethical duties" and "thereby severed from the duties of right" (XXVII/2, 527). As a result, only the other two duties remain for right: In private right or in the state of nature, there is the duty "*neminem laede*," and in the public right of the civil state the duty is "*suum cuique tribue*" (XXIII 386). The *Doctrine of Right* rectifies this fallacious ascription, but only by drawing a distinction, not by inverting the argument. Kant distinguishes "*honestas interna*," a love of honor that is nothing like ambition (*ambitio*: DV VI 420), from "*honestas iuridica*," and assigns only the former to the doctrine of virtue, and the latter to the doctrine of right (DR VI 236). According to ethical honor, a "duty of self-esteem" (DR VI 462, l. 27), one may not offend against the humanity in one's own person or allow oneself to become a mere means (GMM IV 429). According to *rightful* honor, this self-debasement is forbidden only in relation to others and can be integrated within a legal ethics only because of this restricted meaning.

An example of self-debasement that is legally relevant is not mentioned in the passage at hand; the interpreter must therefore resort to justified speculation. One who allows oneself to become the property of another human being, which is permitted only "with regard to animals," undoubtedly violates a systematically first duty of right (cf. §55: VI 345, ll. 31f.). A conceivable argument in support of this conclusion might appeal to the fact that one is one's own property. This is rejected in paragraph 17 with the assertion that someone can be his own master [*sui iuris*], but not his own property, since he is "accountable to the humanity in his own person" (VI 270). The first duty of right is also violated, as mentioned above, by persons who docilely resign themselves to the state of a slave or bondsman (cf. DV §12), or perhaps even by those who submit themselves to a colonization that fully deprives them of their rights.

It is not one's interest in not becoming a slave or bondsman that speaks against enslavement, but a duty: One ought to avoid it happening. However, despite Kant's general disapproval of slavery, including voluntary enslavement (cf., e.g.: "a contract by which one party would completely renounce its freedom for the other's advantage" would be "null and void": VI 283; cf. also VI 348), a thief must endure enslavement (VI 329, ll. 36f.). According to Kant, the perpetrator of a crime violates the duty to rightful honor to such an extent that he "become[s] a slave through his crime"; his children, however, are exempted from enslavement (VI 283/29f.).

The duty to rightful honor is also violated by those who allow themselves be led by the sovereign "into war as he would take them on a hunt, and into battles as on a pleasure trip." Instead, they should claim the right to "give their free assent, through their representatives,... to each particular declaration of war" (VI 345, ll. 37f.).

Rightful honor is thus relevant to both main divisions of right: both to the private right of what is externally mine or yours (the refusal to become a slave or bondsman) and to public right (free colegislation on declarations of war). This underscores the systematic priority of the categorical imperative of right in Ulpian's first formula, for it is on a par with innate right, that is, (the private right to) what is internally mine or yours. In Kant, rightful honor is related to the right of humanity in our own person (VI 236, ll. 23f.) or the innate "right belonging to every man by virtue of his humanity" (237, ll. 31f.). The *lex iusti* (236, l. 24) put in brackets is taken up again in "Innate Right" (*iusti*: 238, l. 2).

Rightful honor can be understood in either a fundamental or a concrete sense. According to the fundamental reading, it requires denouncing the status of having "nothing but duties," forestalling enslavement, and demands self-assertion as an equal legal subject. According to the second, concrete reading, rightful honor requires a person to refuse to allow himself to be voluntarily and consciously deceived or robbed. (Making donations from generosity is obviously permitted.)

7.2. Categorical Imperatives of Private and Public Right?

The duty to assert oneself as an equal legal subject does mark a systematic beginning; but it alone cannot justify legal ethics. Legal subjectivity as a categorical command has to be extended by legal intersubjectivity as an equally categorical obligation; one's original self-esteem must be extended by an equally original esteem for others, so that every being of a legal ability is treated as a being with rights. Since Kant links rightful honor to innate right, and since its content, the universal compatibility of individual freedom, implies esteem for others, one might expect rightful honor to include original esteem both for oneself and for others. Kant does not provide any indication of this sort. He relegates esteem for others to the second formula, perhaps in order to avoid overinflating the content of the first formula or rather to highlight the contrast between the "inner" duty toward oneself and the "external" duty toward others (cf. DR VI 236, l. 10). Kant again has an original interpretation of the formula, according to which the prohibition against wronging someone ("*neminem laede*") is so rigorously valid without exception or compromise that it could prompt us "to stop associating with others and shun all society" (VI 236, ll. 31–33). Due to the prohibition against wronging others, the others become, *e contrario*, persons with rights. And due to the categorical nature of the prohibition, they are persons with inalienable rights, which means that they are equal legal subjects. The categorical prohibition of doing wrong thus amounts to an original respect for others.

Finally, with respect to the third formula – "*suum cuique tribue*" – Kant rejects the customary translation "to each his own" as absurd. His argument – "one cannot give anyone something he already has" – of course assumes that the legal entitlement is previously determined by the second principle, and hence that only its protection is pending in the third. Kant rightly demands the transition to a condition that secures protection, the public state of law. To illustrate, we may point out the distinction between granting and guaranteeing something: According to the second formula, the members of a society grant rights reciprocally by not committing injustice, and according to the third formula these rights are publicly guaranteed.

To what do the imperatives of right implied by the second and third formulae refer? On the surface, the *Doctrine of Right* is divided into two parts, private and public right. The first part, however, is more accurately called "Private Right Concerning What Is Externally Mine or Yours..." (VI 245, ll. 4f.), and is preceded by a "Private Right Concerning What Is Internally Mine or Yours" – thus, the whole is actually composed of three parts. The first part in systematic order is "put in the prolegomena" (VI 238, ll. 21–24), the "Introduction to the Doctrine of Right," simply because there is just one right for what is internally mine and yours. It comes first merely on grounds of its remarkable terseness. This tripartite division may also be read as a criticism of Hobbes. Near the close of chapter 13 in the *Leviathan,* Hobbes states that there is "no Mine and Thine distinct" in the state of nature, "but only that to be every man's, that he can get; and for so long, as he can keep it." And in chapter 15, Hobbes identifies property with what is mine. In comparison, Kant's notion of what is internally mine or yours implies a right that is innate and invariably characteristic of the human being.

Since the first formula relates to what is internally mine or yours, and the third formula to the public rule of law, the second one would seem to belong to what is externally mine or yours. In this way, the entire trio would reflect the proper, tripartite division of the *Doctrine of Right.* The categorical imperative of right would refer to what is internally mine or yours in the first formula, to acquired rights or what is externally mine or yours in the second formula, and to public right in the third formula. This classification, however, is already belied by the fact that the first formula mentions only a part of innate right, self-esteem, but leaves out esteem for others. It follows that the second formula comprises innate right and absolutely forbids wrongdoing, and thus refers to the comprehensive domain of internal and external private right.

Kant's novel interpretation of Ulpian's principles supplements legal ethics with "inner" self-esteem in the first principle, with a comprehensive "external" esteem for others in the second formula, and finally with reciprocal and publicly protected esteem in the third one. The duty to enter a common state of law results from the duty to be "also an end" for others, along with the duty to consider others as ends, which is the equivalent of the prohibition against wronging them. (One might even agree to R. Brandt's oral proposal of linking this tripartite structure to the table of categories in the *Critique* and understanding inner self-esteem as a kind of substance, external esteem for others as causality, and reciprocal esteem as interaction. Kant does not, however, make any such proposal.)

The second principle closes with a provocative, at first glance alienating claim: "even if you should . . . shun all society." It becomes more comprehensible from the famous assertion in the treatise on peace that I can coerce someone "either to enter with me into a condition of being under civil laws or to leave my vicinity" (*Peace* VIII 349, ll. 20–22). What appears there as an authorization ("I may") is articulated here, in the *Doctrine of Right* and similarly in paragraph 42, as a complementary duty: Either one submits to a society under the conditions of moral right or one must refrain from society altogether. To the extent that someone who opts for the latter alternative courts his own destruction, Kant indirectly declares that legal morals have priority over physical survival.

Moral beings have only the alternative of either entering relations of right with one another or refraining from any relations whatsoever. The relation that is devoid of right and in which rights are denied to the persons involved corresponds to a state of nature, and thus suggests Hobbes's famous requirement *"exendum e statu naturali."* But the demand is given a genuine legal-moral, categorical significance in Kant. Kant mentions only the reason for the goal of not "wronging anyone" and its negative side. The negative side, the demand that one leave the state of nature, straddles two options. Kant's genuinely moral theory discloses what Hobbes does not consider and in his pragmatic theory does not need to consider: One can also leave the state of nature by withdrawing from society. (Those familiar with Aristotle's works will recall this alternative in the *Politics*, articulated as the view that one lives like a god if one does not need the community of others in one's own autarchy: I 2, 1253a28f.).

The third, positive principle follows from the second, negative one: Whoever cannot avoid associating with others must enter the public state of law. This duty does not, however, amount to a self-positing of right, as Kersting thinks (1993, 222). It would then state: "[S]ubject yourself to the laws of the state in which you live – you owe it to everyone and everyone has a right to demand it of you." Kant's third duty rather remains entirely embedded in the domain of rational law. It demands the transition from private right to public right, but designates only the locus for the activity of the lawgiver and the positive court. It remains open in the third formula how public right is to be arranged and what the duties of loyalty consist in.

How, then, is the second duty of right to be delineated from the third? In the footnote to paragraph 42, Kant distinguishes between a formal and material concept of wrong. Material wrongs might consist in violations of right such as theft or homicide, whereas remaining in a state of "savage violence" is formally wrong (cf. DR VI 308, l. 5).

If Kant had wanted to delineate clearly the content of the second and third duty by subsuming all of private right under the second duty and all of public right under the third duty, the second would be more precisely rephrased: "Do not wrong anyone *materialiter*." And the third duty would combine the ensuing demand "Do not wrong anyone *formaliter*" with the inevitable means to assuring this end. On the assumption that society cannot be avoided, the following command emerges: "Enter a public state of law." Since there is no limiting qualification in the second duty, the wrong that is prohibited must be understood comprehensively; it includes both what is materially and formally wrong. The third formula explicitly and positively announces what is already implicit and negative in the second formula. Since no one in a lawless state "is assured of what is his against violence" (§42: VI 308), one must enter a "condition in which what belongs to each can be secured to him against everyone else" (VI 237, ll. 7f.). This is a requirement without any restrictions. The corresponding public state of law thus encompasses the entire domain of public right, including not only the single state, but also the right of nations and cosmopolitan law. Its universal validity also supports entering the condition of a world republic and not merely a federation of peoples, as advocated unreservedly by Kant himself (see chapter 11).

The first instance in which Kant recognizes a realization of the decisive meaning of justice is in the third duty, interpreted as a "*lex iustitiae*" (line 8). As still suggested by the conception of the administration of justice, the dissolution of private arbitration and force fully comes to completion only in the public state of law, particularly in the impartial rulings of the court: "The moral person that administers justice is a *court* (*forum*)" (VI 297, ll. 6f.).

Kant concludes with an indication of the logical relation between the three duties of right. He claims that the third group of duties of right contains "the derivation" of external duties of right "from the principle" of inner duties of right "by subsumption" (ll. 11f.). In order to understand this difficult assertion, we should recall that Kant's theory of syllogisms refers to inferences from mediating judgments (*Logic* IX 114, §42). Three components belong to this type of inference: the universal major premise, the minor premise subsumed under it, and the conclusion following from both (*Logic* IX 120f., §58). Kant thus claims that the three duties of right constitute one inference, with the inner duty of right as a major premise, the external duty of right as a minor premise subsumed under it, and the conclusion drawn from both premises as follows. Because one should be a legal person for others and should not wrong anyone, one must – assuming that one cannot avoid society altogether – enter a state of law with every other legal person.

This logical connectedness of the three rules corresponds to the results obtained thus far: Because the first principle relates to what is innately mine or yours, whereas the middle principle relates to what is mine or yours in general, the three duties of right correspond not to the tripartite system of the *Doctrine of Right* but to a system of duties of right that is not discussed elsewhere in the text. One's original rightful honor stands for inner duties of right, since legal self-assertion cannot be enforced. The other aspects of innate right, in contrast, can be enforced, which is why Kant is concerned to avoid identifying the first principle with innate right as a whole. He instead assigns those rights that can be enforced to the broad sphere of the prohibition against wronging others as an external duty. And in the third group of duties of right, the inner duties of right are grouped together with the prohibition against wrongdoing, for they are both secured in the public rule of law.

7.3. A Duty of Right Contrary to Right?

Kant's definition of the first duty of right as an "inner" duty patently leads to difficulties for legal ethics, as it is an ethics of merely external lawgiving. The idea of what is internally mine or yours is not itself problematic, since it denotes merely what is internal relatively, not absolutely. It is the innate, nonacquired component of external relations that is prior to all acquisition (VI 237, ll. 20ff.). The right to nonacquired, not merely external freedom of action in a realm of universally compatible freedom is prior to all acquired and thus fully external legal titles. With the idea of an inner duty of right, however, things begin to get murky, for it seems to conflict with the universal principle of right: "[I]t cannot be required that this principle of all maxims be itself in turn my maxim" (VI 231, ll. 3f.). A disparity in this sense would not be innocuous. It would be incompatible with Kant's principle of division in the *Metaphysics of Morals*, which maintains the equality of both parts side by side, and would instead subordinate the first part, the *Doctrine of Right*, to the second part, the *Doctrine of Virtue*, despite their reverse order in the text. There would be a danger of moralizing right; for duties of right would cease to be ethical duties only in an indirect way, and would instead have a direct ethical foundation.

This formal difficulty involved in an inner duty of right is only aggravated by the content of this right. The other duties of right include both external duties and duties toward others. Legal self-assertion, by contrast, is not only an inner duty, but also a duty toward oneself, and thus rather belongs to a doctrine of virtue for both of these reasons. It is true that self-assertion is a duty toward oneself. Nevertheless, it belongs to right, not as a component of right, but as a preliminary achievement that constitutes right. For this reason alone, it can be seen as the singular phenomenon of a legal duty toward oneself that – while contradicting the system of ordinary duties of right – is not a legal-ethical anomaly.

The inner nature of inner duties of right nevertheless remains problematic: If "inner" means that one must make the duty of right the maxim of one's action, inner duties of right would contradict not only the moral concept and principle of right, but already the very notion of merely external lawgiving. The first principle differs from the second and third principles not in virtue of this formal kind of "innerness," or (juridical) morality. The other three principles may also be conceivably incorporated into one's maxims, so this cannot be what distinguishes them. Kant understands Ulpian's formulae as three aspects of categorically commanded uprightness, which leave the question open as to the reasons for one's uprightness. One's integrity might be due to inclination, *pars pro toto*, or to self-interest, as when (1) one asserts oneself as a legal person from pride, (2) one avoids wrongdoing from fear of penalty, and (3) one wants to enter a state of law because the private enforcement of law is too arduous and risky. The alternative "juridical legality or juridical morality" thus applies to all three categorical principles of right. Juridical morality is not ruled out by any of the principles, but also is not commanded by any of them.

Even when duties of right are fulfilled habitually and thus become a mark of character or demonstrate the virtue of uprightness, they allow for accordance with duty merely from inclination, that is, they do not prohibit mere conformity with right (juridical legality). Kant thus uses another, nonformal and material concept of innerness in order to draw a clear dividing line between the first, "inner" principle and the second and third "external" principles. In legal self-assertion, something happens that may be expressed in action but in content is restricted primarily to the inner realm. The subject takes into account his relation to others, but does not allow himself to be reified or deprived of all rights, and he reflects on others only in relation to himself. Whoever avoids reification or deprivation of rights presents himself as a person who lays a claim to rights.

This implies a legal-ethical insight, the importance of which was not recognized by any theory of right before or after Kant: Right is not naturally given, but must be created. This depends on a threefold achievement by the legal subject, outlined by the three categorical principles of right. In their framework, the three categorical imperatives of right should begin in systematic order with an "inner" achievement – as Kant's concept of rightful honor signifies – namely, one's self-assertion – as the bearer of rights, even if this can be done only in opposition to society. Self-assertion begins with innate right or the compatibility of one's freedom with that of others. The inner duty of right thus does not draw attention to the inner side of right in contrast to its external side. Instead, it contains a self-referential moment that is necessary for constituting a legal subject or legally accountable (imputable) person. Only then are there beings to whom one can direct accusations and prohibitions of injustice (second duty) and of whom one can demand the establishment of a state that ensures the prohibition of wrongdoing. All three formulae, as duties of right, concern the subjective side of right rather than its objective and institutional side. Kant does not put them to use for a constitutional project, but rather is concerned with subjecting natural human beings to the categorical imperative of right, which commands recognition both of oneself and of others as legal subjects.

Since the content of legal self-assertion consists in protest against lawlessness, the first formula implicitly suggests the following inner conflict within the individual. A person subject to the principle of survival can, in competition, insist on being an end for others. The (legal-) moral person can thereby enter into conflict with the natural person. But because one succeeds in becoming a legal-moral person only by overcoming the force of the natural person, the dimension one enters lies beyond physical nature and thus is metaphysical in a literal sense. This domain is the entire sphere of right, and thus is metaphysical not in a theoretical sense but in the double sense of practical metaphysics. First, at issue here are the conditions not for cognition but for practical activity; and second, these conditions are not simply given, but enter the world only by means of practical exertion. If everyone would invariably accept being a mere means for others, there would be no right and, for lack of right, no metaphysics of right.

Whoever wants to be a person in an emphatic sense, albeit in the modest emphatic sense of a legal person, is committed to a metaphysical undertaking. Kant's alienating claim that it is a duty to have a metaphysics (VI 216, ll. 31f., cf. already GMM IV 289ff.) now gains plausibility. Kant's demand is in a provocative way primarily concerned with the recognition of oneself, not of others, and it does not require a – controversial – epistemological position, but a prefatory legal-moral endeavor. Kant's claim that this endeavor is of a synthetic a priori nature is rather secondary and subsidiary. But whether this additional claim is tenable is a separate issue.

PART III

LEGAL MORALS AND PEACE

8

THE NEGLECTED IDEAL

8.1. The Comprehensive Theory of Peace

In the voluminous *Critique of Pure Reason*, Kant emerges as an outstanding theoretical philosopher. His fame as a political philosopher, by contrast, is due to the sketch *Toward Perpetual Peace*, the length of which is equal to roughly 10 percent of the first *Critique*. Its terseness, however, belies its philosophical significance; acute brevity is rather a sign of its remarkable virtuosity.

The text is an eminently political treatise because it uses philosophical means to promote the political, or rather moral-political end of universal and unqualified peace among all states. Although Kant was probably prompted to write the treatise on political grounds by the Basel peace between Prussia and France (April 5, 1795), it is not an occasional essay [*Gelegenheitsschrift*]. It rather contains the main features of a complete legal and state philosophy, along with the principles for putting it into political practice.

The confidence of Kant's line of thought in the treatise on peace attests to the fact that he had been dealing with the issues over a long period of time. A cursory reader will discover Kant as a political thinker only in his later works. But on closer inspection, the portentous concept of a republic is already found in the *Critique of Pure Reason* (B 372ff.; on a political reading, see chapter 12). The first and most decisive publication for the theory on peace, the "Idea" (1784), was published even before the first critical work on moral philosophy, the *Groundwork* (1785). Further occurrences of the concept of peace follow in the "Conjectures" (1786), in the third part concerning the right of nations of the *Common Saying* (1793), and, following the treatise on peace, in

35

the *Doctrine of Right* (1797, §§53–62 and *Conclusion*) and in the *Conflict of the Faculties* (Section 2).

Prior to the treatise on peace, perpetual peace is mentioned as a general goal in the *Proclamation . . . of a Treatise on Perpetual Peace in Philosophy* (1787). It is also pursued by theoretical philosophy in its attempt to overcome those endless controversies among theories on the battlefield of metaphysics familiar from the *Critique* (A viii). In addition, there are two texts that may come as a surprise to those well versed in Kant. The legal order responsible for establishing peace, a "cosmopolitan whole, i.e., a system of all states," is also discussed in the *Critique of Judgment* (1790) under the heading "On the Ultimate End of Nature as a Teleological System" (§83). And the treatise on religion (1793) mentions in the first section a state of "perpetual peace based on a federation of nations united in a world republic" (VI 34). Whereas other modern philosophers are conspicuously silent about peace, it is a fundamental theme not only of Kant's political thought but of his entire philosophy.

As can be expected of Kant, his thoughts in the treatise on peace are not only finely nuanced in their concepts and well argued. They are also embedded in the context of historical experience and even inspired by previous debates on peace. Kant's knowledge of social thought and the history of ideas does not cause him to sidetrack to other topics. He instead proceeds apace to the systematic crux of the matter.

The title of the treatise lends to the impression that it concerns a philosophically marginal topic, since peace was not a fundamental concept of philosophy prior to Kant. This is a surprising state of affairs, since from the beginning of time humankind has expressed the wish that men would tire of war and beat their swords into plowshares, and their spears into pruning hooks (*Isaiah* 2: 4). Unquestionably, Kant's concern for both comprehensive and abiding peace is an existential task of moral significance. But peace in philosophical debates has had to eke out the existence of a wallflower; it is seldom considered, let alone treated in a way commensurate with its importance. Reputable philosophers have produced ample literature on peace in Western thought (cf. Raumer 1953; Janssen 1975; Chaunu 1993; and Höffe 2002a, chap. 8). But among the classical texts of philosophy, there are none that bear the term "peace" in their titles.

This desideratum is even apparent in the great political works of the modern era: in Hobbes's *Leviathan* (although he understands his to be a universal theory of peace), in Locke's *Second Treatise on Government*, and in Rousseau's *Social Contract*. During a period in which Europe was ravaged by war, remarkable approaches to a theory of war emerged – for example, in Locke's *Second Treatise*, chapter XVI. But theories of an international community of peace were lacking. Kant's treatise on peace is a prodigious exception.

Only two reputable thinkers in the Occident have accorded peace more than marginal treatment. Around the dawn of Christian theology, Augustine developed the most important theory of peace for centuries to come in Book XIX of *De civitate dei*. But he places moral-religious issues in the foreground. His focus is on inner peace, especially peace with God, along with cosmic peace. Earthly peace in the sphere of right and law is reduced to an imperfect image. Almost fourteen centuries later, Kant advanced the second pioneering theory of peace from the zenith of Enlightenment philosophy. And he succeeded in uniting the most decisive lines of thought that previously ran parallel to one another: the line of thinking about right and the state inherited from Plato and Aristotle, on the one hand, and Stoic cosmopolitanism, on the other. Kant, however, rejects the mostly apolitical character of the latter. He is familiar with the right of nations as it is discussed in early modernity. Nor is he ignorant of Augustine's idea of perpetual peace, but he no longer reserves it for the hereafter, and instead construes it as a task in this life, or more precisely, as a task of right in accordance with its moral concept. Therein lies Kant's first great innovation: Peace becomes a fundamental concept of philosophy, no longer of theology, and its central concern is legal and political philosophy.

Augustine's moral-religious and eschatological *pax aeterna* (*De civitate Dei* XIX 10–11) is thus transformed into a social and political, but still moral, phenomenon, *pax sempiterna*, or perpetual peace, in the sphere of law and legal ethics. Peace is no longer relegated to the "eternal" life in "some other world," but should instead be established "here on earth" ("Idea" VIII 30, ll. 28 and 18). It also does not prompt a withdrawal from politics, like peace of mind (*ataraxia*) in Epicurean thought. Peace exists in this life, in relations among human beings, not in the inner realm. Finally, peace is universal in the sense that it prevails among all people and not only among the gifted and chosen as in Augustine. (On Augustine's theory of peace, see Geerlings 1997 and Höffe 2002a, sec. 8.2.3; on *De Civitate Dei* in general, see Horn 1997.)

Kant understands the word "perpetual" to mean a particular quality of this life that makes peace unconditional or unqualified. Kant develops an ideal on the basis of this concept of absolute peace that is of decisive importance to international politics: the ideal of a truly global peaceful order that rests on a global legal order.

Despite the existential significance of peace and Kant's exceptional achievements, it is surprising that peace first attained the status of a fundamental concept only in Kantian philosophy. His legal and political philosophy, which is dedicated to peace, was initially discussed intensely over a period of several years. But in German idealism and ever since, it has been pushed to the background (see section 8.4).

In the treatise on peace, Kant uses contemporary peace contracts as a methodological guide. Following their pattern, he presents a set of agreements that consists in six preliminary articles, three definitive articles, two supplements, and a two-part appendix. The second edition (1796) even contains a secret article, which plays on the subtle irony of requiring abstinence from all secrecy.

In its entirety, the treatise covers seven extensive and relatively independent issues: (1) Despite his general disparagement of war, Kant makes the effort to propose war reforms, so long as war remains a reality. War should not be "tamed," since it is absolutely illegitimate except as a defensive measure; but engagement in war should not exclude peace as a possible final goal. This idea of changing war for the sake of peace – or of war reform that plays a functional role in securing peace – has hardly any precursors. The six preliminary rules for carrying out this reform, the "preliminary articles," are directed at political protagonists: heads of state, governments, or parliaments. They point out violations of right that, for the purpose of establishing peace, in part must be stopped at once ("strict laws of prohibition"), in part "contain permissions, not to make exceptions to the rule of right, but to postpone putting these laws into effect, without however losing sight of the end" (*Peace* VIII 347). This "authorization to postponement" signals a theory of moderation and *kairos* that criticizes a policy of rash decision, but unfortunately no further efforts have been taken to develop a theory of this kind up to the present day.

Apart from the basic requirement of an unqualified peace (1st preliminary article), at least three further rules concerning war reform are still topical today. To begin with, standing armies shall in time be abolished altogether; a principle of disarmament should replace that of an arms race (3rd preliminary article). No state shall forcibly interfere in the constitution and government of another state because foreign states have the right to reform themselves (the prohibition of intervention: 5th preliminary article). Finally, since perpetual peace is possible only under the proviso of reciprocal trust, all hostility is to be prohibited "as would have to make mutual trust impossible during a future peace" (6th preliminary article).

(2) The final rules or "definitive articles" contain the core tenets of Kant's theory of peace: the moral and a priori conditions of peace. Kant does not turn to political protagonists right away, but instead considers "social systems," legal and state orders. He also indirectly refers to those who are responsible for them, namely, the constituent assemblies, governments, and the people of the state that authorize them.

Kant sketches a theory of public right that is comprehensive from a legal-moral perspective: (2.1) The first legal-political article discusses the relations between individuals and groups, (2.2) the second article on the right of nations concerns relations among states, and (2.3) the third article on cosmopolitan law explicates the relations between private individuals and groups and foreign states, along with the relations among states that – unlike 2.2 – the states do not owe to one another. The first definitive article thus contains Kant's second major innovation in the ethics of peace. He links the idea of peace to the republic, a political novelty at the time that was first established in the United States and France. However, Kant had already spoken of a republic in the first *Critique* in relation to Plato: CPR B 372ff. (cf. section 12.1). Kant's reflections on the republic thus were influenced not only by the political developments of his time, but also by a long-standing tradition in political philosophy. The second and third definitive articles together constitute the third innovation, the cosmopolitan view of the republic and of peace that was foreign to Plato, on the one hand, and to France and the United States, on the other.

Incidentally, Kant had already spoken of "cosmopolitanism" in the "Idea" eleven years prior to the treatise on peace. The theory of public right it sketches, however, has only two parts. It deals with the civil society corresponding to state right (with the obligation to "the greatest freedom" that "can coexist with the freedom of others"; "Idea" VIII 22) and with the federation of peoples belonging to the right of nations (VIII 24–26), but leaves out cosmopolitan right.

The global peaceful community that is required at the intermediate level seeks not only to end one war but to "end *all war* forever" (*Peace* VIII 356). Following the model of the domestic securing of peace, a world republic according to its positive idea is requisite (VIII 357), but it would differ from a "universal monarchy" in which all states coalesce into a single state. In his plea for a federation of peoples that always expands as a "negative surrogate" or second-best option, Kant argues that states would otherwise not concede to renouncing their sovereignty.

Kant did not first conceive this idea in the 1790s, since he had already made a note of "the final completion: a federation of peoples" twenty years beforehand (*Reflection* 1499, XV 783). In the treaty on peace, he understands the federation of peoples to be a continuing free association that is formed "solely for the purpose of maintaining themselves in peace, among themselves and collectively toward other states" (VIII 383). The *Doctrine of Right* (§61) makes reference to a permanent state congress and explicitly distinguishes it, as a "coalition of different states which can be *dissolved* at any time," from the United States of America (VI 351). Kant's guideline is rather taken from the States-General, such as the assemblies of elected delegates from the seven provincial states that belonged to the Republic of the United Provinces of the Netherlands at the time. The federation of peoples was in any case conceived not as a federal state but as a confederation that could be dissolved at any time. This makes it difficult to reconcile with the task of unqualified peace (see chapter 11).

(3) The termination and culmination of public right in cosmopolitan law does not supplant "national" civil law, but rather supplements it. Kant adheres to a complementary, not exclusive cosmopolitanism. Since this undermines Hegel's criticism in the *Elements of the Philosophy of Right* (§209, remark), one might wonder why Hegel, who was younger, did not have a more discriminating position. Even Hegel's direct criticism of Kant's theory of peace (§§330–340, esp. §333) lacks philosophical and political acumen (see section 8.4).

Whereas the right of nations is based on the recognition of relations which states owe to one another, cosmopolitan law concerns relations that are not owed, namely, transactions in the wide sense of *commercium*: voluntary, not exclusively economical exchange. However, cosmopolitan law concerns not the positive relations themselves, but only the small section of relations that actually are owed, since they, like right in general, are linked to an authorization to use force. Kant's cosmopolitan law, namely, consists in the authorization to offer engagement in commerce without eliciting hostile treatment. This kind of right – unlike philanthropy – depends on reciprocity. The legitimating basis of right is a theorem in Kant's theory of property. Since "all nations stand originally in a community of land, though not of rightful community of possession (*communio*) ... or of property in it," they each have a prior subjective right: the authorization "of offering to engage in commerce with any other" (MM §62).

Kant is here emphasizing a qualified right of cooperation: The trades-man may offer his goods, just as the researcher may offer his knowledge or even the missionary his religion – but neither partner in the trans-action may become violent. As long as the offer is made on foreign territory, the person making the offer merely has visiting rights, not the right to hospitality. This is the case regardless of whether individuals, groups, firms, or an entire people or state are at issue, or whether eco-nomic, cultural, tourist, or political interests are being pursued. In all cases, one may knock on others' doors, but one does not have a right to enter. As in Bacon's *New Atlantis*, a community may combine its gen-erosity toward foreigners with a ban on immigration. Moreover, it may prohibit not only certain types of goods and services, but even trade altogether. Attempts to establish economical autarchy in a "closed com-mercial state," such as those proposed by Rousseau (*Projet de constitution pour la Corse*, 1764) and later by Fichte (1800) and Friedrich List (*Das nationale System der politischen Ökonomie*, 1840) are just as valid from a legal-moral standpoint as a system of customs and dues that protects the national economy from undesired competition.

To be sure, there may exist national-economical considerations that caution against long-term damages; there may also be contraindicating grounds that alarmingly envision the loss of economic, cultural, and political autonomy. It is crucial that the state is not required to justify its protective economic policies to other states. Even if their coopera-tion would result in a overwhelming net advantages, there is no moral-legal command that a state must avail itself of them. Kant's legal morals remain nonpaternalistic; they allow a state to relinquish benefits or even to do itself damage. Undoubtedly, self-isolation from the outside world is not a legitimate reason for a just war. Kant would have harshly criti-cized the cession of Hong Kong forced by Great Britain after the Opium War (1840–1842) and the opening of Chinese harbors for commerce, along with the U.S. forced opening of Japanese harbors for commerce in more recent times.

Regardless of whether cooperation is successful, both parties should be protected. The murder, enslavement, or theft of newcomers and, conversely, the subjection, exploitation, or enslavement of locals are not permitted. Kant's harsh reckoning of the colonial politics at the time is politically relevant. According to Kant's criteria, virtually all of the colonies established in modernity, ranging from South, Central, and

North America to Africa and Australia, are clear examples of injustice, since "they counted the inhabitants as nothing" (*Peace* VIII 358).

Kant's qualified rights of cooperation consist in more than the merely negative prohibition of unjust colonization, and in positive respects they are more than international private rights, notably, the right to commerce. Since rights of cooperation comprise research, culture, and tourism, they in fact amount to a demand that is particularly topical today in the age of globalization. All people have a modest right to a comprehensive community of cooperation, namely, universal visitor rights, but not the right to hospitality. This does not mean, however, that they must relinquish personal and collective particularities. Kant thus already combines a right to universal cooperation with a right to individual difference.

(4) According to Kant's politico-sociological claim in the first definitive article, primarily two motives promote the establishment of a global peaceful federation: the negative motive of experience with the terror of war, and the positive motive of republicanism. Republics – which approximate constitutional democracies or democratic juridical states [*Rechtsstaaten*], but not all states with a division of power – avowedly have little inclination to wars of aggression. And according to the principle of imitation, the republican constitution instituted in *one* state will soon be assimilated by other states. Kant does not trace the inclination to peace among democracies back to the heightened moral sensitivity of their civilians. Exemplary of his clear-headedness, he merely appeals to the capacity of democracies to allow their citizens more opportunity to pursue their self-interests (for criticism on this point, see chapter 10).

(5) The first supplement ("On the Guarantee of Perpetual Peace") supplements the moral theory of peace with a teleological theory of nature. By drawing on ideas from his philosophy of history, notably in the "Idea" and the *Critique of Judgment*, Kant outlines a social history of mankind that is determined solely by nature, in particular by the discord among human beings, but also by peace as a final end. He here turns to legal and state orders in the sense of social systems and their "naturally necessary" development, on the one hand, and to politicians and theoreticians of politics, on the other hand; for they can no longer excuse their disinterest in a global peace order by presuming that it is unfeasible.

Heraclitus's renowned fragment declares war (in the wider meaning of tension and conflict) to be the mother of all things, that is, of all nature, even of its subhuman parts (Diels and Kranz, Fragment 22B80).

Kant limits his scope to human beings. He believes that discord is the decisive factor in the general development of culture ("Idea," 7, proposition: antagonism; cf. chap. 9). Discord, namely, drives people to settle "even into the most inhospitable regions" (*Peace* VIII 363), advances culture (cf. CJ §83, V 388ff.), and even serves moral purposes, since it promotes altruism for the sake of the respective community and, in particular, prompts the transition from the state of nature to the rule of law and civil state: War compels people "to enter into more or less lawful relations" (*Peace* VIII 363).

War here manifests the cunning of (human) nature as a means to the final end of the abolition of war. But even if war is abolished, this does not mean we should fear social entropy, the slow stagnation of global society, for peace does not entail the dissolution of the multiplicity and rivalry between languages and religions or confessions, nor does it diminish commercial competition. The global rule of law and civil state is not *solely responsible* for global peace. Apart from political relations, there are also social and, above all, economic relations. But one does not have a right to enter these relations – they instead arise from voluntary action. The impetus for entering them is called the spirit of commerce according to Kant's second, socioeconomic thesis on the development of a global society. And "since the power of money may well be the most reliable of all the powers (means) subordinate to that of a state" (*Peace* VIII 368), a driving force toward globalization lies in the spirit of commerce or, we may extrapolate, in the benefits afforded by any cooperation whatsoever. The spirit of commerce, however, leads only to a world society and not to a federation of peoples, nor to a world republic.

The treatise on peace thus brings together four aspects of the securing of peace in a clear order of precedence: (a) The leading goal consists in the establishment of a federation of peoples or a world republic (see below, chapter 11). (b) The republican or democratic constitution of single states aids the establishment of a federation of peoples. This principle of democratization (in the sense of a democratic juridical state) is accompanied (c) negatively by "all the hardships of war" (*Peace* VIII 350) and (d) positively by the spirit of commerce, for it "cannot coexist with war" and "sooner or later takes hold of every nation" (VIII 368). The "great artist nature" thus makes use of the natural discord between human beings in order to "let concord arise even against their will" (VIII 360). Human beings come together in single states from assuredly selfish motives, and these states, in turn, first wage war with one another. But then, after time, they learn to live together peacefully due to their interest in commerce and prosperity.

The interplay of all four aspects not only ensures that all war is outlawed without qualification or reservation. Since the spirit of commerce causes an increase in prosperity, negative peace or the absence of war culminates in a positive peace. Peace of this sort is generally well known from diverse cultures, ranging from Greek *eirênê* to Hebrew *shalom* and Roman *pax*, up to Germanic *fride* (cf. Janssen 1975 and Höffe 2002a, chap. 8; see further bibliographic references in the latter).

8.2. "Kingly People"

(6) In the second supplement, Kant engages in a theory-praxis discussion in order to underwrite a partial relationship between philosophy and political power. Under the heading "Secret Article for Perpetual Peace," he demands no less than the abolition of all secrecy and instead encourages free and public discussion "about universal maxims of waging war and establishing peace." In view of international political practice, this demand is revolutionary, comparable to the Copernican turn effected by the epistemology and theory of objects in the *Critique of Pure Reason*. Kant confronts secret diplomacy, which as a practice was not restricted to his epoch, with the principle of publicity. This principle applies the general demand for publicity, or in the *Critique*, the demand that "everything" must submit to "free and public examination" (A XI, footnote), to national and international right. Every maxim of state right and of the right of nations must be examined as to its inner probity. And every maxim that does not withstand this test because it can be successful only in secrecy is prohibited by legal morals.

(7) The continuation of the theory-praxis discussion in the two-part appendix on "morals and politics" finally takes up a motif from the introduction: the conflict between philosophers "who dream a sweet dream" and statesmen proud of their worldly wisdom (*Peace* VIII 343). To the extent that Kant settles this conflict, he also bridges the gap between philosophy and politics.

The establishment of peace on this front is already discussed in the second supplement, where Kant responds to Plato's principle of the philosopher-king, according to which either philosophers must become kings or the so-called kings presently in power ought to engage in sincere and thorough study of philosophy, for otherwise there can be no end to the devastation of states. The core of Kant's response to Plato consists in a distinction. It corroborates both Plato's intention of promoting reason to its realization and his assumption of the compatibility between (moral) theory and (real) praxis (cf. Kant's *Common Saying* and *Conflict*). But it also separates the project of defining moral principles from their real application and entrusts philosophy only with the former task. In this way, Kant applies the division of labor that he espouses in general (cf. GMM IV 388f. and "Idea" VIII 21f.) to the political sphere. Political activity does not fall under the competence of philosophers, but its principles do; practical concretization and execution, in turn, are incumbent on the rulers.

By virtue of their moral character, the philosophical elements absolutely precede all other factors. As theoretical principles of peace, however, they do not provide instructions for political realization but rather depend on that power of judgment that is allegedly missing in Kant but here again is shown to be present (see chapter 3). Moral-political prudence is needed that passes judgment "as favorable circumstances arise" (*Peace* VIII 378) but that "takes the principles of political prudence in such a way that they can coexist with morals" (372). Kant illustrates this by the moral politician (VIII 372 and 377) and opposes him sharply to the political moralist, "who frames a morals to suit the statesman's advantage" (372). Kant calls "morals" that in this way have been subjected to self-interest the "twistings and turnings of an immoral doctrine of prudence" (375).

Following Kant's requirement of consulting philosophical maxims at the beginning of the second supplement, the following statement appears in the concluding paragraph, clearly in allusion to Plato: "It is not to be expected that kings will philosophize or that philosophers will become kings; nor it is to be desired, however, since the possession of power inevitably corrupts the free judgment of reason." (Hence, the "intellectuals," as Kant writes Kiesewetter in these weeks, should not "make common cause with the politicians' trade"; October 15, 1795, *Correspondence* XII 45.) Kant then corroborates Plato's principle: "Kings or sovereign [*kingly*] peoples (i.e., those governing themselves by egalitarian laws) should not, however, force the class of philosophers to disappear or to remain silent, but should allow them to speak publicly. But that kings or sovereign [*kingly*] people (ruling themselves by laws of equality) should not let the class of philosophers disappear or be silent but should let it speak publicly is indispensable to both, so that light may be thrown on their business" (*Peace* VIII 368).

The fact that, for Kant, philosophers have a capacity to give counsel (VIII 368f.; cf. *Conflict*, I. Section, 4: VII 35), recalls the well-advisedness [*eubolia*] of Platonic philosopher-kings (*Republic* IV 428b). But unlike in Plato, their capacity to advise extends not to the entire domain of political rule but to a small, albeit fundamental sector. And therein lies Kant's first, epistemological [*wissenstheoretisch*] argument for the division of labor between philosophy and politics: They must be divided because the cognitive competence of philosophers does not extend to concrete politics. Philosophy does not grasp the conditions of reality or train the experience and judgment belonging to this competence, but it does discriminate what is feasible or effective. For this reason, Kant does not recommend employing philosophers as political advisers. But he recommends close attention to the "maxims of philosophers about the conditions under which public peace is possible" (*Peace* VIII 368). As legal-moral principles of human coexistence, these maxims correspond to the principles of political justice. Thus, Kant's version of the principle of philosopher-kings is tantamount to the commitment of politics to elementary principles of justice.

According to Plato, recognition of the good is inherent in knowledge of the idea of the good (*Republic* X 618c-d); such recognition is action-guiding and all action is guided by recognizing a good. Kant's second argument, which plays on corruptibility, takes aim at this assumed unison between the *principium diudicationis* and the *principium executionis*. Even if philosophers had unlimited competence in giving counsel, they should still be denied political rule, since otherwise their actual competence in the free judgment of reason would be corrupted.

Plato would repudiate this objection with the argument that "his" philosophers' reason is impervious to corruption, since it is what rules the soul (*Republic* VI 484aff.). Platonic philosophers have the distinctive feature of relating to themselves practically in such a way that they are invariably directed toward the good and just. They do not serve particular interests, nor are they constrained by them, and they defy all fame and power (cf. *Republic* I 347d, VI 499b-c, VII 521b, VIII 539e). Kant would reply that an absolutely assured rule of reason or complete eradication, instead of mere subduing, of power is conceivable but not realizable for finite rational beings such as human beings. He is here evidently indebted to Rousseau, who, in the *Social Contract* (chap. II, 7), speaks of a higher reason that perceives all passions of human beings and itself has none. Reason of this kind is reserved for the gods.

Kant's argument in response to Plato is thus ultimately anthropological in nature and extends the anthropological component of moral philosophy, which Kant does not subsume under (empirical) anthropology (see section 5.2): Good rulers in a strict sense, that is, incorruptible rulers, do not exist, even if they are in Plato's sense free from the immense dangers of corruption, such as personal property and the predilection for supporting the well-being of one's own family over general well-being. Even in communities of women or children or in cooperatives, man is still made "from such warped wood" ("Idea" VIII 23; *Religion* VI 100) that he "will always misuse his freedom if he does not have anyone above him" ("Idea," ibid.). By the same token, if the philosopher is granted power, he will be in danger of losing his intellectual independence. Plato, too, cautions against corruption through power (*Republic* VI 491b-e) except in the case of the rule of philosophers. His ideal notion of the philosopher explains why he does not place any restrictions on their rule. Only in the *Laws* does he acknowledge that the rule of laws is a necessity due to the corruptibility of all human beings (IX 874e-875d; cf. III 631cff., IV 713c-714a).

Kant's skepticism may ultimately have its source in his theorem on radical evil, which irretrievably devastates Plato's expectation of reconciling morals and individual wellness in this life (cf. *Republic* II 357d-358a and IX 576bff.). According to Kant, human beings have a propensity to swerve from what is morally commanded for the benefit of self-gratification (see above chapter 4). This propensity, with commensurate force, will cause the corruption of the free judgment of reason.

Kant parts with Plato on a further point. Whereas only few people are suitable for philosophical activity according to Plato's *Republic*, "universal...human reason" is sufficient for philosophical reflection in Kant's view (*Peace* VIII 369). A democracy of reason thus replaces Plato's aristocracy of spirit (acquired from schooling in mathematics and dialectics). Common human reason surely cannot manage without schooling. But this does not entail intellectual aristocracy for Kant; philosophers do not possess any special capacities or insights and thus have no special rights. Deprived of office and privileged insight, philosophers are no more than the champions of "universal reason itself, in which everyone has a voice" (CPR, "Doctrine of Method," Chap. I, Sec. II: B 780). The treatise on peace also attaches importance to "universal...human reason" (VIII 369). To ensure that everyone is heard, universal freedom of speech is mandated in the second supplement of *Perpetual Peace*. Whereas Plato attaches importance to philosophical friends – the supreme, unwritten doctrine is accessible only to a closed circle of the initiated – Kant adheres to the principle of publicity and even grants it a transcendental status (*Peace* VIII 381).

Incontestably, the point at issue in the theory of peace is not so much theoretical reason, but practical, "morally legislative" reason (*Peace* VIII 369). Kant is thus indebted to Plato in a crucial respect. Plato reserves the throne not for professional philosophy instructors, but primarily for the idea of the good. Kant endorses the requirement inherent in the idea of the good, namely, that morals should rule public affairs. He also agrees with Plato on a second point: Morals cannot be derived from experience, but are the result of abstracting from experience. Kant therefore rehabilitates Plato's notion of ideas in the *Critique of Pure Reason*; concepts are needed that, at least in the moral sphere, transcend possible experience (B 369–373). In line with the analogy of the cave, insight into the ideas and ultimately into the idea of the good can be attained only after a turning of the soul [*periagôgê*] (*Republic* VII 515c). In Kant's words, the regency of morals is bound to a "true reform in one's way of thinking" ("What Is Enlightenment?" VIII 36) and to a "revolution in one's disposition" (*Religion* VI 47).

People who submit themselves to the reform and heed to the principles of legal morals are awarded an honorific title that most perfectly expresses the democratization of the principle of philosopher-kings. Kant calls them "kingly people" (*Peace* VIII 369), because they submit their coexistence to right and right to morals. Accordingly, the *Doctrine of Virtue* asserts that a person of true, intelligible virtue is not only "free," "healthy," and "rich," but also "a king" (VI 405). For Kant, kings are truly moral persons, which may be either natural persons ("human beings") or collective persons ("people").

In the treatise on peace, the people take the place of Plato's philosopher-kings – outstanding individuals are replaced by the entirety of those who are both affected by and responsible for the affairs of the state. Undoubtedly, a people may be conferred the honorary title of a "kingly people" only if it submits itself to the requirements of legal morals. Kant does not justify any democracy whatsoever, but a democracy committed to legal morals, which only by fulfilling this condition is a "kingly democracy." If it is to be legitimate, it must rule itself according to "laws of equality" (*Peace* VIII 369) and ensure that "no one can rightfully bind another to something without also being subject to a law by which he in turn *can* be bound in the same way by the other" (first definitive article, VIII 350).

A people is kingly if every citizen is equally a king, but not in the sense of absolutist rulers unbound by laws. The citizen also does not need to be a truly moral person. It suffices that, as a legislator (directly or mediated by representatives), he does his utmost to support laws that do not conflict with legal morals and, as a "subject," to obey these laws. These conditions are commands of legal morals. Thus, "kingly people" are primarily distinguished not by their uncommonly advanced education, as Plato's kings with respect to mathematics and dialectics, but by their justice, which Plato also considers ultimately decisive (although he defines justice differently).

Kant devised his fourth innovation, the democratic interpretation of the principle of philosopher-kings, long before the treatise on peace. Already in the *Critique of Pure Reason*, in the very passage in which he rehabilitates Plato's concept of the idea, Kant transforms the personal requirement "that a prince will never govern well unless he participates in the ideas" into a criterion divested of all personal morals: A "constitution providing for the greatest human freedom according to laws that permit the freedom of each to exist together with that of others" is a "necessary idea, which one must make the ground . . . of all the laws" (CPR B 373). Thus, already in the *Critique*, the just king is replaced by the just constitution of a people, now taken to be kingly.

8.3. Kingly Humanity

Since the human craving for peace is as old as humanity itself, it is not surprising that Kant's treatise on peace enjoys remarkable and in fact reputed precursors. For instance, the *Essay towards the Present and Future Peace in Europe* (1693) by William Penn, the Quaker and founder of Pennsylvania, was published at the end of the seventeenth century. A generation before, Comenius, the bishop of the Bohemian parish, sent a room document entitled "The Angel of Peace" (*Angelus Pacis*) to the members of the "English and Dutch Peace Delegation." Again, in a prior generation at the time of the Thirty Years War (1635), the Duke of Sully contrived the grand design (*Grand Dessein*) of a "universal, very Christian republic," which was to be led by a senate of sixty members. Its disputes were to be arbitrated by a supreme court of law.

More than a century before, while confessional tensions precipitated the Schmalkaldic War in Germany, Sebastian Franck penned the *Little War Book* (1539) in defense of pacifism. Even earlier, Erasmus had written *The Complaint of Peace* (1517). And in the late Middle Ages, Marsilius of Padua stands out as the author of *Defensor Pacis* (*The Defender of Peace*, around 1324). One should also recall Dante's *Monarchia* (around 1310), the writings of Pierre Dubois (1306), and the Bohemian king George of Podiebrad (1462–1464), and especially Augustine's *De civitate Dei* (413–426, esp. XIX 10–13 and 26–28).

The notion of peace thus is not new; and it is such a "natural" concept that it did not need to be invented by any author. In Kant's century, a French secretary at the Utrecht Peace Congress, the Abbé Castel de Saint-Pierre, came out with the *Projet pour render la paix perpétuelle en Europe* (1713–1717), which was soon widely discussed. Rousseau (1756/1761 and 1756/1782), notably, made detailed extracts of it and wrote a probing commentary, but it is not mentioned in the *Social Contract*. Others, such as Voltaire (*De la paix perpétuelle*, 1769), ridiculed the plan as unrealistically zealous. They derided not the idea of peace itself, but rather the hope of realizing it in political institutions. Voltaire, skeptical toward political institutions, but also blind to their utility, places his hope in progressive enlightenment, growing tolerance, and the pressure exerted by changed public opinion.

What makes Kant exceptional is not the occurrence of the idea of peace in his writings, but its distinct profile. This includes Kant's innovations with respect to previous proposals of peace plans, which are partly mentioned above: Kant does not pursue any political interests. Further, he develops a purely philosophical argument; he is just as remote from Erasmus's and Franck's appeal to the New Testament as from Augustine's relegation of peace to the hereafter. Kant does not anywhere conceal religious motives; in the treatise on religion, the idea of peace is explicitly described as "philosophical" and opposed to a "theological" chiliasm (VI 34). Further, Kant refrains from all political zealotry and acknowledges conflict as a fundamental element of the political sphere. Peace does not rule where vain love and friendship hold sway, in an eternal never-never land of freedom from conflict, but where conflicts are treated according to legal-moral principles. This is bound to a clear restriction. The peace Kant discusses is, as a mere protection of life and freedom, a legal task.

Kant removes other restrictions with ease. What humanity until now had known of peace was like a small isle in the great ocean of violence and war: Peace was both temporally and spatially limited. Wherever there was domestic peace or even fortress peace, national peace was lacking; and whenever national peace reigned, there was no peace transgressing national borders; and even from an international perspective, "ecumenical" peace across all countries and cultures was inconceivable. Kant's predecessors, banished from their countries by the division of confessions and other inner European problems of war, write only about Europe and in particular almost only about Christian states. Soloviev, in the *Short Stories on the Antichrist* (1900; 1984, 54) still discussed "peaceful cooperation" only of "all Christian peoples and states." The "possible" addition of "Moslem princes" to the eternal peace pact among the "24 Christian states of Europe," as in the writings of the Abbé Saint-Pierre, was considered a generous act of mercy.

Kant rejects all of these restrictions and instead vindicates a moral universalism of right and peace, that is, a global, both temporally and spatially universal peace. It is no coincidence that Kant's treatise is the most renowned plan for peace. Its four innovations and, in particular, the connection between the republic as a political innovation at the time and a truly global perspective, give rise to a plan of great political courage. If humanity would recognize it by establishing a legal order according to moral principles not only within states, but also between them, then it would, as a whole, attain the status of kingliness.

Kant's treatise on peace contributes not only to political thought. It also contains a social utopia, or rather a (realistic) vision that is still compelling today for two reasons. First, it awakens latent utopian energy and overcomes that resigned loss of hope and vision that robs life of all magnificence and impoverishes the world. The experience that "human beings in general, or heads of state in particular, . . . can never get enough of war" (*Peace* VIII 343) is confronted by morally legislating reason, which "delivers an absolute condemnation of war as a procedure for determining rights" (VIII 356).

The treatise is also compelling because it allays the fears of Friedrich Wilhelm von Schütz, a contemporary critic and formerly passionate exponent of revolutionary ideas, who wrote that "the idea of a perpetual peace cannot be realistic" (in Dietze and Dietze 1989, 299). Kant no doubt perceives this danger, and thus mentions "philosophers, who dream that sweet dream" (*Peace* VIII 343) and the possibility that the goal is "merely chimerical" or a delusion (VIII 368). In the treatise on peace he does not succumb to illusions of wishful thinking with respect to the good of human beings or the sagacity of their sovereigns. Instead, he expressly demonstrates that perpetual peace is not "an empty thought" (VIII 372) and "no empty idea" (VIII 386). Even those who find Kant's proof dubious cannot deny that the chances for realizing peace considerably increase under Kantian conditions.

A first condition amenable to realization rests on giving up the notion of a comprehensive utopia. In contrast with Augustine or with the first stage in the development of the Platonic polis (*Republic* II 369b–372c), Kant does not defend a comprehensive ideal of peace. In Plato's elementary polis, human beings live in peace not only with other human beings, but also with the gods, or even with nature (cf. Höffe 1997, chap. 4). Kant does not consider most of these dimensions of peace. Whereas Plato binds social peace to inner or personal peace, Kant places peace in the domain of right, where reference to personal attitudes is immaterial. The following dimensions are left out of Kant's conception of peace: (1) the peace of man with himself, that is, inner or personal peace, (2) its extension or deepening in religious peace in or with god, and further (3) peace in and with nature, ecological peace, and (4) that cosmic peace that has been so important since Augustine, in which all things attain a proper locus within a hierarchically constructed world order (*De civitate Dei* XIX 12f.). (5) Only social peace remains to be considered.

Even this dimension is understood in a moderate way. In German, the expression "Friede" (peace) is related to "free" [*frei*], "to wed or woo" [*freien*], and "friend" [*Freund*]. A derivative of the Indo-Germanic root *prî* – to love or to care for – it "originally refers to a state of love and care, with greater emphasis placed on the aspect of mutual help and support than on emotional attachment and affection" (Janssen 1975, 543). The meaning of *Friede* later was narrowed down to (6) a negative social peace and signified only the (usually temporally restricted and spatially limited) deterrence of violence. Kant's (7) political and more precisely legal concept of peace leaves aside the first four dimensions and denotes something in between the comprehensive social concept and an extreme contraction of it: On the one hand, violence is deterred without any temporal restrictions or territorial limitation, while on the other hand, a moment of active help is added, but it is restricted to the single task of safeguarding right. In all three definitive articles in the treatise on peace, a negative concept of peace predominates: legal security.

The second aspect that is amenable to the realization of peace lies in the very concept of right: As mentioned above, Kant renounces the idyllic vision of the cessation of all conflict. The decisive anthropological fact of "unsocial sociability" is confirmed in the first supplement.

Although passions such as "the desire for honor, power or property" are "far from admirable in themselves," they resist the human "tendency to laziness" and induce him to take the first steps "from barbarism to culture" ("Idea," Fourth Proposition). Kant thus does not only allow for conflicts but even welcomes them; but he condemns force as a means of resolving conflicts.

As a further aspect amenable to realization, the first supplement introduces the "great artist nature," which makes use of the natural discord between human beings in order to let "concord arise . . . even against their will" (*Peace* VIII 360): Human beings unite from assuredly selfish motives in single states that at first wage war against one another, but after time, particularly due to interests in commerce, they learn to live in peace (see above, section 8.1).

The fourth aspect amenable to realization is meant to contrast with former utopian visions such as Thomas More's *Utopia* and the vast array of political novels that emulate this model in the sixteenth and seventeenth centuries. Because they give free reign to social and political imagination, they are rightly called "*voyages imaginaries*," or fictional voyages. Kant strongly opposes them by explicitly maintaining that the "sweet dream" is the dream of "philosophers," that is, precisely those whose métier requires them to employ concepts and argumentation. In Kant, reason rather than the imagination travels far. It elevates perpetual peace to the status of an "immediate" legal moral duty (*Peace* VIII 356, l. 4; cf. 362, l. 9; 364/9; 378, ll. 19–22). Apart from wars of self-defense (345), "war" is absolutely condemned "as a procedure for determining rights" (356). This categorical imperative of peace establishes peace that is in a moral respect *eo ipso* perpetual. The motto adhered to by most states stems from the Roman military theorist Vegetius (A.D. fourth century): "If you want peace, prepare for war" [*Si vis pacem, para bellum*]. Kant substantially counters this with the principle: If you want peace, prepare for – political – justice [*Si vis pacem, para iustitiam*]. In his own words: "[S]eek ye first the kingdom of pure practical reason and its *justice*, and your end (the blessing of perpetual peace) will come to you of itself" (*Peace* VIII 378).

8.4. Truncated Influence

Kant's text elicited an uncommonly swift and intensive response. Whereas a second edition of the first *Critique* only appeared six years following its publication, the treatise on peace, despite its doubled circulation, was already reprinted in the span of a few weeks: The first 2000 copies were followed by a further 1500. And the second edition hit the market already in the following year. The *Critique of Pure Reason*, the most important work of modern philosophy or, according to Schopenhauer, the "most important book ever to be written in Europe" (*Letters*, no. 157), was not a literary success like the political sketch *Toward Perpetual Peace*. Four further editions of the latter appear during Kant's lifetime, in the span of almost ten years until 1804. Another dozen follow before the outbreak of the First World War; in the subsequent forty years, twenty further editions are published (Raumer 1953, 162), and numerous others follow suit.

The popularity of the author was undoubtedly greater than that of the text. Kant was familiar with his own worth; he demanded payment of four "Reichstaler" per printed sheet of the first *Critique* (Vorländer 1992, chap. 9, p. 81f.), whereas he demanded ten for *Toward Perpetual Peace* (Letter from August 13, 1795, to the Königsberg publisher Nicolovius, *Correspondence* XII 35). Even this sum, however, is not "a fortune," as it corresponds to about a month's salary of an elementary school teacher.

The text was, moreover, perused and discussed intensely. Closer friends – such as Kiesewetter and Erhard, Stäudlin and Sophie Mereau, a "professor in Jena" – responded to it in epistolary reports. Even more important were the reviews by several highly competent authors that were published in Germany and in neighboring countries (cf. in Buhr and Dietzsch 1984, 61ff.). Whether the text was greeted with laudatory or even enthusiastic appraisal or, as was the case with Wilhelm von Humboldt, reserved judgment ("In all, I cannot regard the treatise as very important": letter to Schiller, October 30, 1795; similarly on December 11, 1795) – it became the talk of the day in intellectual circles. Even leading supporters of revolutionary France saw Kant as a sympathizer (cf. Azouvi and Bourel 1991, 65–83).

The phase of reviews was followed by that "classic German peace debate around 1800" (Dietze 1989, 58) that in large part was broached by discussions about Kant. In the *Philosophical Journal*, one of the two editors, Fichte himself (1795/1966, 221), wrote that "the comfort and ease of the presentation" should not mislead the reader into denying the proper importance of the work's main idea, which it "has in our estimation," namely, that this idea "lies in the essence of reason, that reason absolutely demands its own realization, and that it thus belongs among those purposes of nature that are to be preserved, not destroyed." Although Fichte claims to have only a "few words to add" to Kant's treatise, he diverges from Kant on two points. He puts "another municipal authority," the ephorate, at the side of the executive power and says more clearly than Kant that a federation of peoples is "merely an intermediate state" for the "securing of peace" and that the true end lies in a "international state."

In the same year, Friedrich Schlegel put pen to paper. In the *Essay on the Concept of Republicanism Occasioned by Kant's Treatise on Perpetual Peace*, he unleashed polemical pyrotechnics against Kant's thesis that democracy is necessarily despotic and that republicanism can be established only through gradual reform. Schlegel starts out with admiring esteem for Kant, but concludes that Kant's political thinking does not withstand close scrutiny, since his definitions of legal or civil freedom are only "minimal." The – admittedly unattainable – "maximum would entail an absolute equality of the rights and obligations of all state citizens and thus would make an end of all rule and dependency" (*Kritische Friedrich-Schlegel-Ausgabe* VII 13). The criticism of Kant inherent in the first part of this sentence is undoubtedly persuasive; Schlegel confronts Kant's limitation of active citizenship with the following argument: "[P]overty and *supposed* corruptibility, womanliness, and *supposed* weakness are not legitimate reasons for denying the right to vote" (ibid., 17). However, the identification of equality of rights with freedom from rule is dubious. Schlegel's attempt to eradicate all rule per se both within states and among states, and thus to establish a powerless world society of free and equal peoples, contradicts Kant's assessment that "law and freedom, without authority," produce anarchy, which in turn violates the command to establish a public legal order (*Anthropology* VII 330).

The younger Joseph Görres had his word two years after Fichte and Schlegel. Misjudging its genuine moral status, he interpreted the categorical imperative of right merely as a social pragmatic command. One would think that Görres's views were influenced by the utilitarian Bentham, if it were not for the fact that *A Plan for a Universal and Perpetual Peace* (1786) was published posthumously under the title *Principles of International Law* (1843). Görres agreed with Bentham's fundamental tenet of common well-being: "The end of all peace is the happiness of the people, and the first requirement for the achievement of this end is stability. Peace only rightly deserves that name if it guarantees the people prosperity for the unlimited duration of their existence" (in Dietze and Dietze 1989, 315). According to Kant, an interest in welfare is indeed among the causes of peace. Its actual end, however, consists not in collective welfare ("bliss of the people") but in right, and right is committed to securing the universal coexistence of individual freedom. Other ends are justified only by right defined in this way, that is, they are "functional" for right.

German intellectuals – ranging from Görres and Schlegel to Humboldt (who, in the aforementioned letter to Schiller, detected a "much too stark democratism" in Kant) – already had difficulties with Kant's republicanism at the time. They questioned public powers that are committed to nothing other than right and the principles of human freedom, to common lawgiving and the equality of citizens (*Peace* VIII 349f.). Even Friedrich Gentz distanced himself from Kant, who had previously been his tutor. He nevertheless compiled the treatise *On Perpetual Peace* (1800). But as evinced by his translation of Edmund Burke's *Reflections on the Revolution in France* (1790) into German (1793), he rejected republicanism, a pillar of Kant's theory, under the influence of Burke's conservative criticism of the French Revolution.

Other intellectuals at the time, such as Schelling, were not even receptive to the idea of an international peaceful order of law. Hegel already endorsed the contrary position in his essay on natural right (1802/1803), asserting that war, not only peace, is "absolutely necessary." Since he links war with the "moral sanity of a people," he claims that perpetual peace would reduce all peoples to "perpetual silence" (*Works* II 481f.). Hegel does not budge from this assessment. Almost two decades later, in the *Elements of the Philosophy of Right* (1821, §333) he almost literally repeats it and in this way subjects the principle of his legal philosophy to a regrettable limitation. Freedom is a right on the national level, but it is revoked on the international level.

One might criticize Kant as the adherent of a tradition reaching from Rousseau, the Encyclopedists (cf. the article "war"), and Adam Smith all the way back to Latin (e.g., Tacitus, *Germania*, chap. 7f.) and Greek antiquity (e.g., Aristotle, *Politics* VII 15, 1334a26). In this tradition, war is considered morally advantageous as a regenerative factor. Thinkers of the tradition, however, do not intone an "original encomium of war," but only praise those virtues necessary for war, notably, courage. They support war only on grounds of its expediency for virtue. Smith, for example, does not justify war as such, but sees it as the best way to practice the important virtue of powerful and rigorous self-control. The gentle virtues of humanity, by contrast, ripen under the soft rays of unperturbed peace (*Theory of Moral Sentiments*, 1759, Part 3, chap. 3).

It is true that Kant expresses "high esteem for the warrior" in the *Critique of Judgment* (§28). However, he explicitly demands that "he at the same time display all the virtues of peace, gentleness, compassion," which at most find feeble resonance in Smith. This supplement is the first indication of why Kant sees "something sublime" in war. For "a long peace causes the spirit of mere commerce to predominate, along with base selfishness, cowardice and weakness, and usually debases the mentality of the populace." War assuredly does not have a moral worth as such. On the contrary, it is "the source of all evil and corruption of morals" (*Conflict* VII 86). In order to have "something sublime," it must, according to Kant, fulfill strict conditions and at least be "conducted with order and reverence for the rights of the citizens" (CJ, §28).

In post-idealism, as in Schopenhauer or Marx, the idea of a global peaceful order plays as minimal a role as it did in Hegel. Nietzsche even has Zarathustra teach in his "discourse with the kings" that "you should love peace as a means to new wars. And the short peace more than the long" (p. 74). In Rawls's Kantian-inspired *Theory of Justice* (1971) and in his second major work, *Political Liberalism* (1993), it is seen as a vain undertaking to search for a theory of an international legal order (unlike Rawls 1993).

The same surprisingly holds for critical theory (and even for Bloch). In a century of two world wars and innumerable regional wars, critical theory claims to have unleashed utopian energies. But whether we consider Marcuse or Horkheimer, Adorno, or even Habermas's legal philosophy (1994) – silence on the topic of an international peace order is persistent and tenacious. (Since then, however, Habermas 1995 has appeared.) This deficit does not have a merely contingent explanation. Both in critical theory and in Rawls, the legitimation of public powers or legal ethics receives much too short shrift.

This is not much different in works of legal philosophy in the twentieth century. The conception of the right of nations appears in Radbruch's *Legal Philosophy* (1932, §28), in Kelsen's *Pure Doctrine of Right* (1934, 1960, chap. VII), and in Hart's *The Concept of Law* (1961, chap. X), but surprisingly without the notion of a global peace. (Kelsen wrote only one journal article: "The Strategy of Peace," 1944.) In

Luhmann's legal theory, both the right of nations and the notion of peace are nowhere to be found. This discovery proves Hegel's words to be true in a thoroughly trivial sense: The owl of Minerva does not take flight before the break of dawn. Philosophy offers so little preparation for urgent problems of life that it tends to aggravate the danger of reacting in a more moralizing than discursive way to them.

9

THE "IDEA": LEGAL PROGRESS

Civilization today demonstrates conflicting attitudes toward the civil religion of the Enlightenment, the idea of progress. Its exaggeration of Rousseau's skepticism has made the contribution of scientific-technical progress to the purification of morals doubtful. It also views this progress as endangered by menacing side effects that escaped Rousseau's attention. On the other hand, it strongly supports the sciences, medicine, and technology, and justifies these disciplines by their net benefits. Moreover, it fosters better legal and state relations, with emphasis on establishing the rule of law instead of brute force between states. And it also looks forward to considerable progress in this sphere.

Kant may be consulted in discussions about these conflicting attitudes. In his philosophy of history skepticism merges with optimism about progress, and Kant rejects any claim to exclusiveness on either side. Just as the first *Critique* seeks to resolve the conflict between rationalism and empiricism or skepticism in theoretical philosophy, the "Idea" strives for a peaceful solution to the conflict between optimism and skepticism in thinking about progress. Once again, peace is substantively defined as a middle position and methodically determined by a concise critique, or reflection on the appropriate form of knowledge. Whereas the procedure of critical thinking about progress, including the privileged status of legal progress, does carry conviction (section 9.1), doubts arise about its exact contour: Legal progress is said to aim only at a federation of peoples (section 9.2). It both is driven forward by a natural mechanism and is associated with moral maturation (section 9.3).

9.1. Critical Thought and Progress

(1) *Legal Progress*: Like Rousseau in his *First Treatise* (1750), Kant rejects the assumption that the progress of art and science contributes to the improvement of morals (cf. seventh proposition, VIII 26, 17ff.). However, he revises Rousseau's narrow vision. The first proposition of the "Idea" already incorporates art and science in the improvement of the human being: "[A]ll the natural capacities of a creature are destined sooner or later to be developed completely and in conformity with their end." Their importance is qualified, however, by the three ways acknowledged by Kant of developing natural capacities: cultivation, civilization, and moral maturation.

These three ways are ranked in hierarchical order and recall Kant's three imperatives. Kant understands art (*technê, ars*) as skill (cf. CJ, §43) and relates it to the "use of means to all sorts of discretionary ends" (GMM IV 415). Cultivation through art and science thus seems to be a mostly technical procedure. The second way is the civilization of customs. If it is not taken "to the point of excess," it will lead to "love of honor and outward propriety" (ll. 25 and 26), and thus at least indirectly to social well-being. This gives it the status of a social-pragmatic imperative. The categorical imperative finally leads to the third way, that of moral maturation: "the slow and laborious efforts of citizens to cultivate their minds" toward a "morally good attitude of mind" (ll. 28 and 32).

Kant expresses frank approval of the first stage of progress: "[W]e are cultivated to a high degree by art and science," whereas his approval of the second has a critical undertone: "[W]e are civilized to the point of excess" (l. 22). "But we are still a long way from the point where we could consider ourselves morally mature" (ll. 22f.). At the same time, Kant avoids the fallacies of a limited perspective. He does not consider his own epoch to be a reckoning of all epochs, whether for better or for worse. He does not believe in the decline of civilization, nor does he consider the present to be the "completion of history."

Both restrictions on art and science and on the achievements of modernity enable Kant to confront Rousseau's skepticism toward progressive thinking with his own skepticism. His skepticism is enlightened, but of a modest and critical form. It is attenuated by a third point, which, after the events of the twentieth century, is especially relevant today: Kant champions legal progress and its crowning in an international peaceful order. Factors that make a philosophy of history seem ridden with difficulties are missing. For instance, Kant does not construct history from the blueprint of a speculative logic, nor does he neglect concern for the individual.

(2) *Reasoned hope*: Since "progress" is a historical concept, it should be relegated to the competence of historians. Insofar as they still even venture to ask the question about progress or the related question as to the meaning of history in general, they appeal to readily accessible material: single events, chains of events, and groups of events. Since their microperspective does not allow them to discover meaning, historians such as Koselleck (1997) have advocated meaninglessness, understood not as a belief in negative meaning or the progression of disaster but as a dismissal of the question about meaning altogether. One might endorse the alternative macroperspective, directed at vast time spans, perhaps even at the entire history of humankind. But history as a science – as those in the discipline rightly contest – is not capable of this vision. It is nevertheless somewhat hasty for historians such as Wehler (1999) to speak of the "hubris of the philosophy of history," unless they mean its "control over definitions," or its claim to decide exclusively on what counts as the writing of history.

Here, too, Kant emerges as an interesting interlocutor, since he already anticipates the objection. He takes on the superlative macroperspective of a "universal history of the world" (VIII, l. 2; cf. 30, l. 29), but explicitly removes it from the task of "history proper, that of *empirical* composition" (cf. 30, ll. 30f.). A universal history can be seen only from a "different angle," which "a philosophical mind . . . might be able to attempt" (ll. 32f.). Counter to the obvious objection that history is then reduced to untamed speculation, Kant demands that a philosophical mind be "well acquainted with history" (l. 33). Even if philosophy takes on a perspective different from the study of history, it does not renounce the shared minimal precondition of experience. Its "different angle" clearly indicates, however, that philosophy consciously avoids the great error of many philosophies of history, the conflation of the "speculative" and the "empirical."

Philosophical history even provides the "prospect of a future" (30, ll. 14f.) without claiming prophetic powers in either of two familiar senses. In the introduction, Kant mentions a future Kepler and Newton (18, ll. 14–17). But he does not intend to voice a "theoretical," truth-revealing prophesy, which would be able to predict the future objectively based on social research akin to the method employed by natural science. An objective prediction, namely, would not be compatible with the object, the "free exercise of the human will" (17, l. 7). Nor does Kant call forth that "moral-practical" prophesy of wisdom familiar from religious texts, which in the face of a menacing future of pragmatic decline urges present society toward *metanoia*, or to a radical change in attitude for the benefit of the good.

Kant believed that his era was in a bad state with respect to right and law, but he did not consider it to be bad through and through. It was bad because on an *inter*national level between states, violence and war were predominant. But it was not entirely bad, since there already were states that *intra*nationally were subject to right and law. The second and more fundamental difference is that for Kant, the better future ("the comforting prospect," 30, l. 14) is expected not from moral or religious individual endeavors or from *metanoia*, but from a path that eases the burden of personal morals for the individual. Human beings "neither pursue their aims purely by instinct, as the animals do, nor act in accordance with any integral, prearranged plan like rational cosmopolitans" (17, ll. 27–29). This path is thus not affected by the overburdened concept of the "end of redemptive history [*Heilgeschichte*]." Kant's alternative concept of progress is neither quasi-mechanical nor planned; he calls it the purpose of nature and defines it as the mediation between man's nature and his freedom. The purpose of nature anticipates Hegel's "cunning of reason," which shows that the latter term is not entirely novel. Kant also offers a more modest alternative. On Kant's view a finality or final causality is at work behind the backs of active agents. From the microperspective there certainly is situational meaning in history. But in contrast to an optimism that distorts reality, Kant finds that "in the great world-drama ... despite the apparent wisdom of individual actions here and there, everything as a whole is made up of folly and childish vanity, and often of childish malice and destructiveness" (17f.). He nevertheless seeks to discover a purpose of nature "behind this senseless course of human events" (18, ll. 8f.) and for which there is a special way of knowing. Progress that is brought about by a purpose of nature is neither the concern of objective knowledge nor an individual moral performance, but rather that for which we have "grounds for hope" (30, l. 14; concerning "hope," see also 17, l. 6, and 23, l. 37).

One might raise the objection against Kant's philosophy of history that it lacks the more advanced, critical notion of teleology developed in the third *Critique*. In fact, substantial thoughts on this issue may be found in the *Reflections* from the 1770s, such as in no. 1396: "Through civil coercion all seeds unfold without exception. This is the destiny of mankind, not of the individual, but of the species" (XV/2 608). And Reflection no. 1423 states that "man is an animal that needs to be educated. [...] One generation must educate the next. And only the species as a whole, not the individual, achieves its destiny. As an animal that is self-preserving and human, man is made for society. Man is only secure and at ease in society through the exercise of coercion and he needs a ruler" (XV/2 621). In the 1770s, Kant even articulated the final goal of legal and state theory. In his "Sketch for the Anthropology Society" at this time, the following note can be found: "When peoples establish law and common powers among themselves, external security is founded" and "a federation of peoples" replaces "barbarism" (XV/2 790, Reflection no. 1501).

The fact that substantial thoughts already originate from the time before the third and even before the first *Critique* does not prove that they are of a precritical nature. In the 1770s, namely, critical philosophy was gradually taking shape. Moreover, the critical nature of Kant's thoughts can be decided not by the content of statements such as "progress of the species," but only by their methodical placement, which is not thematic in the *Reflections*. Instead, the "Idea" reprises the relevant insights of the *Critique* that concern the interconnectedness of a critique of objectivity claims and an epistemological critique.

With respect to the critique of objectivity claims, Kant denies that teleology is an objective feature of the course of history. Nor does he accept the ontologization of teleology that would make nature anthropomorphic. Nature is not an agent or quasi-agent that determines ends and follows them. Kant would agree that the criteria that define the human species do not contradict a human being's self-assessment as a being capable of reason (against Schnädelbach 2000, 54), but he does reject the interpretation of the *species* as a rational agent. The *Critique* defines teleology as an exclusively regulative, and moreover heuristic idea, not as a constitutive one (B 715f.). By the same token, the purpose of nature in the "Idea" provides only a "guiding thread" that does not replace "history proper, that of empirical composition" (30, ll. 30f.). The concept of a purpose of nature incidentally does imply final natural causality, which again recalls Aristotle (see chapter 2), since it corresponds to the three-fold meaning of his *physis*. Like Aristotle, Kant is concerned with (a) a seed in which all to come is already enclosed, (b) the unfolding of the predisposition, and (c) the completion of this unfolding.

With respect to Kant's epistemological critique, in turn, the cognitive relation is characteristically modest: The purpose of nature, which contributes to progress, can only be the object of hope (CPR B 832) or of (rational) belief, which is strictly distinguished from knowledge (B 848ff.). To be sure, Kant did not write a "Critique of Hope," but in this essay he develops the concept of hope as a characteristic form of rationality (cf. Conradt 1999), in the sharpest conceivable contrast to hope understood as an affect (cf. *Anthropology* VII 251–253; CPrR V 74; *Conflict* VII 86). The *Critique* places this rationality in the context of morals and religion, but it may with equal justification be placed in the historical and legal spheres.

(3) *The federation of peoples as an idea*: The methodical determination of the federation of peoples as an "idea" (VIII 24, l. 28) gives it the very status that in the treatise on peace is granted not to the federation of peoples but to the world republic. Kant is aware that the idea was ridiculed as "wild and fanciful" when it was marshaled by its earlier advocates, the Abbé St. Pierre and Rousseau (ll. 28f.). The accusation of zealous daydreaming [*Schwärmgeisterei*] this suggests was in fact common ever since the movements of the reformers. In their spiritual piety, they championed such goals as the baptism of adults, rigid Church discipline, and a community of property, and they wanted to realize the kingdom of god on earth. In Kant, the concern with accusations of zealotry [*Schwärmerei*] is an important theme ever since the *Critique*, where it is taken in a wide, not merely religious sense. In the "most general sense," zealotry is "an overstepping of the bounds of human reason undertaken on principles" (CPrR: "On Incentives," V 85; cf. *Anthropology* VII 191), or "a delusion of being able to see something beyond all bounds of sensibility" (CJ V 275). As such it is akin to mother wit (*Anthropology* VII 203) and the shifting of meaning (*Anthropology* §10), which in an "enlightened age" generally cannot "appear" (*Prolegomena*, Appendix, IV 383). Kant discusses a version of zealotry specific to political theory in the section entitled "On Ideas in General" in the *Critique*. He cites the view of the Platonic republic that has "become proverbial," namely, that it is a "supposedly striking example of a dream of perfection that can have its place only in the idle thinker's brain." He then goes on to refute this view (B 372).

In the *Critique*, Kant already substantially defines the idea of the state as a "constitution providing for the greatest human freedom according to laws that permit the freedom of each to exist together with that of others" (B 373). It is methodically defined as the opposite of a dream, namely, as a pure concept that "has its origin solely in the understanding," that "goes beyond the possibility of experience," and thus "is an idea or a concept of reason" (B 377). Ideas "first make the experience (of the good) itself possible, even if they can never be fully expressed in experience" (B 375). Kant specifically refers to the idea of the state as an archetype that is necessary, not "drawn from experience," and that induces government and legislation to come ever nearer to possible greatest perfection, or to come in agreement with the idea (B 373f.) Thus in the seventh proposition when the federation of peoples is treated as an idea, Kant is emphasizing precisely that reason plays a role in social coexistence, and that the law and its public protection bestow a state character on the idea of a federation of peoples through two definitional elements: "law-governed decisions of a united will" and a "united power" (VIII 24, ll. 26f.). The seventh proposition assumes that the concept of an idea is familiar from the first *Critique* and is merely concerned with refuting the possible objection of fanciful zealotry (ll. 28ff.). The ninth proposition corroborates the refutation by fending off speculations that the history spoken of in the "Idea" has a novelesque or fictional character ("novel," 29/10; "a work of fiction," "Conjectures" VIII 109; cf. CJ, "General Remark" following §29, V 273, l. 6). Kant opposes the "Idea" to the tradition that began with Thomas More's *Utopia* (1616) of political novels that open the floodgates to the social and political imagination in "*voyages imaginaries.*" These include the Gargantua and Pantagruel novels by Rabelais (1532–1552), Campanella's *Civitas solis* (1602/1623), Harrington's *Oceana* (1656), and later Swift's satire *Gulliver's Travels* (1726), Schnabel's *Insel Felsenburg* (1731) and F. L. von Solberg's *Insel* (1788). Contrary to this tradition, Kant understands his aim of a federation of peoples to be a product not of the imagination but of legal morals and of practical "reason" (cf. VIII 24, l. 21).

According to the first *Critique*, ideas have the further property of being endlessly approachable but never completely attainable – as suggested at B 373. In the "Idea," Kant likewise writes that "nature only requires of us that we should approximate to this idea" (VIII 23, ll. 24f.; cf. 27, ll. 28f.) The relevant argument is famous: "[N]othing straight can be constructed from such warped wood as that which man is made of" (23, ll. 22–24). It is important for Kant's epistemic claim to recognize that the statements in the "Idea" are called propositions, which Kant understands not as arbitrary or problematic (possible), but as assertoric judgments (*Logic*, §30).

In the second Untimely Meditation on the "Advantages and Disadvantages of History for Life" (1874), Nietzsche draws the much-cited distinction among three species of history: a monumental, antiquarian, and a critical species of history. Kant's philosophy of history certainly cannot belong to the second species. He is not concerned with "love and loyalty," "piety," and "thanks," nor with "tending with care that which has existed from of old" (Nietzsche, *Untimely Meditations*, 72f.). His conception shows more proximity to the monumental species of history, since the principle of legal progress can determine ends to be pursued with firm resolve by the "being who acts and strives." But Kant does not stress the importance of "models, teachers, comforters," of great statesmen of the past or of institutional achievements such as the Greek or Roman republics. Instead, he alludes to the necessity of wars and the potential willingness to forge peace that is inherent in this necessity. Kant's philosophy of history thus belongs to the critical species of history, not only in his own, critical-rational sense, but also in agreement with Nietzsche's understanding. Those who are suffering or in need of liberation may "break up and dissolve a part of the past" (ibid., 75). Kant, however, maintains that if war belongs to the past it can be dissolved by the future of (eternal) peace. The dissolution does not proceed in the way described by Nietzsche as "an attempt to give oneself, as it were *a posteriori*, a past in which one would like to originate in opposition to that in which one did originate" (ibid., 76). For Kant, history does not rewrite itself, but makes perspicuous the incentives inherent in human nature, which we have "reason to hope" may be overcome.

9.2. A Contradiction in the Federation of Peoples

Kant's difficulties lie elsewhere. They concern not the methodical determination of progress but its substantive definition – and even then, Kant's difficulties do not have their source in the first propositions of the "Idea," which we may swiftly recount here. First, Kant puts forward an evolutionary theorem not in anticipation of Darwin for the whole of nature, but only for individuals and species. All natural dispositions of a creature are destined sooner or later to be developed completely and in conformity with their end (first proposition). He then applies this general theorem to the human being and claims that human natural dispositions are developed only in the species as a whole, but not in the individual (second proposition). Nature has willed that human beings produce everything entirely by their own initiative (third proposition), and their incentive for doing so lies in unsocial sociability (fourth proposition). The untamed, wild, or brutal freedom appears as "antagonism" between human beings ("unsocial"); but due to the disagreements this arouses, human beings concede to the limitation of their freedom through socialization ("sociability"). Kant significantly restricts his attention to spontaneous, thoroughly selfish passions, but their collective interaction brings about something new. And this reveals Kant's ingenious approach: Egoism, competition, and war, all of which are familiar reasons for skepticism against progress, are collectively referred to as antagonism and they become the driving force of progress. Unsocial sociability thus has a providential power: "All the culture and art which adorn mankind and the finest social order man creates are fruits of his unsociability. For it is compelled by its own nature to discipline itself" (VIII 22, ll. 32–34).

The propositions following the first four general ones are concerned with the precise aim to be pursued. Since this aim consists in a complete civil constitution that, in contradistinction to religious eschatology, is achieved "here on earth" (30, l. 18; cf. l. 28), the section on legal philosophy begins with the fifth proposition. In the same framework, the seventh proposition discusses in two paragraphs of almost equal length the international and interstate legal and state orders. The first paragraph roughly corresponds to the second definitive article of the treatise on peace ("the right of nations shall be based on a federalism of free states"), and the second paragraph roughly corresponds to its first supplement "on the guarantee of perpetual peace," whereas cosmopolitan right is still outstanding. The more precise contours both of a global legal order and of the driving force leading to it pose certain difficulties.

The modern age has called the state of coexistence while lacking any legal form the "state of nature." Although Kant does not use this expression, he describes the counterpart to the state of cosmopolitanism ("world citizenry") as an international state of nature. He speaks of "unrestricted freedom" (24, l. 10) and "the unsociableness of men, and even of the large societies and states" (ll. 13f.), of "wars, tense and unremitting military preparations" (ll. 16f.) and the "barbarous freedom of states" (26, l. 1), and especially of a "lawless state" (24, ll. 22f.; cf. 25, l. 29: "lawless freedom").

Since law is in force in already "established states," but only within the states, the international state of nature is only a residual state of nature. If coexistence without right or law altogether is a primary state of nature, and coexistence in which public powers or authorities do not exist is a secondary state of nature (cf. Höffe 1994, chap. 10, and 2002a, sec. 4.1), then the residual state of nature in the "Idea" appears to be secondary. From the contrastive concept of a federation of peoples, we may infer that Kant views "security and rights" as already given (24, l. 14; in ll. 16 and 35 only "peace and security"), but still dependent on judgment and power. "Security and rights" can be decided not by right itself but by the parties concerned. In the international state of nature, private justice thus reigns in two respects: in the interpretation of "security and rights" and in the practice of instituting them.

Calling the subjects concerned "savages" (24, l. 23) might evoke a second deficiency in them, a deficiency of development in addition to their legal deficiency, a lack in cultivation and civilization. Kant, however, understands the "savages" to be human beings that do not like to be constrained (l. 33); he is referring only to their legal deficiency or lawless freedom.

From the perspective of the treatise on peace and the *Doctrine of Right*, it is unclear why Kant designates the "cosmopolitan state" (26, l. 10) as the alternative to "unrestrained freedom" (22, ll. 21f.). In the former works, cosmopolitan right is the second section of inter- or supranational right, whereas the "Idea" is concerned with precisely the other section, the right of nations. But Kant translates "*societas civilis*" (in French, "*société civile*," and in English, "civil society") with "*bürgerliche Gesellschaft*" ("bourgeois society") and understands it not as a civil society in today's sense, as a society of citizens, but rather as any form of coexistence in a legal and state form. The expression "cosmopolitan" extends this social form to the entire world; a globally comprehensive civil society, a global or world state, is "cosmopolitan."

This interpretation is supported by Kant's employment of the expression "cosmopolitan." In the "Idea," it appears only in three passages with the exception of the title, and once in each of the three final "propositions": (1) The seventh proposition calls the international state of law "cosmopolitan" and entrusts it with the task of "general political security" (26, ll. 10f.). This task is assigned not to the respective states themselves but to a "united power" that acts in compliance with "the law-governed decisions of a united will" (ll. 26f.). (2) With the supplement of a "universal" cosmopolitan existence (28, l. 34), the eighth proposition emphasizes the difference between Kant's view and that of Abbé St. Pierre (see section 8.3.): Instead of resting content with a European solution, Kant is seeking an all-comprehensive, global solution of the future "without precedent in the past" (28, l. 29). (3) The concept of the "cosmopolitan goal" (31, l. 4) in the ninth proposition shows that there is something in the global solution that makes it "the highest purpose of nature" (l. 34). In all three passages of the "Idea," "cosmopolitan" designates neither a subjective right, the cosmopolitan right of the *Peace*, nor an objective (cosmopolitan) right, the sum total of all laws regulating subjective cosmopolitan right. "Cosmopolitan" rather has a double meaning: It designates both the political, legal state and the goal of establishing it.

According to the fifth proposition, "a perfectly just civil constitution" is characterized by a double superlative. The general task of right and law, "freedom under external laws," should be combined "with irresistible force" and "to the greatest possible extent" (22, ll. 16f.). Since this task depends on the lawful external relation of states according to the seventh proposition, this relation among states in the cosmopolitan condition should contribute to the double superlative. There are two conceivable ways it could do so. If the endangerment of personal rights through war were overcome, the cosmopolitan state would have a subsidiary and complementary influence on domestic law. The cosmopolitan state would help it resolve its task of safeguarding rights. The seventh proposition, however, contains no indication of this sort, but rather suggests another possibility: Every state, even the smallest, carries the responsibility for the "security and rights" of their subjects (24, l. 24). Kant's meaning is that a civil constitution determined by laws is complete only when it exists not only among individual human beings, but also among states.

Kant's views may be convincing up to this point. The difficulties become apparent in the details. Since the international state of nature is only a residual state of nature, the world state that abolishes it bears only residual responsibilities. The already existing states are not to be dissolved in the world state, but brought into legal coexistence. The subsidiary world state thus attains a federal character for the benefit of its own subsidiary character. Kant does not, however, mention a federal but state-like world organization. The federation of peoples he refers to (24/23 and 26) rather has no state character according to the treatise on peace (see chapter 11). Now, a "world state without a state" or ultra-minimal world state does not perform what the seventh proposition demands: that "even the smallest" state can expect "security and rights . . . from a united power" (ll. 24ff.). Does Kant's proposed solution of a federation of peoples thus contradict its task of publicly securing rights?

Kant clarifies the conception of a federation of peoples as a *foedus amphictyonum*, which alludes to the unification of Greek city-states or peoples. Amphictyonies are less than legal-political confederations. They are loose confederations like the famous Pylaean-Delphian amphictyony. But since they still have common laws and common powers, the federation of peoples in the "Idea" is a more ambitious organization than that in the treatise on peace. According to the ideal of the amphictyony, it must have the character of a state, since it possesses both elements that define the civil state or statehood according to Kant's late legal philosophy in the *Doctrine of Right* (e.g., §8): It has both a general collective will and this will has the power that provides the desired security to everyone. In anticipation of this development, the "Idea" speaks both of laws "of a united will" (24, l. 27) and of its "unified power" (ll. 26). Only in virtue of the federation of peoples' state character can it fulfill the task of "general political security" (26, l. 11) and, analogously to the single state, ensure not only negative peace or the absence of war, but also positive participation in peace, "in which every state, even the smallest, could expect to derive its security and rights not from its own power or its own legal judgment, but solely from this great federation" (24, ll. 24–26). An amphictyony, however, has only a highly restricted sphere of competence. It does not get involved in the inner affairs of the confederate states, but rather is confined to the limits set by minimal statehood.

The second paragraph of the seventh proposition now draws attention to "the danger, lest human energies should lapse into inactivity" (26, l. 11), which threatens the cosmopolitan condition. If cultural progress arises from antagonism and the latter is subdued in the cosmopolitan condition, stagnation is a likely danger. Kant does not say, however, "that" all energies threaten to become inactive. He rather maintains that the cosmopolitan condition itself is "not completely free from danger, lest" they become inactive (l. 11), which means, as expressed by the finality in the word "lest" (*damit*), that it always remains threatened. This permanent danger distinguishes the cosmopolitan condition from the familiar civil condition. It also indicates a grave legal deficiency: There is no security to be had about global state security. Kant ascribes an inherent fragility to the developmental goal of not allowing "the energies" to become inactive.

If this solution is convincing, it likewise would have to hold for single states, which, in order to prevent the inactivity of energies, also would have to put up with a fragile single statehood. But juridical states do not choose this option, for it would endanger what must not be endangered, the rule of law. Instead, they merely restrict the tasks performed by the state to allow room for competition, and thus for the development of energies. The same strategy may be applied to the cosmopolitan condition. If the (always federal) world state is given only modest state tasks, then states could still compete with one another and reciprocally prevent the stagnation of energies.

A glance at Kant's further elaboration on the federation of peoples seems to indicate that he did not achieve a final stance or clarity on this issue in the "Idea." His remark that there is "common external agreement and legislation" (25, ll. 6f.), or more than merely a contract between states, speaks for a (minimal) world state. This does not contradict the fact that the result is "like" a "civil commonwealth" or state (25, ll. 6f.). For, due to its minimal statehood, the world state docs not attain the full state level of an ordinary state, but is only similar to it. The indication that the structure maintains itself "automatically" is to be taken with a grain of salt (l. 8). It means that the state is guided not by the public powers but by a "secret mechanism" (29, ll. 13f.; cf. the *Anthropology*, which in relation to the history of the species speaks of a "mechanical device of Providence," VII 330). This is to be understood as a system of "actions and counteractions" (25, l. 21; cf. 26, ll. 13f.), which is regulated by the "law of equilibrium" (l. 9) and results in a "concert of powers." The "united power" that appears in the same passage (ibid.) is characteristic of statehood, but it is assigned only a secondary and subsidiary responsibility. Since the united power only "reinforces" the law of equilibrium, Kant assigns original responsibility to this law: primarily to ensure the balance of powers for the security of states, and only secondarily to establish a federation of peoples.

This multilayered solution may be considered realistic in the sense of contemporary realism in political science, which views the states as the prior agents in the international scene and accords at best a subsidiary role to international organizations (e.g., Morgenthau 1948; Waltz 1979; on criticism, see Höffe 2002a, sec. 9.1). But only contingent conditions can bring about the type of equilibrium Kant envisioned, and it would not in normal circumstances cover all states. Small states in particular could become the shared prey of the large ones. Further, there is no stability in the equilibrium; and if it is lost, a federation of peoples with merely secondary responsibilities would not be capable of its restoration. Finally, the equilibrium does not bring about the lawful condition between states, which would constitute the perfection of the civil constitution (cf. 24, ll. 2f.). It follows that Kant's order of precedence must be reversed: The cosmopolitan condition is first achieved only in the federation of peoples – provided that it is established as a minimal and federal world state. One may hope for a subsidiary and preliminary situation of global equilibrium, since it would then be easier to win the consent of single states.

9.3. Mechanism plus Moral Maturation

The second difficulty with the "Idea" arises in connection with the force that compels mankind to establish a cosmopolitan state, since this force is inseparable from morality. Kant rightly does not believe that natural dispositions are fully developed at the two lower stages of cultivation and civilization, but that moral maturity is achieved only at the highest stage (moral maturation). This urges two questions: If the tasks of right and state are limited to "freedom under external laws" (22, l. 16), how can they relate to the highest level of progress, that of the inner cultivation of the citizens' minds (26, l. 28); how can they be concerned with the "morally good attitude" of citizens (l. 32)? And second, how can the moral disposition, the performance of an individual person, rely on a social order that has the authority of enforcement?

The fact that, for Kant, there is a link between the perfection of right in the cosmopolitan legal order and the perfection of the person in morality, and thus that the two fundamentally different forms of social and personal development are somehow connected, seems to pose problems in three respects. First, the connection would contradict the second proposition or at least qualify the thesis that the natural dispositions, which in human beings aim at the use of reason, develop completely only in the species as a whole, not in the individual. The moral disposition, namely, belongs to the individual and results from the development of the faculty of desire, its proper natural disposition. This development is of crucial importance to reason. Second, the federation of peoples is in danger of becoming utopian in the negative sense if it can be realized only when many, or perhaps virtually all human beings have acquired a moral disposition. Third, Kant seems to run the risk of impairing the meaningful division of right and morals, or of juridical legality and juridical morality (see above, section 5.3).

Before these problems can be addressed, we must first consider a question that arises with respect to the mechanism as a premoral element of the driving force: How probable is the developmental emergence of the "automaton" [*Automat*]? The same cause supposedly accounts for the mechanism leading to the cosmopolitan condition and for the legal form regulating single human beings. This cause is "unsociability" (24, l. 7): As long as the states remain in "unrestricted freedom" (l. 10), and in "unsociability" [*Unvertragsamkeit*] (l. 13), "inevitable antagonism" (l. 15) and "discord" (25, l. 24) arise, which prepare the way for grave evils – for "wars," "tense and unremitting military preparations" and the "resultant distress... even in the midst of peace," along with devastations and even the complete inner exhaustion of powers (24, ll. 16–21). Because of these evils humans attempt to arrive at "a condition of calm and security" (ll. 15f.). Since this condition is reached by acknowledged self-interest, the first, premoral driving force is pragmatic in nature, or from the perspective of single states, selfishly pragmatic. Enlightened self-interest, however, does not achieve what Kant is aiming at: that "every state, even the smallest," can expect its own security and rights; the stronger states would still victimize the weaker ones from self-interest.

On closer inspection, Kant takes three possibilities into consideration. They all amount to processes that develop behind the backs of human agents and independently of their decisions. The first possibility, which foresees a purely causal mechanism governing the process, reckons with "lucky accidents" (cf. 25, l. 28, "rule of blind chance"). However, it is improbable that the contingent interplay of efficient causes or "Epicurean concourse" (l. 9) should produce a constellation of states that "can survive in its existing form" (ll. 13f.). (Kant had already rejected Epicurus' atomism, according to which all material things are formations that emerge from the purely contingent collision of atoms, in his precritical work on the *Universal Natural History and Theory of the Heavens*, I 227.)

The second, more demanding possibility assumes providence in nature, which is also ascribed great importance in the second work on the philosophy of history, the "Conjectures on the Beginning of Human History" (VIII 120ff.). The "regular course" of nature leads our "species gradually upward from the lower level of animality to the highest level of humanity" and develops its capacities "by a perfectly regular process within this disorderly arrangement" (25, ll. 16–20). Since the development benefits the species, Kant discusses it from a social-pragmatic or utilitarian perspective.

According to the third possibility, "nothing rational" emerges from "all these actions and counteractions," that is, nothing that will benefit human well-being (ll. 20–22). It is even possible that they prepare for "a hell of evils to overtake us, however civilized our condition," because "barbaric devastation . . . might perhaps again destroy . . . all the cultural progress hitherto achieved" (ll. 24–27). The possibility of no progress whatsoever may be seen in connection with Moses Mendelssohn's *Jerusalem* (1783), but there is nothing in the latter that expresses the "hell of evils, however civilized our condition."

Kant himself promises a middle position, namely, that "barbarous freedom" can lead to evils among states just as it does among the savage (individuals). These evils include arms expenditures, wars, and the continual preparedness for war that compel them to find "a law of equilibrium" and "a cosmopolitan system of general political security" (26, ll. 1ff.). But Kant neglects the problem of the incompatibility among different states' enlightened self-interests. Even if every state were interested in the abolition of all war, it would not disadvantage the most powerful states to come together in a "federation of powerful nations" and to leave out all other states that, due to their weakness, do not threaten them.

International organizations that guarantee every state, even the smallest ones, "security and rights" are thus not entirely legitimate. In order to redress this deficiency, one might make moral maturity a requirement. Whereas this is a foreign element to legal and state theories, it is recurrent theme in the "Idea." The sixth proposition (23, l. 23) expresses the view that the good will is needed, the result of successful moral education. The legal order, an institution bound by the limits of external action, is thus brought into connection with the inner requirement of morality. But this convergence is restricted to the task mentioned in the fifth proposition of "establishing a perfectly just civil constitution" (22, l. 18). The deficiency discussed in the seventh proposition can be redressed only by an exceptional moral maturation, one that applies not to individuals but to states. The juridical morality of collective subjects or states, and thus a "collective juridical morality," commands the more powerful states to acknowledge the "security and rights" of even the smallest states.

Even if this moral assumption is compatible with right as an external lawgiving, it is at least incompatible with the aforementioned antagonism, which has nothing to do with morality. A question also arises concerning the order of causes: How can collective juridical morality be the cause of a just legal order and at the same time its effect? A "good will" (23, l. 29) is portrayed as a necessary condition in the sixth proposition, whereas its equivalent, the moral-good disposition, appears as the result of a just constitution in the seventh proposition (26, l. 32). According to Kant, every community should actively educate its citizens in order to produce moral-good dispositions (ll. 28 and 31). Kant does not, however, require a reciprocal relationship: Citizens of a prior, weaker stage of moral education might urge the states to relinquish "their vain and violent schemes of expansion" (ll. 26f.), just as states that have become nonaggressive may instead apply their resources to the moral education of their citizens.

A further problem lies in the lack of a distinction between legality and morality: Why shouldn't it be sufficient for the global legal condition to be established merely on grounds of the desire for honor and external respectability? As soon as the states forgo applying their resources to "vain and violent schemes of expansion" and begin to guarantee "security and rights" to smaller states, the cosmopolitan condition sought for has already been achieved. Kant's counterargument – "all good enterprises which are not grafted on to a morally good attitude of mind are nothing but illusion and outwardly glittering misery" – has the very kind of moralizing character that he himself criticizes in his *Doctrine of Right* (§C): "[T]hat I make it my maxim to act rightly is a demand that ethics makes on me" (VI 231).

The solution considered above from the *Doctrine of Right* also is more convincing in substantial respects than that of the "Idea": The development of humanity as a whole is not completed in the "civil" state of single states and in their coexistence, the cosmopolitan condition, unless the rule of law culminates in morality. The danger of zealotry that inheres in the requirement of morality is nevertheless to be avoided: No demands are made that could not be fulfilled "here on earth" (VIII 30) among beings made from "such warped wood" as human beings (23). Later, in the treatise on peace, Kant rather places his confidence in republicanism, since it allows citizens' self-interest to come into play. But even this solution is not without problems (see chapter 10).

One might now accede to one of Kant's weaker claims and maintain that right is an insufficient but necessary condition of morality.

According to Socrates' maxim "it is better to suffer injustice than to commit injustice" (cf. *Republic* I 353d3–354a11), it is possible to have a morally good disposition even when there is no justice in the polity. Right no doubt supports morality, but is not a necessary condition of it. Incidentally, Socrates' maxim is not an owed duty. One cannot require of individuals or states that they suffer injustice, but one can demand that they acknowledge security and rights.

10

PEACE I: ARE REPUBLICS PEACEABLE?

Eleven years after the "Idea," moral maturation ceased to be a necessary condition for peace in Kant's writings. In the treatise on peace, Kant mentions the "malevolence of human nature, which can be seen unconcealed in the free relations of nations" (VIII 355), thus recalling the contrastive concept of the moral good. But he no longer has a theory of education or of moral maturation conducive to this end. Instead, a new idea or thesis appears that later became prominent in the theory of international relations. It may be traced back in the history of ideas to Kant's "First Definitive Article" in the treatise on peace (e.g., Doyle 1983). In its untainted form, it is a thesis of contemporary political science: Democracies are peaceable. According to the weaker thesis, democracy is a comparative concept and the *extent* to which a state is democratic is causally linked to its aversion from war. The weaker thesis is usually supplemented by the even more cautious claim that this connection becomes efficacious only in relation to other democracies.

There are two sides to this claim. The proper claim is that democracies *are* peaceable (with the aforementioned limitation); a further claim taken from exclusive right is that *only* democracies, not authoritarian states, are peaceable. (On the extended debate, see Singer and Small 1972 and 1982; Doyle 1995; for an overview, see Maôz and Russet 1993 and Brown, Lynn-Jones, and Miller 1996; Schumpeter 1919 is already significant; see also Höffe 2002a, sec. 9.3.)

The appeal to Kant is not obvious for two reasons: On the one hand, Kant is concerned with a republican constitution and refuses "confus[ing] it with a democratic constitution (as usually happens)" (*Peace* VIII 351, ll. 21f.). On the other hand, his theory of peace is part of a normative, and moreover moral theory, a legal ethics that defies the empirical approach of political science. According to Kant, the republican constitution arises from the "pure source of the concept of right" (l. 2). It thus arises from the moral concept that, to augment his challenge even further, appears within a metaphysical framework. The section devoted to the republican constitution contains unambiguously metaphysical elements: It speaks of "higher beings" (VIII 350, ll. 25f.), of the "citizen of a state in a supersensible world" (l. 27), and of "divine laws" (ll. 28f.). If contemporary appeal to Kant is not misplaced to begin with, Kant must be able to fulfill two conditions: His concept of the republican constitution, in short, of a republic, must be compatible with modern democracy (section 10.1), and his arguments must remain independent of large sections of his legal ethics, in particular of its metaphysical components (section 10.2). Only if it can be shown that both conditions are met may we enter into more fine-grained and substantial debate with Kant (section 10.3).

10.1. Kant's Concept of the Republic

At first glance, Kant's concept of the republic seems transparent; it is already defined in the first sentence of the first definitive article by three elements. But the concept loses clarity in two further definitions that appear in the course of the article. These definitions contradict the other three elements and are not even compatible with one another. Kant thus makes three attempts to define the concept of a republic and mentions five elements that belong to republics, but he does not address the problem of the coherence of the three approaches and their five elements.

The first three elements correspond to the three fundamental roles that natural persons must adopt with respect to right and law. Kant tacitly assumes that the only conceivable roles are as follows: (1) As members of a society (prior to law) and as human beings, persons create legal relations among one another; they become legal subjects to each other. (2) They are equal subjects of a single common legislation, the medium in which legal relations subsist ("subjects," *Peace* VIII 349, l. 11); they are legal subjects with equal rights. (3) And in the community thus created, equality is a right; those subject to legislation are equal citizens of the state (cf. VIII 351, l. 14: In the republican constitution, the "subject" is also a "state citizen").

Before Kant explains the normative element of each of the three roles, he first shows that they "are based" on a "postulate" (VIII 349, ll. 12ff.), a universal legal and state precept. Since the state of nature, due to its "lawlessness," denies "security," there is a legal moral duty (cf. "must," l. 23) to leave it for the sake of a "condition of being under civil laws." Common law replaces private caprice, and public constraint replaces private justice [*Privatjustiz*]. Both aspects characterize a legal and state order. Similar to his interpretation of the second and third Ulpian rules, Kant might be thinking more specifically of the following alternative: Either one avoids society altogether or one enters into society with others in which the property of each is secured from all others (see chapter 7). In line with the topic at hand – "a human being (or a nation)," Kant says clearly enough that the state of nature to be overcome is a state not only among individual human beings, but also among peoples.

Strictly speaking, the following alternative again presents itself: A nation either will avoid society with all other nations and even leave their vicinity (ll. 21f.) when the states "already wrong one another by being near one another" (354, l. 5) or will enter into a condition of law with them. There are three aspects (ll. 25ff.) of the latter, more common option of not avoiding society but instead giving it a legal form, that is, a civil (349, l. 24) or "rightful constitution" (l. 25) that overcomes the state of nature. Consequently, there is a threefold state of nature. The universal command of law and government is to be fulfilled by three composite commands that correspond to the three definitive articles. The state of nature among human beings is overcome by state civil law and its republicanism. The state of nature among nations (as states) in relation to one another is overcome by the right of nations and its federalism of free states. Finally – as a new addition to the "Idea" – the state of nature among "individuals and states" (l. 31) is overcome by cosmopolitan law and its principle of hospitality.

Within the framework of the first composite command, the primary concept of the republic is characterized by "principles of freedom." They amount to "the warrant to obey no other external laws than those to which I could have given my consent" (VIII 350, ll. 16–18). This first criterion of a republic corresponds to a rigid consensus theory or to a legitimating individualism that demands consent, or more precisely, the worthiness of consent ("could have given"), not the actual consent of each of those affected (Höffe 2002a, sec. 2.3). The criterion is composed of two parts, but Kant does not spell them out. Of primary importance are those affected, which means *formaliter* that all force ultimately issues from them, the people as defined by political theory. And external, or rather *all* external laws (cf. doing "no wrong to anyone," VIII 350, l. 17) must be amenable to consent, meaning that the criterion is to be fulfilled not only *formaliter*, but also *materialiter*. Every legislation proposal is saddled with the burden of proving that it deserves the consent of those affected (already in the essay on the Enlightenment, VIII 39, ll. 13–15). And since Kant says "I" and "my" determination (ibid.), this criterion is to be understood distributively, not collectively: At issue here is the consent of every single individual affected and not – merely – that of all those affected together.

The second criterion of a republic comprises the "principles of dependence" and corresponds to the principle of the juridical state, since it subjects all fellow legal subjects to the same "common legislation" (VIII 349, l. 11). According to the third criterion, the "law of equality," citizens of the state are equal members of the legislative power, which for Kant is the result of their mediation through representatives. By linking the three criteria, Kant devises a republic that is a democracy in today's sense. According to the first criterion, all force emanates *formaliter* from those concerned, the people; and the community is free *materialiter*. According to the second criterion, a juridical constitution belongs to the community, and – as asserted in the third criterion – all citizens cooperate representatively, but equally in its legislation.

An objectionable element of Kantian legal ethics can be found in the *Doctrine of Right* (§46, similarly in the *Common Saying* VIII 294). It reduces a large number of legal subjects to mere passive state citizens and thus gainsays modern democracy. The requisite "equality of all state citizens" in the treatise on peace, however, does not make allowance for such discrimination; Kant is thus "more democratic" here than in the *Doctrine of Right* and the *Common Saying*. The later *Anthropology* also defines the republic without this favoritism. Kant here develops the relevant connections between the three concepts of law, freedom, and (public) power, without any reference to merely passive state citizens. Whereas anarchy consists in "law and freedom without authority," despotism in "law and authority, without freedom" and barbarism in "authority, without freedom and law," the republic – the only "true civil form of government" – is singled out by the merging of all three concepts into one: "authority, with freedom and law" (VII 330f.). The republic is thus distinguished from anarchism by its (public) authority, from despotism by its freedom, and from barbarism by the connection it establishes between authority and law.

In the treatise on peace, not only the freedom rights at issue in the first principle but all three principles have the status of "innate and

inalienable rights belonging necessarily to humanity" (VIII 350, ll. 23f.).
According to the systematically primary definition of the republic, it is
characterized by human rights that here possess more than freedom
rights alone. Kant is also familiar with a plurality of human rights, and
although the *Doctrine of Right* mentions only one, in substance it makes
allowance for more (see sections 1.3.2 and 6.5).

In a second attempt to define the republic, Kant introduces the division of powers, albeit only as the "separation of the executive power
(the government) from the legislative power" (352, ll. 14–16). Perhaps
an independent jurisdiction is given no mention because it is taken
for granted. Since this second approach leaves aside the prior definitions, the aspect it introduces might appear exclusively valid. Political
scientists in fact tend to focus on it alone. But we would be well advised
to consider the second approach as a supplement to the first one and
not as an alternative, because more importance seems to be attached
to the prior approach both in the text and in substance. The republic
would then be defined thus far by two principles: human rights and the
division of powers.

Kant might mean that consensus is needed only in principle: The
laws, notably the articles of constitution, must be generally amenable
to consensus. In his explanation of the peaceable nature of republics,
however, Kant demands the agreement of state citizens as a fifth element
in the definition of republics. Important decisions of a government such
as the decision to go to war require the actual consent of state citizens.
Therefore, Kant endows democracy with a participatory character in
an emphatic sense. And since this element again is complementary, we
can assert the following intermediary conclusions.

Kant defines the republic through five or, given the double meaning of the first element, through six elements. In slightly more modern
terms, these elements consist in (1) the people as the origin of all force,
(2) freedom rights, (3) the juridical state and (4) the participation of
the people in lawgiving, (5) the division of powers, and (6) due to
the emphasis on the cooperation of the people, participation in an
emphatic sense. Kant's republic thus has less kinship with communitarian republicanism than with an ambitious conception of the democratic
constitutional state as a free, juridical state and participatory democracy.
So contemporary political scientists are not mistaken in applying Kant's
point about the peaceable nature of republics to today's democracies.
They would, however, have to add the restriction that democracy in the
narrowest sense – that is, mere national sovereignty – does not suffice.

10.2. A Separable Thesis

The institution of a global peaceful order or federation of peoples is, according to the "Idea," only minimally established by a moral accomplishment or by moral maturation. Enlightened self-interest is more important: In order to overcome the roots of misery and evil to which states are driven by antagonism, one should leave the international state of nature and establish a federation of peoples (see chapter 9). According to this argument, all states have an inclination toward peace, and it is motivated by self-interest. This is seemingly in conflict with the thesis on the peaceable nature of republics in two respects.

First, not any state whatsoever, but only republics are considered peaceable. And since republics are defined by moral criteria, morality is required over and beyond self-interest. Morals and the good will, as elements foreign to right in the "Idea," do not enter the treatise on peace; the latter is solely concerned with a morals of legal institutions or with a legal morals. Kant also adduces a new argument that surely does not thwart, but rather supplements the line of argument in the "Idea" by filling an unnoticed gap in its reasoning. Kant appeals to misery and evil in the "Idea" as powers that promote peace, but in this work he is not aware that statesmen causally responsible for misery and evil must not also be their victims. On the contrary, as Kant recognizes in the doctrine on peace, the so-called cabinet wars at his time show that the perpetrator "gives up nothing at all of his feasts, hunts, pleasure palaces, court festivals, and so forth," and thus can "decide upon war, as upon a kind of pleasure party, for insignificant cause" (VIII 350; cf. DR §55: "the sovereign . . . leads them into war as he would take them on a hunt, and into battles as on a pleasure trip," VI 345).

Republics, by way of contrast, are considered peaceable because those affected must give their consent, that is, an explicit agreement based on inner conviction (cf. Grimm and Grimm 1854/1984, I, 1398). "They would have to decide to take upon themselves all the hardships of war (such as themselves doing the fighting and paying the costs of the war from their own belongings, painfully making good the devastation it leaves behind, and finally – to make the cup of troubles overflow – a burden of debt that embitters peace itself, and that can never be paid off because of new wars always impending" (*Peace* VIII 351). The *Doctrine of Right* (§55) takes up part of this argument in its assertion that whoever must devote their belongings and their life to the purpose of war has a right to "give their free assent, through their representatives, . . . to each particular declaration of war" (VI 345f.). Accordingly, this is not a distributive right of each individual, but a collective right of the people by means of a majority decision: Only voluntarily can one risk losing one's property and ultimately one's life.

Second, Kant significantly does not appeal to the higher morals of democratic citizens in his thesis on the peaceable nature of democracies. He makes no mention of a comprehensive sense for law that would relegate all conflicts, including those between states, to a third, neutral party. Nor does he appeal to genuine peaceableness. Kant does not irrationally assume a fundamental aversion to all violence among citizens or their political parties, associations, and institutions. He thus retracts the moral requirement in the "Idea" and takes only enlightened self-interest into account, in this way reinforcing instead of qualifying its importance. Without mentioning a positive interest in commerce, he appeals to a negative interest, the same that appeared in the seventh proposition of the "Idea": People have an interest in avoiding the misery of war.

Instead of citing an ambitious civil virtue or sense for law in connection with peaceableness, or republican and democratic integrity, Kant merely appeals to the capacity of democracies to promote the unfettered rule of citizens' self-interest. Whereas war is decided by those who are least afflicted by it in nondemocracies, the decision makers in democracies are those who impersonally or personally suffer. Kant adduces this as an additional legitimation of the republic; as for its moral justification, he adds its functional role in securing peace: "[I]n addition to the purity of its origin – its having arisen from the pure source of the concept of right – the republican constitution does offer the prospect of the result wished for, namely, perpetual peace" (*Peace* VIII 351, ll. 1–4). In order to gain a voice themselves, the victims of arms races and war must be legally equal subjects of the war-waging collective subjects, that is, of the states. However, the argument considers only the offensive parties who wage war, and not those who are attacked.

Kant's claim about the peaceable nature of republics is compelling to empirical political science because its normative components are modest and virtually uncontroversial. The claim rests almost exclusively on the argument from enlightened self-interest. Kant's highly complex and even metaphysical ethics of right and peace are left out of consideration. The theorems of natural right and their precedence over positive right, of a (single) innate right, of private and public right, of the intelligible relation that is property, of the earth as common property originally shared by all human beings, and of the categorical imperative of punitive justice – these and many other doctrines (see above, chapters 6 and 7) are not relevant to Kant's argument. Even those demands discussed in the second and third definitive articles for a federation of peoples and for the reduction of world citizen rights to visiting rights, not rights of hospitality, do not play a role. The two-part argument suffices: In republics, war is to be decided by the citizens or by their representatives, and for this very reason republics lend an ear to self-interest. If their peaceable nature, considered normatively, is grounded exclusively in self-interest, it does not need morals and does not belong to Kant's *ethics* of right and peace. The argument retains a single moral element from institutional morals, which consists in the democratic demand that those affected must give their consent.

10.3. Skeptical Considerations

Contemporary debates in political science deploy two ways of explaining the peaceable nature of democracies. According to the so-called normative explanation, democracies solve external conflicts according to the same schemes as internal conflicts. Accustomed to resolving internal (domestic) conflicts by means of legal forms, and hence without recourse to violence, democracies then apply this procedure to the external (international) arena and so act peacefully in their international relations. According to the second, "structural" explanation, the decision structures that predominate in democracies are averse to war.

Whereas Kant's theory is usually considered a normative explanation (e.g., Maôz and Russett 1993, 625), the text testifies to the contrary. It does not comply with the typical scheme of conflict resolution for republics: the abolition of force through right. The issue of grafting this scheme onto external relations is pertinent to the second and third definitive articles but does not apply to the first. Whoever takes this lack of normative explanation to be indicative of a structural explanation will comprehend only half of the treatise on peace. This is because Kant, on the one hand, links the decision to wage war to the consent of those concerned, while, on the other hand, he asserts that these people will reject consent on grounds of self-interest. Precisely this second claim qualifies the validity of the thesis on the peaceable nature of republics, but this goes unnoticed by Kant. In fact, Kant places so much trust in the peaceableness of republics that he asserts in the second definitive article that the republic "by its nature must be inclined to perpetual peace" (*Peace* VIII 356, ll. 18f.).

Kant is correct with respect to two issues only: First, the argument from democratic consensus, or in short, the democratic argument, is tenable. Only republican or democratic constitutions grant decision making to those who suffer, although, as mentioned, only to those on the side of the aggressor, not also to those being attacked. Second, the argument that hinges on the grave nature of war, or more generally on self-interest, is tenable. On the basis of the democratic argument, deciding on war is no longer the "easiest thing in the world." From both arguments, however, the desired outcome of a robust peaceableness, or the "prospect of the result wished for, namely, perpetual peace," does not follow (VIII 351, ll. 3f.). According to the first preliminary article, perpetual peace consists in an unqualified and perpetual peace that, as suggested by the term "prospect," is highly likely to be realized. This anticipation, however, is not warranted by Kant's arguments. Instead, they relativize the thesis on peaceableness in both directions: First, the assumption that democracies are peaceable at all and, second, the claim to exclusivity, that is, that only democracies are peaceable.

Let us begin with the second relativization. At least in our contemporary age, deciding on war is by no means the "easiest thing in the world" for nondemocracies. Since wars, in particular, endanger the advantages of peace, including advancements in economics, science, and culture, Kant's empirical assumption that one "gives up nothing at all" for war is invalidated. Even if the impoverishment of a country does not impair the luxurious living of its political elite, domestic revenues will diminish when salaries are reduced. Due to the effects of war, other financial sources, such as the exploitation of raw material, are impeded. Hence, the absolute "nothing at all" is clearly mistaken. Besides, nondemocratic states are providing for more and more of the welfare needs of their citizens and thus are assuming some measure of subsidiary responsibility for economic policies. As a second counterargument, one may add that modern weapons and continual expenditures on arms are so costly that they cannot be afforded over time without a flourishing economy. Above all, the destructive effects of modern weapons, such as atomic bombs, mean that wars using them can no longer be seen as "pleasure parties" by the dictators deciding on them "for insignificant cause." In short, both the development of the state's responsibilities and the development of weapons diminish the exclusive entitlement of democracies to peaceableness.

On the other hand, the republican constitution ensures only that the decision to initiate war is very difficult, which entails far less than comprehensive peaceableness. The difficulty of deciding on war extends only to that degree of peaceableness covered by enlightened self-interest. Self-interest in no way speaks against all wars if one (1) trusts more in weapons than in troops, (2) places only voluntary, not conscripted troops into service, (3) wages war only against weaker opponents, (4) additionally profits from a surprise attack and moreover (5) aspires toward economic profit, especially through the transportation of arms or the annexation of rich raw material assets, or toward the geographically strategic advantage of an extended sphere of influence, and even (6) will allow costs of waging war to be paid, and perhaps overpaid, by one's allies.

As a consequence, a second intermediate conclusion seems inescapable: On the one hand, Kant's arguments lead to a more modest and realistic thesis. Since democracies are conducive to the realization of citizens' self-interest and only few wars promise a net benefit, democracies are *hesitant* to go to war, but not *fundamentally adverse to war*. If they are nevertheless fundamentally peaceable, then they must possess a genuine moral element over and beyond enlightened self-interest. This might be anchored in the integrity of democratic citizens or in their sense of right and justice. But since this is not the case to any reliable degree in the majority of democratic populations, one would be well advised to consider argumentative strategies unburdened by claims of morality, in particular those that appeal to international regulations and organizations (see chapter 11).

With respect to the first relativization, contemporary political scientists tend to simplify Kant's complex arguments. If dictators and totalitarian regimes were transformed into liberal democracies, as commanded by law and legal ethics, wars would become obsolete. But two lines of argument speak against the thesis of "worldwide peace through worldwide democratization" (more extensively in Höffe 2002a, sec. 9.3.2).

Along the *first* line of criticism, historical experience urges skepticism. The French Republic already devastated Europe with a war that was by no means free from hegemonic pretensions. The older democracy of the United States of America expanded toward the West, paying no heed to the indigenous people; it also annexed a series of states from Texas, Arizona, Nevada, and Utah to California and New Mexico. Nor did Great Britain's democratic development impair its plans to gain

world power. Kant assumes that every state has a natural interest in hegemony. The corresponding "craving of every state (or of its head) is to
attain a lasting condition of peace in this way, by ruling the whole world
where possible" (*Peace* VIII 367; cf. *Religion* VI 34). This does not need to
be imperialist in the sense that the extension of power as such is willed.
The craving to rule the world is already sufficiently accounted for by
that "natural" interest in security, familiar from Hobbes, that leads man
to "force, or wiles, to master the persons of all men he can" (*Leviathan*,
chap. 13). Kant rightly transfers this familiar idea to the unfamiliar
domain of relations between states. Oddly, he does not apprehend the
consequence of skepticism this induces toward the peaceableness of
republics.

The suggested counterexamples – along with many others from the
Middle Ages and classical antiquity – certainly do not meet the standards
of democracies today. Nevertheless, recent modesty about restricting
peaceableness to liberal democracies is not a sufficient ground for inval-
idating Kant's claim. At least to begin with, the aforementioned wars
were so widely supported that even "more democratic democracies"
would have consented to them.

Surely, already for argumentative reasons, experience as an "Is" cannot vitiate the normative principle of self-interest as an "Ought." But
experience teaches either that the self-interest of citizens is not contra-
dicted by every war or that the contradiction is not sufficiently apparent.
Democracies have at best an *inclination* to peace; they are, as mentioned,
hesitant to go to war, but not adverse to war. Under certain conditions,
supposed democratic pacifism may change abruptly into its opposite,
democratic imperialism. And sometimes one occurs in the name of the
other: Sermons of democracy may veil economic interests.

Statistics confirm that democracies are at least as susceptible to war
as nondemocracies. In the period from 1945 onward, Great Britain,
France, and the United States were at the top of the list of belliger-
ent nations (according to Gantzel 1995), whereas in the period from
1816 to 1980 the ranking was headed by France and followed succes-
sively by England, Russia, Turkey, Italy, and China (Singer and Small
1982, 294). Counterexamples even speak against the weaker claim that
democracies are not peaceable per se, but only toward other democracies. Following the French Revolution, France was granted financial
support not by the more democratic Great Britain but by Prussia, her
very opponent. And in the years 1812–1814, Great Britain waged war
against the (relatively) democratic United States, which in turn waged

war against the confederate states to prevent their independence. Even the German-British rivalry in the nineteenth century arose not from the opposition between their forms of government but from a conflict of interests of no relevance to democracy. And the arms race between India and Pakistan did not first begin with military rule in Pakistan.

According to a *second* line of criticism, Kant's arguments are in part unconvincing, and in part they lack sound empirical assumptions. If the war is not waged at the state's borders, the citizens will feel less hardship. The impact will be even more reduced if war is waged against a clearly weaker enemy. Furthermore, wars may be profitable; they might either cause growth in prestige and power or divert attention away from internal political difficulties. Wars may also be avoided from causes that are independent of democracies, such as the development of weapons. Due to the disastrous consequences of mutual assured destruction, there are only losers in an atomic war. Finally, the hitherto peaceable nature of democracies might diminish as soon as familiar antagonisms, such as that between East and West, melt away and most states become democratic. Today it is already evident that the remaining hegemonic power is employing its preponderance for the benefit of its own self-interest.

Skepticism thus seems unavoidable. Up to now, experience with democracies and the arguments put forward for their peaceableness do not allow us to expect worldwide peace from worldwide democratization. Even if the democratization of all states is helpful, and moreover commanded on legal-moral grounds, one can hardly anticipate world peace without globally binding protocols and equally global organizations, along with their right to public enforcement.

PEACE II: FEDERATION OF PEOPLES OR WORLD REPUBLIC?

11.1. A Contradiction?

In the three definitive articles of the treatise on peace, the conditions for perpetual peace are spelled out according to the three fundamental forms of public right: the right of the state, the right of nations, and cosmopolitan right. However, as announced in the title of the corresponding section and in the headings of the preliminary articles, peace "among states" is of primary concern here (VIII 343 and 348). Since the second definitive article is dedicated to international peace, its three and a half pages (354–357, l. 18) constitute the core of the entire treatise. Its fundamental claim that there should be a federation of peoples and not a fusion into a state of nations (354, ll. 8f.) is nevertheless beset with difficulties.

Already the first argument, which points out the analogy between nations "as states" and individual human beings, underscores the need for a state of nations. The second paragraph announces a historical-factual impediment: In every state, majesty – or sovereignty – consists "just in its not being subject to any external lawful constraint at all" (ll. 24f.). But the third paragraph explains this fact by the viciousness of human nature. The fourth paragraph distinguishes only three kinds of relations among states, and these culminate in the federation of peoples. The first kind of relation designates war or victory, but is self-defeating: Where there is no tribunal, conflicting legal claims are resolved not by juridical procedures and right but by force. The second kind of relation, a "peace pact (*pactum pacis*)," does signal an important advancement; but it can end only "a current war," "not a condition of war." The third kind of relation between states seems most adequate for peace: "a federation of a special kind," a "pacific federation (*foedus pacificum*)," would seek "to end *all war* forever."

The next two paragraphs 5 and 6, however, do not only support this pacific federation or federation of states. They also point out grave shortcomings. Since public laws are lacking, the pacific federation turns out to be a "free federalism" that would be well advised to "accommodate [itself] to public coercive laws" and thus to become a world republic. In the last sentence of the second definitive article, the status of a pacific federation is reduced to such an extent – it is only a negative surrogate of a federation of peoples – that a fourth kind of relation is urged: Instead of a federation of peoples, there should be an international state (VIII 357, l. 10) or a world republic (357, l. 14). The decisive question for the second definitive article remains: Is the initial demand for a "federation of peoples, not international state" compatible with the concluding remark about the "federation of peoples as a negative surrogate"? (On a discussion of recent literature, cf. Cavallar 1992; see also Höffe 1995b; Gerhardt 1995; and Merkel and Wittmann 1996.)

First, several incontestable points should be recalled. In the expression "right of nations," or Latin, *ius gentium*, one might misread "*gentes*" in a literal sense as denoting communities of the same origin or ethnically homogenous groups. If this were the case, Kant would be concerned with rights of ethnic groups: of clans, tribes, and other "natural communities." Their rights might include the right to leave a state union and to establish a separate state. Although this kind of authorization was already topical at the time, for instance, in relation to the War of Independence in the newly founded United States of America, Kant does not take it into account. His interest is directed exclusively at "nations as states" (*Peace* VIII 354, l. 3), thus not at "*gentes*" in the sense of "blood related people" but rather "civitates," those people in the sense of citizens that are referred to in the constitutional language of the following principle: "All force is issued by the people." Whether states are ethnically homogenous or heterogeneous is of no relevance here (on the concept of an "enlightened nation state," cf. Höffe 2002a, sec. 6.3). To avoid misunderstanding, one could rename the "right of nations" the "right of states" (cf. DR §53), understood as the right regulating the coexistence of single states. Skeptical toward unnecessary coinages (see CPR B 368f.; cf. also CPrR V 10), Kant rather adheres to the customary reading of the right of nations as the right that settles disputes between states.

According to both Hugo Grotius's highly influential work *De iure belli ac pacis* (*The Law of War and Peace*, 1625) and the Peace of Westphalia (1648), which was of great importance to the classical conception of a right of nations, the supreme state authority of the sovereign gives him the right to go to war [*ius ad bellum*]. The consequence of this is obvious: States that insist on sovereignty give the impression of "an arena full of wolves, each of whom claims the space for himself, and who, incapable of killing or driving each other away, temporarily prowl around one another, hissing and growling, reluctant to tolerate their situation" (Radbruch 1932/1999, §28).

As in the entire treatise on peace, the second definitive article decidedly renounces this kind of right: "The concept of the right of nations as that of the right to go to war is, strictly speaking, unintelligible" (VIII 356, ll. 35f.). Kant's rejection supports a radically new right of nations; a right of nations that plays a functional role in securing peace (a pacific right of nations) takes the place of a warlike right of nations. The preliminary articles still concern war and warfare, so one might still suspect residues of a "right to go to war" and a "right in war" [*ius in bello*]. The articles, however, rather endorse war reform for the purpose of promoting peace. The sixth preliminary article, concerning right in war, puts forward only prohibitions, not permissions. It prohibits all action that make peace impossible by undermining trust and that let "hostilities... turn into a war of extermination" (VIII 346, ll. 31f.). And the fifth preliminary article categorically refutes the two possible justificatory reasons for a war: The inferiority of a foreign state and a civil war in a foreign state. "No state shall" – here in the sense of *may* – "forcibly interfere in the constitution and government of another state."

This does not constitute a satisfactory argument against the problems with humanitarian intervention today. Kant does not discuss the possibility of genocide or its apparent preliminary stages: ethnically or religiously inspired massive human rights violations such as rape, pillaging, expulsion, and homicide. In these cases the exceptional right of necessity [*Notrecht*] may be defensible. (Cf. Höffe 2000a; on controversial assessment, see Lutz 2000 and Merkel 2000.)

Kant has a good reason strictly to reject a warlike right of nations: Whoever takes the liberty to go to war contradicts the legal-ethical basic principle of "universally valid external laws limiting the freedom of each" (Peace VIII 356, ll. 37f.). Laws would then be replaced by "unilateral maxims" and right would yield to "force" (357, l. 1). Since a war is won only by the side that is comprehensively stronger, and since victory and defeat depend solely on relative power, reason declares that "war as a procedure for determining rights" is "absolutely condemned" (356, ll. 2f.; cf. 349, ll. 35f.). Kant does not adhere to an extreme pacifism that makes no allowance for self-defense. In the third preliminary article, he takes for granted that the citizens of a state will also use arms "in order to secure themselves and their own country against attacks from without" (cf. VIII 345). Kant's usually sober prose, however, is interrupted by the dramatic tinge of a philosopher: The condemnation of war, he writes, comes down "from the throne of the highest morally legislative power" (356, ll. 2f.).

One might have expected a different position from Kant's writings on the philosophy of history in the 1780s. They suggest that Kant does not only perceive evil and misery in war, but also sees it as a contribution to the cultural progress of humanity ("Idea" VIII 24 and 26, "Conjectures" VIII 121). In the treatise on peace, this positive contribution is still maintained. Even if war is categorically condemned in a moral respect, Kant still acknowledges that it presses any nation whatsoever to "form itself internally into a state" (*Peace* VIII 365, ll. 36f.). In the *Peace* as well, war is employed by the cunning of nature as a means to its abolition. Kant diverts from a merely pacific right of nations only in the *Doctrine of Right,* where he elucidates a threefold right with respect to war: a right to go to war (§56), right during a war (§57), and right after a war (§58). In all three cases, however, at issue is not the rigid, moral concept of right, but rather violence as a characteristic of the state of nature (cf. for §56: VI 346, l. 12, and for §58: VI 348, l. 14, whereas §57, like the fifth preliminary article, is concerned with principles of warfare that enable overcoming the state of nature, VI 347, ll. 5–9).

Kant unambiguously opposes ambitious claims to sovereignty in his time with the rejection of a right to go to war. He otherwise reacts "conservatively" toward them, at least with the proposal of a federation of peoples, since he does not urge from the states any renunciation of sovereignty. But this conflicts with the analogy between states and individuals, according to which there is an international state of nature that is to be overcome in the same way that the conventional, "national" state of nature is overcome and replaced by a public civil state. Since states "already wrong one another by being near one another," each of them, "for the sake of its security, can and ought to require the others to enter with it into" a state "in which each can be assured of its right" (*Peace* VIII 345, ll. 5–8). Otherwise, they have "to leave my vicinity," as the footnote preceding the definitive articles adds (349, ll. 21f.; this requirement corresponds to Kant's interpretation of the second Ulpian rule – see section 7.2).

According to the international state of nature argument, the establishment of a state-like union is already needed between existing states, and in the ideal case, it would be a federation of republics bound together in republican fashion. The establishment of this collective body is a duty in a legal-moral sense. Since it overcomes the international state of nature, it does not appear as something that states mercifully grant to one another, but rather belongs to what they may "demand" from each other (354, l. 6). The legal-ethical analogy between single states and individuals in any case entails that states owe a republic of a second order to one another: a republic that is composed of communities that are already in the form of states, that is, a world community in the sense of a republic of states or world republic.

This world republic cannot exist without a minimal state form. Although Kant's federation of peoples should have a "constitution similar to a civil constitution" (l. 7), it lacks a state form. It is an ultraminimal world state (UMWS) with respect to its governing structure. Therefore, the thesis about the federalism of free states in the second definitive article is clearly incompatible with the analogy it rests on. According to the former, a state form is rejected, but if the analogy is to hold, a state form is required. Just as a legal community of individuals ensues only from the renunciation of freedom, there is a legal community of single states only if the states duly renounce part of their sovereignty.

11.2. A Modest World Republic

In the first supplement (*Peace* VIII 367, l. 14), Kant elucidates the notion of a "universal monarchy" as a single state that progressively enlarges to global dimensions. This kind of homogenous world state (HWS) or world realm is not the requisite world republic. The second definitive article rightly denies that "different states" should be "fused into a single state" (354, ll. 14f.). For since the states already guarantee legal-morally commanded legal security, there is no legal-moral requirement for them to dissolve. On the contrary, the world republic requisite for the purpose of legal security is a state of states, a *civitas civitatum*. And in accordance with its political ethical core, this state of states consists in secondary and complementary statehood.

Its authority and power may be derived from Kant's analogy. As long as states are analogous to individuals, the individual states or primary states may act and refrain from acting at their own discretion, under the proviso that they do not encroach on the rights of other individual states. The first definitive article may answer the ensuing question of what exactly their rights consist in. All force is issued by the people – whether "the people" consists in the primary republic of natural individuals or in the secondary republic of individual states, in which case the people are the totality of primary republics. And the "condition of being under common civil laws" (VIII 349, l. 21) is characterized by freedom rights, the rule of law, and the participation of the people in legislation, along with the division of powers and emphatic participation (see section 10.1). There is even a legal-moral claim or innate right to all of these principles.

In this way a novel kind of human right emerges; it is new with respect not to its content but to its addressee. It consists in a "human right of states," or in short, a state right, and has primarily two aspects (on a substantial and detailed debate, see Höffe 2002a, Part III): As individuals in relation to one another, states have the right to life and limb and to property. This first state right primarily demands territorial integrity and security. Moreover, individual states have a right to political and cultural self-determination. Precisely because the primary states or single states have additional responsibilities to fulfill, the secondary state or world republic is assigned only a narrow range of powers; it is a minimal world state (MWS).

Within the framework of the legal-moral fundamental task of arbitrating conflicts without the rule of force, the international legal community has only the remaining responsibility of overcoming the residual state of nature. The tasks of the state familiar to us – such as those concerning civil and penal law, labor and social law, the right to language, religion, and culture – all these responsibilities of primary states are removed from the jurisdiction of the secondary state or world republic. But this must be qualified, since additional powers and responsibilities of the secondary state may be derived from the cosmopolitan right discussed in the third definitive article.

Within the framework of the second definitive article, only that state form is legitimate on Kantian premises that is an intranational watchman state or minimal state with a highly restricted sphere of tasks. A world organization that arrogated to itself more responsibilities than that of securing international peace would violate the state right to (political and cultural) self-determination. Kant takes this right to be so basic that he already articulates it in the preliminary articles.

According to the second preliminary requirement, "no independently existing state . . . shall be acquired by another state through inheritance, exchange, purchase or donation." And according to the fifth preliminary requirement, no state, and thus no state of states, "shall forcibly interfere in the constitution and government of another state." Following the analogy between state and individual, the world republic may, however, interfere where single states contradict the legal-ethical principle of freedom that can coexist with the freedom of others, or universal tolerance, as it applies to the right of nations.

11.3. Ideal or Surrogate?

Although the international task of protecting territorial integrity and political self-determination has the dignity of a human right and calls for a minimal world state (MWS), Kant rejects this as a solution. Both in the thesis of the title and in the first paragraph of the second definitive article, he espouses a federation of peoples without any renunciation of sovereignty, that is, an ultraminimal world state (UMWS). He envisages neither a common book of public laws (*Peace* VIII 356, ll. 13f.) nor an authorized tribunal (of arbitration). The federation of peoples is made up of sovereign partners that maintain their sovereignty entirely. Their conflicts are regulated not by an impartial third party but by the partners themselves, that is, by the individual states.

One advantage this solution affords is self-evident. The misuse of power is a danger in every state, but must not be feared in a community without a state. Hopes placed in state authorities likewise are discarded: There is no expectation of secure legal protection. This lack of all public force may be welcomed by the individual states in their attempts to guard their sovereignty. But as a solution to the problem of legal security it contradicts the fundamental thesis of Kant's ethics of the state: that legal disputes are to be settled by an impartial and sufficiently powerful third party. Agreements are no doubt better than direct force, and better than war. But if the appropriate instruments for securing agreements in a legal form are missing, the legal solution is a solution without security, and this means that the right established does not have the final say. Right in this sense is provisional and represents only a transitional stage to the proper task of safeguarding rights in a legal form.

The usual criticisms of a world republic weigh its advantages against its disadvantages, thus drawing up a cost-benefit analysis. Kant argues more fundamentally: He maintains that the idea of an international state is self-contradictory (VIII 354, ll. 9f.). On hearing the word "contradiction," those well versed in Kant will recall the antinomies of the first two *Critiques*. Since Kant calls perpetual peace the highest political good in the *Doctrine of Right* (VI 355, l. 30) and since the concept of a highest good leads to the "dialectic of pure practical reason" (CPrR V 110ff.), one might expect a corresponding subsidiary dialectic of pure practical reason *with respect to right and law*. But there are no hints of this dialectic in the treatise on peace. The contradiction Kant claims to find in this work is not at all speculative, but is supposed to inhere in the *concept* of an international state (*Peace* VIII 354, ll. 9ff.). Since the myriad peoples in this kind of state are subjected to a single lawgiver, they would fuse into a single people. This contradicts the task at hand of securing the peaceful coexistence of different peoples.

This argument correctly underscores the right of nations to retain their idiosyncrasies in the same way that individuals may retain them in individual states. The "fusion" of peoples into a single, homogeneous people of the state is prohibited. Kant, the founder of a universalistic ethics, may thus incite criticism of the "(hyper-) globalist" position that purports to be universalistic. "(Hyper-) globalism" acknowledges the existence of individual states only as transitional stages to a single global state. It argues that individual states have a derivative significance and that a primordial right is merited by (natural) persons alone (Beitz 1979, 53, 181f., among others). After some time, the individual states should, on this view, lose their character as original juridical entities and confer their monopoly of force on a world state. But from a legal-moral perspective, one might object that a world state in this sense would deprive the individual states of a legitimate right to self-determination, that is, of the right of a people to organize themselves into individual states. This right follows from the primordial right of the individual persons and is limited merely by the commensurate rights of other groups of persons and by the individual states that organize them. The world state is entitled to settle legal conflicts between states that arise from the transgression of this limit, and according to the second definitive article, it has no entitlement to do more.

According to a further argument in support of a world state, many states today owe their existence to accidental developments, and no small number of them still confront resistance from their subjects. From this fact, however, one may conclude only that a people has the right to revise the state formations in place, but not that there is a right to criticize those states that profit from an overwhelming consent of their citizens, nor that there is a right to fuse all individual states into a single world state. On the contrary, a homogeneous world state would violate state rights. An international state, by contrast, would not dissolve the peoples of the primary states, but rather only contest their exclusive right to a state form. It would develop as a secondary state or state of states.

To see a contradiction in the fact that the second element, the state of states, cancels out the first element, the statehood of individual states, is to think in terms of the overly simple alternative: either full sovereignty or none. In truth, there are numerous intermediate stages, and the international state designates one that is defined by an especially marginal renunciation of sovereignty, one that is not far from allowing full individual sovereignty. There is no contradiction in the concept of an international state, but only in that multilayered sovereignty that has long been familiar to us from the concept of a federal state. Since there were already prominent examples of federal states in Kant's era – the Netherlands, Switzerland, the United States of America, and finally the German Reich – it is surprising that Kant became "totally absorbed by" the alternative between an ultraminimal state form or federation of peoples, on the one hand, and a homogeneous world state form or universal monarchy, on the other hand. He does not take into account the intermediate stage of a federal world state.

If Kant's analogy between states and individuals is accurate, there are only two possibilities. *Either* the imperative of individuals to renounce their freedom in leaving the state of nature already involves a contradiction. The advantage of securing right and peace must somehow come about without the disadvantage of the renunciation of sovereignty by those affected. It would then suffice to live together on the basis of contracts, without a state. *Or* there can be no assurance of the rule of law without a certain renunciation of sovereignty. But then the idea of international statehood, so far from being self-contradictory, is a condition that makes possible the state of international lawfulness. If Kant espoused the first option of a federation without force, he would be an advocate of utopian freedom from rule or anarchy, as supported by such illustrious thinkers as Burke the younger (1756) and Schlegel (1796). The latter's ideas were even "occasioned by the Kantian treatise on perpetual peace" (see section 8.4). Proudhon, Marx, and the Frankfurt School later follow suit, but they give a picture of a nonpolitical or even apolitical utopia. And more important, such utopian visions are

expressly rejected by Kant, who understands anarchy to be the dissipa-
tion of all legal protection, which is why any state whatsoever is morally
better than no state at all (*Peace* VIII 373, ll. 3of.). For the same reason,
Kant considers "lawless freedom" to be a sign of savagery. Whereas savages prefer "a mad freedom to a rational freedom," "civilized peoples"
that are "each united into a state" must "hasten" even in their relations
to one another "to leave such a depraved condition, the sooner the
better" (354, ll. 16ff.).

In agreement with this line of thought, Kant admits in the final paragraph of the second definitive article that the positive idea of a right of
nations can be realized only in a world republic or international state
and that the federation of peoples signifies only a "*negative* surrogate"
(357, ll. 13ff.), that is, a substitute that does not fully achieve the desired
goal. Since there is an incessant danger that "the stream of hostile inclination that shies away from right" might break through (ibid.), precisely
that aspect is lacking that is required by the title concept of perpetual stability, namely, the unconditionality of peace. Kant was obviously aware
of the requirement: "In accordance with reason there is only one way
that states in relation with one another can leave the lawless condition,
which involves nothing but war; it is that, like individual human beings,
they give up their savage (lawless) freedom, accommodate themselves
to public coercive laws, and so form an (always growing) *international
state*" (ll. 5–11). This solution to the problem of war deserves a moral
status ("in accordance with reason"), and is even the only solution available ("only one way"). The fact that single states "already have a rightful constitution internally" (VIII 355, ll. 36f.) does not imply that they
"have outgrown the constraint of others to bring them under a more
extended law-governed constitution in accordance with their concepts
of right" (ll. 37f.). They have outgrown only the external constraints
from other states that demand changing their internal constitution. In
internal relations, where the state of nature has been overcome, they
are free; but in external relations, where the state of nature continues
to exist, they are not yet free.

Is there in fact a contradiction in the concept of an international
state? Undoubtedly, *one* contradiction cannot be overlooked. From a
historical-factual viewpoint, only few states are prepared to renounce
their sovereignty as required. In light of the history of totalitarian
regimes in the twentieth century, the lack of readiness cannot be discredited as a sort of obstinacy on the part of states. So long as there is
no shared consciousness regarding the morality of right and law on a

global level, or so long as there is no willingness actually to act on the basis of a shared legal consciousness, a world state is in danger of allowing force, not law, to govern. There is also the danger that the conflicts that were previously dealt with by foreign policy and that become the domestic conflicts of a world state would be decided by a majority on the basis of self-interest, with even less consideration for the rights of all. Finally, the hope that a dictatorship might be overthrown from the outside would effectively disappear.

Against the background of this sort of worry, the depth of Kant's awareness of the issues is once more made evident. He is familiar with the most important arguments against a world republic. He does not discuss the simple alternative: international state of war or a world republic. Rather, he brings into view three alternatives to the practice of war. Besides an ultraminimal world state (UMWS), he considers a federation of peoples, a federal and minimal world state (MWS), and universal monarchy as a homogeneous world state (HWS). Even if other expressions are preferred today, or additional subsidiary determinations introduced, no substantially different possibilities have been developed to replace these three options already familiar to us from individual states. Whether they are natural persons, societies, associations, or individual states, those affected either enter free agreements without renouncing their freedom of action, in which case they make contracts that are accepted only by the federation of peoples and comply with a favored catchword among political scientists: "governance without government" (Rosenau 1992). Or they agree to renounce their freedom of action to a considerable extent, which leads to dictatorship or despotism and, on the international plane, corresponds to a homogeneous world state with regard to state rights.

Kant confronts the third option of a universal monarchy with three counterarguments that have lost none of their force today. First, there is the danger of a "soulless despotism" (*Peace* VIII 367, l. 16) and "graveyard of freedom" (ll. 26f.), or what we would call a totalitarian dictatorship. Second, a universal monarchy would "deteriorate into anarchy" (l. 17) and all legal protection would be lost. Finally, a global centralized state would be ungovernable (ll. 14–16).

These arguments are to some extent convincing if they are understood as expressions of pragmatic considerations. They issue from demands of political prudence, in particular, the thought that with regard to the formation of an international state, heightened caution is in order. But they do not amount to fundamental objections. The dangers of dictatorship and of ungovernability are no different at the level of individual states, and yet such dangers do not discredit every state form whatsoever. They merely call for reliable protective measures that are to be employed even more rigorously in a world state with its far greater dangers. Such dangers amount to a pragmatic caveat, but they do not provide an argument against the principles. Kant's republican idealism in his conception of a world republic in any case aims at a moral conception of the state. This avoids the danger of "soulless despotism" from the start and thus also bars the subsequent danger of deterioration into anarchy. Furthermore, "prudent institutions" should be able to cope with the danger of ungovernability.

Kant's assertion about the contradiction inherent in the concept of an international state may be interpreted in two further ways, although neither is especially convincing. According to one interpretation, Kant identifies the international state in the second definitive article with the universal monarchy in the first supplement, as also shown by his caution against fusion in both passages (VIII 354, l. 15, and 367, ll. 12f.). An international state with minimal state tasks is, however, substantially different from the homogeneous state of a universal monarchy. The idea of the right of nations contradicts a homogeneous centralized state only because it abolishes the "separation of many neighboring states independent of one another" (367, ll. 8f.). The minimal world state, on the contrary, reinforces separation in the form of far-reaching independence of states.

According to the other interpretation, Kant has an actual contradiction in mind: In conformity with "their idea of the right of nations," the people "do not want" absolute state sovereignty or an international state (VIII 357, ll. 10–12). This contradiction is in fact evident. In order not to give in to it and hopelessly declare all to be lost, Kant offers a negative surrogate at the end of the second definitive article. Kant develops a "second-best strategy" to avoid the pure state of war even in a situation in which the states refuse to renounce any sovereignty: This strategy is to enter contractual agreements without a state character, that is, to establish a *federation* of peoples instead of an international state.

Agreements are no doubt better than a state of war. But since a federation lacks the instruments requisite for securing that which is to be agreed on, namely, world peace, there can be peace only with reservations and qualifications, which according to the first preliminary article is a mere cease-fire. Without the "sword of justice," a federation remains a (modified) state of nature. In place of a project that awakens hope, this gives us a half-hearted solution of trusting in the peaceable nature of republics, which cannot be justified either by Kant's arguments or by historical reality (see section 10.3).

A subsidiary and federal world republic is no longer half-hearted. It accommodates world citizens not according to that exclusionary and problematic understanding of cosmopolitanism in Hegel's *Philosophy of Right*: a "fixed position . . . in opposition to the concrete life of the state" (§209, Remark). In a homogeneous world state one is a world citizen *instead of* a citizen of a state. The federal world republic, on the contrary, defies the simple alternative of "single state or cosmopolitanism." Its world citizenship does not dissolve national citizenship but rather is complementary to it. One is primarily German, Russian, Senegalese, or a U.S. citizen, secondarily European, African, or American, and thirdly a world citizen or citizen of a federal world republic. If continental intermediate stages of citizenship are introduced, as according to the model of the European Union, citizenship may even be threefold. Kant's moderate political cosmopolitanism (Kleingeld 1998, 347) is more precisely both a complementary and subsidiary cosmopolitanism.

11.4. Evil in Relations among Different Peoples

Kant uses a concept in the treatise on peace that might contain an argument *against* the idea of a world republic, even though Kant does not introduce it as such. It has virtually disappeared from philosophical discourse since the beginning of the twentieth century (see section 4.1), and is thus overlooked by the majority of interpreters (excluding Laberge 1992). In Kant, the expression does not appear as by accident, but in four important passages.

Already in the first preliminary article, Kant speaks of the "evil will," which "makes use of the first favorable opportunity" to start war anew. The second definitive article says of the "malevolence [*Bösartigkeit*] of human nature" that it is greatly veiled in a condition under civil laws and under the coercion of the government, but that it "can be seen unconcealed in the free relations of nations" (VIII 355, ll. 3f.). A few lines later, Kant voices the hope that the human being will "eventually become master of the evil principle" (ll. 13f.). Finally, the "Appendix I" stresses that within a state "a certain malevolence rooted in human nature" may still "be doubted," whereas it "is quite undisguisedly and irrefutably obvious in the external relations of states to one another" (VIII 375, ll. 25–31). And the treatise on religion links this malevolence to radical evil, since it does not discover any clear testimony for it in the "external condition of peoples" (VI 34).

Is there an argument against a world republic lurking within the concept of evil? Whether with respect to individuals or states, Kant designates what is radically evil as that which is evil at the root (Lat. *radix*), unlike extreme malice. Since it is inborn, radical evil cannot be overcome. But it is a propensity, not a predisposition, which leads persons to submit (moral) duty to (sensible) inclination when they come into conflict, and to favor force over right in living with others. Within a state, this propensity is "greatly veiled" when persons adhere to moral duties of a juridical nature in fear of punishment. This is not the case in international relations, due to the lack of any "common external constraint." The profusion of wars is sufficiently clear evidence of the malevolence "rooted in human nature" or of human willingness to use violence. (On the connection between the "maxim of violence in human beings" and their "malevolence," see also DR §44.)

Therefore, whoever denies any chance of peace between states fails to see that states are merely malevolent, but not morally corrupted, and that malevolence or evil is not a predisposition, but merely a propensity. Kant does not harbor the hope, for instance, that individual states might at some point give up their willingness to use force completely. This kind of fantastical optimism might also easily be used to criticize Kant's realism by those skeptical about peace. But Kant is in fact more discerning about political reality and is aware that states "at least verbally" pay homage to the concept of right. Instead of simply using warfare out of sheer cynicism, they "always duly" cite reasons to justify war (*Peace* VIII 355, l. 13). This allows us to infer that they retain signs of moral sensitivity or even evince a fact of legal reason.

The Europeans in the epoch of the Enlightenment understood themselves to be members of "civilized peoples" that look down with contempt on the indigenous people of America, the "savages," because they "struggle unceasingly" (354, l. 17). As already mentioned in the introduction (section 1.4), Kant disparages both positive self-assessment and negative assessment of others and by virtue of this impartiality emerges as a resolute world citizen. Nor does he invoke the contrary cliché of the *bon sauvage*, or the good savage, who associates with others of his kind in pure harmony and concord. Kant rather assumes a state of "lawless freedom" as the state in which, on his view, Europeans live together. He therefore refers to "European savages" who differ from their counterparts in America not by their higher moral standards but by their more selfish prudence. Whereas some savages "eat up their enemies," the Europeans "know how to make better use of those they have defeated": They would rather make them "subjects" for the benefit of waging "even more extensive wars" (354f.).

Belligerence among Europeans is not only "greatly veiled," but also "unconcealed" wherever a "common external constraint" is lacking. Conversely, a global state proves to be necessary in order to counter the radical evil of individual states in the same way that it is countered among natural individuals. A sanctioned legal order is needed not in order to stamp out evil altogether but to prevent it from remaining unconcealed, and thus to make it at least accessible to juridical legality. The legal order thus conceived, or henceforth international statehood, is envisioned by the following statement from the first supplement: "The problem of establishing a state, no matter how hard it may sound, is soluble even for a nation of devils (if only they have understanding)" (*Peace* VIII 366, ll. 14f.). In order to establish the republic of peoples, the peoples must not overcome their "natural egoism" and "eradicate" radical evil "root and branch." The moral maturation of states articulated in the seventh proposition of the "Idea" is not mandatory. It is sufficient that the peoples adhere to enlightened ("understanding") self-interest as it suggested by the expression "devil." For, as an argument from Hobbes's *Leviathan* (chap. 13) shows, no state can be so weak that it is unable "through cunning or in cooperation with others" at least to endanger the strongest state considerably, if not destroy it.

If one acknowledges Kant's principle of legal ethics, the moral exigency of right and state, and the analogy between individuals and states as a justificatory reason in the second definitive article, then the ultraminimal world state (UMWS) proves to be a sensible intermediate goal despite the malevolence of states. But it is not suited to lead to the ultimate goal, since it lacks any state form. The second option Kant considers, the homogeneous world state (HWS), however, lays claim to an overly excessive state form. As a consequence, an intermediate option is needed, a state republic with a minimal world state form (MWS). A world republic demands the ceding of state sovereignty, but only to a minimal extent. The world republic cannot deny its responsibility to protect the individual states and safeguard their right to self-determination. But with respect to antagonism between and not within states, it is the world republic that deserves sovereignty: Right culminates in world right and the public safeguarding of rights culminates in the tasks of a subsidiary and federal world republic.

THE CRITIQUE OF PURE REASON: A COSMO-POLITICAL READING

12.1. Three Motives

For Kant, politics is an executive doctrine of right. As the embodiment of state prudence, it must conform to morals or, more precisely, to legal morals. Whoever denies this requirement and "frames a morals to suit the statesman's advantage" is called a political moralist, whereas a moral politician acknowledges the requirement (*Peace* VIII 370ff.). "Right must never be accommodated to politics, but politics must always be accommodated to right" ("Supposed Right" VIII 429). According to the first definitive article, moral politics requires that "every civil constitution in states must be republican," which corresponds less to communitarian republicanism than to a democratic constitutional state or a constitutional democracy (see section 10.1). An interpretation that applies this requirement to the first *Critique* is "political" and investigates whether reason, as it is treated here, has a republican character. Since Kant's legal morals first reaches completion in the cosmopolitan dimension, in the right of nations and in cosmopolitan right, the political reading merges with a cosmo-political reading.

A cosmo-political reading seems prima facie surprising, since the project of the *Critique* is continued in the *Metaphysical Foundations of Natural Science,* and not in the *Metaphysical First Principles of the Doctrine of Right,* where legal morals are developed. Further, the *Doctrine of Right* refers back to the *Groundwork* and to the second *Critique,* but scarcely to the first *Critique,* apart from its general critical program. According to the division of rational knowledge (B 868), the first *Critique* pertains to nature, understood as "everything that is," whereas the *Doctrine of Right* concerns "that which should be." Nevertheless, three motives speak for a political reading: a textual ("philological") and a systematic motive, along with a motive from the history of philosophy. (The republican character of other theorems, for example, the "kingdom of ends" in the *Groundwork* and the "kingdom of spirits" in the treatise on religion, are not considered, whereas "common sense" [*Gemeinsinn*] in the *Critique of Judgment* is relevant.)

(1) The first *Critique* already invites a (cosmo-) political reading by its political references. Important key words appear such as the Platonic republic (B 372–374), civil legislation (B 358, 372ff.), a constitution providing for the greatest human freedom (B 373), and perpetual peace (B 780). The references are, however, too cursory and accidental to justify a proper political reading.

Another reference, the supposition that we are "legislative fully a priori in regard to our own existence" (B 430), pertains to morals but not to legal morals. This restriction also applies to the famous intention of the first *Critique* to make room for morals and to ensure that we "can sever the very root of materialism, fatalism, atheism" (B xxxiv). A further reference is no longer accidental and is thoroughly political: "If governments find it good to concern themselves with the affairs of scholars, then it would accord better with their wise solicitude both for the sciences and for humanity if they favored the freedom of such a critique" (B xxxivf.). But this concerns the merely political precondition announced by Kant's oft-repeated demand for the freedom of the sciences (e.g., *Religion*, preface to the first edition; *Peace*, Appendix II; *Conflict*, Section 2), "by which alone reason's investigations can be put on a firm footing" (B xxxv). The political reference here does not pertain to reason itself, nor to the way it is determined.

(2) Three elements are of decisive importance to Kant's moral political theory. (a) The theorem of the state of nature describes this state, in agreement with Hobbes (B 780), as a state of war (B 779) and "of injustice and violence" (B 780). (b) Right overcomes the state of nature and is secured by public right, which has a republican character. (c) The significance of the constitution of this republic lies no longer in makeshift peace, but in unqualified perpetual peace. Starting with the "battlefield of these endless controversies," which is called metaphysics (A viii), all three elements may consistently be found in the first *Critique*. In the first chapter of the "Doctrine of Method," in the second section of the "Discipline," Kant even expressly makes reference (1) to "the state of nature" (B 779f.) and war, (2) to the alternative "peace of a state of law," and (3) to its achievement of "perpetual peace" (B 779f.).

The state of law is achieved when reason makes its "assertions and claims valid" no longer through war, but rather through a "trial." The execution of the critique in the form of a juridical procedure is well known, but the fact that this already demonstrates republican reason is ignored. Metaphysics in the state of nature and in the plural, however, is superceded by metaphysics in the state of law and in the singular, and the appropriate juridical procedure itself has a metaphysical character due to its fundamental philosophical significance. Interpreters of Kant are equally unaware that the subsequent question as to who sets the rules of the trial is answered by key political terms: The third chapter in the "doctrine on method" speaks of the "government of reason" (B 860), of its "legislator" and "legislation" (B 867f.), of the "legislative" (B 875), and of its "office as censor" (B 879). One should also note that the dictum of metaphysics as the "queen of all the sciences" (A viii) is ascribed to the theory of reason by the monarch ("queen"). If these passages are taken together, the first *Critique* contains a considerable number of political references.

Even followers of Kant often question the importance of Kantian architectonic; they occasionally attribute it to excessive pedantry. For Kant, however, substantial tenets are at issue, not external aspects such as elegance, simplicity, and unity. Architectonic has to do with an aim that is internal to reason, and it too has a political character. Reason should not submit to something alien, but rather should assume regency. This claim to the "government of reason" (B 860) is indebted to Plato. But Kant turns from the scholastic concept [*Schulbegriff*] of philosophy in the sense of "a system of cognition . . . as a science" to the cosmopolitan concept [*Weltbegriff*] of philosophy as "the science of the relation of all cognition to the essential ends of human reason" (B 866f.). In this respect philosophy does not merely comply with the judicative understanding of the title concept and thus does not merely perform judicial criticism. It takes on the office of censor as no mere addition, but even beyond this becomes the "legislator of human reason" (B 867; cf. the *Vorlesung über philosophische Enzyklopädie*, 33). It of course does not govern a political community – in this sphere Kant espouses the division of labor between politics and philosophy (see section 8.2). Philosophy should rather have unlimited rule over "the scientific community" (B 879) or epistemic republic. And because humanity as a whole belongs to this republic, it has a cosmo-political character. The following cosmo-political reading seeks to trace out the expectations that are thus awakened.

Kant's republican understanding of philosophy has its source in his precritical phase. Soon after he began writing on metaphysics, on December 31, 1765, he wrote a letter to the mathematician and philosopher friend Johann Heinrich Lambert. This letter may be read as a version of the first *Critique* in a nutshell. In the letter he complains of the "devastating disunity among supposed philosophers." The reason is that "we lack a common standard with which to procure agreement," a theme that he takes up again in his *Announcement of the Programme of his Lectures for the Winter Semester 1765–1766*: "The reason for this divergence is the fact that, whereas in the former science there is a common standard, in the latter science each person has his own standard." Finally, he calls the task and end of philosophers to "make their efforts agree" (*Letters* X 53: Nr. 32). It is not difficult to uncover all three elements of Kant's cosmo-political legal ethics in these statements: Disunity alludes to the epistemic state of nature, and the lack of a common standard corresponds *ex negativo* to the epistemic state of law. Agreement, in turn, suggests epistemic peace.

(3) The third motive from the history of philosophy is more challenging. As is well known, the criticism of modern philosophies of subjectivity was initiated as a movement in German idealism and is still continued today. It has been carried out by highly different approaches, ranging from those of Schelling and Hegel to Marx and Nietzsche ("The subject' is a mere fiction": *Fragment from the Autumn of 1887*, no. 9 [108], *Kritische Studienausgabe* XII 398), to American pragmatism, Wittgenstein, Heidegger, and Foucault, and finally to analytical philosophy, Apel and Habermas, and to the different approaches by Rorty and the sociologist Luhmann.

Descartes is not considered the only advocate of the incriminated philosophy of subjectivity. Many scholars, foremost Apel and Habermas, classify Kant's first *Critique* under what they generally refer to as the "methodological solipsism in modern philosophy of mind" (Kuhlmann 1987, 145). According to their charge of solipsism, Kant understands by reason a consciousness that is the capacity of cognition from the perspective of the solitary individual. This view is diametrically opposed to the notions of consensus, discourse, and an ideal communication community. The philosophy of consciousness ascribed to Kant is overcome by linguistic pragmatics, by transcendental pragmatics in Apel (1973 and 1976), and by a somewhat more modest universal pragmatics in Habermas (1976). (The following criticism of the solipsism charge is taken from Höffe 1996a.)

As a rule, the charge of solipsism is considered so patently justified that it is thought enough just to mention the transcendental apperception and its status as the "highest point" (B134) in the domain of theoretical philosophy (ethics remains outside of consideration here). The charge, which has become an *opinio communis,* has itself been exempted from "critical scrutiny." But a closer reading of the first *Critique* prompts weighty suspicion. Before we finally concede to the view that Kant supports the conception of "a thoroughly self-transparent, . . . rational subject, immediately capable of truth, which qua rational subject is essentially pure, extramundane, and thus untouched by history and social praxis, that is, in principle solitary" (Kuhlmann 1987, 144), we would be well advised to unfold the criticism and to ask whether the first *Critique* in fact contains the incriminated position (on Habermas, cf. Höffe 1987, on Apel, cf. Höffe 1990).

A cosmo-political reading of the *Critique* must consider the solipsism charge because the leading concept of republicanism is a social phenomenon. Thus, republican reason has a social and consequently antisolipsistic character. A republican reading of the *Critique* should expect to find not only textual, but also systematic elements as supportive evidence from sections dealing with the fundamental program of the critique. These include the title and the motto of the first *Critique,* its two prefaces, and the architectonic in the "Doctrine of Method." In advance, we should make a distinction to which we will recur in the course of the following investigation. The expression "methodological solipsism," which is used profusely in the literature, can denote either an empirical or logical subject, and it can refer to motivations, social theories, or linguistic and epistemic theories:

(a) As a concept referring to *motivations,* antisolipsism is acknowledgment not merely of personal interests, but also of the common good.
(b) A *social* theory is antisolipsistic according to which relations to other subjects are essential to individual subjects. According to a "logical" variant, subjects are constituted only in and through intersubjectivity. And according to the more empirical ("communitarian") variant, there are no atomic individuals unconnected to all other individuals. Instead, human beings are members of a common enterprise that has in part a communal, in part social character, develops certain life forms (cultures, civilizations), and in the end

comprises all of humanity, including the past and future – against which the communitarians voice skepticism.

(c) According to Wittgenstein's private *language* argument, there is no language whose words "refer to what can only be known to the person speaking; to his immediate private sensations" (*Philosophical Investigations*, §243). Wittgenstein here explains that a pure and fundamentally private or secret language, not a merely temporary private language, is impossible.

(d) Finally, Apel, Habermas, and other pragmatic critics of Kant challenge a theory of knowledge that is based on reason and detached from contingent viewpoints. This position is antisolipsistic to the extent that it plays on historical and cultural commonalities, such as on the way patterns of perception change (Habermas 1981). And since the commonalities are also peculiarities, the theory of knowledge obtains a communitarian character – although perhaps without being noticed as such, and *à contre-coeur*.

12.2. "Critique" Instead of "Meditation"

The fact that Kant sharply criticized Descartes as the leading authority in the philosophy of subjectivity may awaken doubts about the charge of solipsism confronting Kant. He adopted at least four elements from Descartes. The radical turn he intended thus does not break with every element from the tradition; a circumspect new grounding of philosophy proceeds more cautiously.

Kant adopts from Descartes the view that fundamental philosophy must come to grips with the dominant form of skepticism. Descartes takes aim at early modern versions of ancient skepticism, whereas Kant criticizes above all Humean skepticism. Furthermore, like Descartes, Kant wants to overcome the traditional form of metaphysics, but not metaphysics altogether. Any fundamental criticism of metaphysics, at any rate, tends to lead to a new metaphysics. Third, the new sketch of metaphysics is carried out as a "*discours de la méthode*." In an almost literal translation of Descartes' title, the first *Critique* describes itself as a "treatise on method" (B xxxii, cf. B 24f.), but in fact adopts a method different from that of Descartes. And whereas the *Discourse* is preliminary to Descartes' main fundamental work of philosophy, the *Meditations*, the first *Critique* is already Kant's main work, not the *Metaphysical First Principles of Natural Science*. Finally, Descartes attaches importance to the public domain and to the mutual exchange with others working in the same field, since "we should collectively progress much further than any one in particular could succeed in doing" (*Discours*, 6me partie, p. 39). According to Kant, the "shared participation in the same science" can lead to "literary friendship" (to Garve, August 7, 1783: *Letters* X 315). Kant is thus not a straightforward critic of Descartes. The basic intention, entire construction, and method of the *Critique*, along with its substantial assertions, however, demonstrate that Kant adheres to a clearly anti-Cartesian and antisolipsistic position.

Descartes and Kant articulate their distinct methods in the titles of their fundamental works of philosophy: Descartes expresses methodological solipsism, whereas Kant stresses his denial of it. But they both perform a similar thought experiment. In Descartes' form of "meditations," however, it is executed by the first person singular. The exemplary viewpoint of all thinking beings is expressed by the "I," but *in concreto* it is remote from the entire world and refers only to René Descartes; it doubts all acquired knowledge and discovers a first, unquestionable foundation. And this foundation remains in the first person singular: "... *dubito ergo cogito ergo – qua res cogitans – sum*" ("I doubt, therefore I think, therefore I am a thinking thing"). Kant's thought experiment, on the contrary, has the form of a "critique" that, as a juridical procedure, is a social enterprise and dismisses the pragmatics of methodological solipsism, or the turning back of the first person singular on himself.

The *first antisolipsistic aspect* of the first *Critique* thus concerns its method and consists in the replacement of meditations by a court of justice. Taken alone, the method is only a legal, not a political process. As a procedure that eliminates war among philosophers and instead establishes peace, it belongs to public right and is politically significant. The outstanding importance of a court is alluded to in the *Doctrine of Right*, which in §36 designates the courthouse [*forum*] as a "moral person that administers justice."

12.3. For the Benefit of the Common Good

In the course of the court trial, Kant analyzes Cartesian thoughts and adheres to a clearly anti-Cartesian position. Paragraph 25 of the transcendental deduction and the chapter on the paralogism directly concern not the question of solipsism, but rather the possibility of cognition independent of experience. Those aspects of Kant's work that are relevant to the question of solipsism, however, disarm the charge against Kant.

First of all, Kant not only discusses Descartes and, more generally, rationalism. He also confronts rationalism with the opposing position of empiricism and skepticism, thereby staging a conflict, that is, a genuinely social situation. Now Kant could "magisterially" resolve the conflict so that only the topic would be social, whereas the method would be solipsistic. In fact, however, he already begins settling the controversy communicatively and discursively by the very way he constructs the procedure of a critique of reason.

O'Neill (1989, chaps. 1–2) already correctly interprets the first *Critique* by recourse to Hannah Arendt (1982) and Hans Saner (1967/1983) as a social and even political, but by no means solitary enterprise. One of her arguments, however, cannot win credence. It asserts that the motto from Bacon in the second edition is already remote from Descartes' solitary introspection. Bacon's remark "*in commune consultant*" is to be translated not, as in O'Neill, by "discuss together," but more liberally as "consult on the common good" or, following the *Editio princeps* of Bacon's *Instauratio magna*: "join in consultation for the common good." Near the close of the first *Critique* in the "Doctrine of Method" or, more precisely, in the last paragraph of the "Architectonic," this proposed interpretation is supported by further assertions. Here, the motives of the motto and both prefaces are incorporated and articulated in the way they are ultimately to be understood in the first *Critique*. This is also a passage that does not change from the first to the second edition of the first *Critique*. Kant appeals to the "common good" of the scientific community and to its "chief end, that of the general happiness" (B 879). This no doubt contains a social and, unlike the trial, even clearly political motive. The *second antisolipsistic* and *political aspect* in the first *Critique* is thus motivational; according to its motto, the critique serves the common good.

It is widely acknowledged that Descartes, as an important scientist and philosopher, adopts from Francis Bacon the idea that science is committed to the common good. The first part of the *Discourse*, namely, alludes to what the sixth part demands with all possible clarity: ensuring the common good of all human beings ("*bien général de tous les hommes*"). Bacon and Descartes have a social and technical understanding of this social pragmatic task committed to the common good. The sciences should serve to relieve people of work, prepare for risks, and promote health. Kant is less ambitious in the first *Critique*. Its value is more than merely internal to philosophy, but it excludes the common political community and concerns only the scientific epistemic community. Both prefaces announce two fundamentally different elements for the benefit of that community's common good. Instead of relief from work or physical health, the first preface concerns the resolution of those contradictions in which reason inevitably involves itself (A vii f.), and the second preface deals with ways of thinking such as materialism, fatalism, and atheism, which could become generally injurious to the public (B xxxiv; cf. B 494, et al.). In the former, Kant pursues an inner epistemic and theoretical interest, whereas he also pursues a moral-practical interest in the latter.

Motivational antisolipsism is corroborated by the beginning of the motto from Bacon. Being "silent about ourselves" and allowing only facts to be voiced (*"De nobis ipsis silemus: De re autem…"*) articulates negatively what is positively maintained by the concept "common good": All people should renounce personal interests and wishes. In this way, the common good prevails *eo ipso*.

12.4. A Democratic Discourse

Discourses or treatises that rehearse the pros and cons of a problem were already composed by Descartes and, later, by Rousseau. Apel and Habermas adopt this understanding of the "discourse," since they speak of "discourses" only where validity claims are no longer naively assumed, but rather become the discussed topic of debates in search of renewed, henceforth rationally motivated consent. With respect to metaphysics or foundational philosophy, the first *Critique* has a discursive character in precisely this sense. It is first manifest in the way it discusses the chief controversy among philosophers. This controversy turns out to be so fundamental that it requires setting aside the tasks of traditional philosophy and first clarifying its entailments and limits. The discursive character of the first *Critique* is further evinced by that criterion of science to which philosophy is also subjected. The perpetual antagonism appears to be a nuisance when measured against the yardstick of science. This leads to the *third antisolipsistic* element, which is taken from *social theory* and has a political character. Scientists pursue a "common aim" and investigate ways to attain their aim "to achieve unanimity" (B vii). The entire work is guided by this goal of democratic consensus. Kant attaches importance to "agreement" (B 766) not only in the (second) preface, but also retrospectively in the "Doctrine of Method," which is verbally identical (excluding minimal exceptions) in both editions.

The first *Critique* is discursive also because it seeks to resolve disputes not by means of a superior brand of dogmatic knowledge but through a (philosophical) court of justice. It is indebted to Bacon in this respect, too, since the latter demands of all science "lawful evidence" (*Novum Organum*, aphorism 98). Bacon makes evidence a requirement for normal sciences only, whereas Kant also applies it to the philosophy of science, namely, transcendental critique. Moreover, the metaphor Kant uses to illustrate the critique suggests its discursiveness: The critique sets out to survey the land of reason (B 294).

Since a court of justice accommodates academically educated professional judges, and thus experts, discourse theory might announce misgivings as to whether this conflicts with their assumption of fundamental equality. But one can invalidate these suspicions with respect to the rational process. Kant's general statements about the enlightenment also obtain for the enlightenment of theoretical reason: "[N]othing is required but freedom, . . . namely, freedom to make public use of one's reason in all matters" ("What Is Enlightenment?" VIII 36; cf. *Peace*, Appendix II; *Conflict*, section 2.8). Hence, special esoteric knowledge is of no avail and solely general reason is required, even if it is at times only dimly present. Academically trained professional philosophers are not the sole administrators in the trial of theoretical reason. Conducted as a "free and public examination" (A xi), it takes the equality of all people for granted.

Habermas invoked G. H. Mead (1983, 75) in the course of calling for an ideal exchange of roles for ethics. Kant not only had answered this call long before Mead, but also had put forward the idea in the distinctive form of an exchange of roles with a genuinely universal significance. It is most naturally expected in ethics, where Kant actually explains with great precision that the "dignity (prerogative)" human beings have "over all merely natural beings brings with it that he must always take his maxims from the point of view of himself, and likewise every other rational being, as lawgiving beings (who for this reason are also called persons)" (GMM IV 438). But the exchange of roles also appears in the first *Critique*. Since the trial of theoretical reason dismisses the "private validity of the judgment" (B 849) and instead concerns reason alone, all persons must – again with the qualification: in principle – act out each of the roles of the prosecutor, defendant, and judge. Kant is clear enough on this point in the "Doctrine of Method" when he declares that the "claim" of reason is "never anything more than the agreement of free citizens, each of whom must be able to express his reservations, indeed even his veto, without holding back" (B 766f.).

The enlightenment philosopher's enterprise does not require expert knowledge, affiliation with a special social standing, or an official charge, whether granted by divine or human mercy. At the same time, an aspect of reason comes to the fore that again shows Kant's proximity to Descartes and is the sixth point of convergence with the latter's *Discours*, this time with the first section of that work. Reason is something that the human being has in common with everyone of his kind and that enables him to gain knowledge, but this knowledge transcends erudition acquired in the closed study. This insight has an even longer history reaching back beyond Descartes. More than three centuries before Kant and almost two centuries before Descartes, Nicolas of Cusa prompted laymen [*idiota*] to speak their minds. In the three treatises *De sapientia* (On Wisdom), *De mente* (On the Mind), and *De staticis experimentis* (On Experiments Using the Scale), the protagonist (the "idiot") is not restrained by the straitjackets of school learning or a ministry, is unprejudiced, and thinks freely. Likewise, no experts on reason are present in Kant's trial of reason, but rather laymen and in principle only laymen.

The first *Critique* merely implicitly presupposes what Kant makes explicit two years later in the motto of the essay on enlightenment: "*Sapere aude!* Have courage to make use of your own understanding!" (This, too, might recall Bacon and the frontispiece of the *Novum organum*, in which a ship ventures out on the boundless ocean of knowledge.) The presupposition, like the leitmotif of the *Critique*, has two sides: The theoretical task of using one's own understanding requires a practical and even moral exertion. It consists in a personal but not private precondition (and is thus indifferent to the question "solipsism: yes or no"). That preconditon – courage – makes possible the willingness to engage in a critique of reason. And the lack of such willingness likewise can be traced back to a moral, this time negative "exertion": that one remains a minor [*unmündig*] out of indolence (ibid.). The first *Critique*, on the contrary, takes up the challenge of thinking for oneself.

Where reason is concerned, everyone is a judge or even a judge at the constitutional court, as long as all are able to summon up the aforementioned courage and demonstrate precision and patience. This is corroborated by Kant's method of presentation. The first *Critique* restates certain positions from the history of philosophy, since otherwise there would be no problem or antagonism among philosophers to make the trial or discourse necessary. Just as judges should be informed about the reasons for and substance of the trial in customary juridical procedures, philosophers should be likewise informed in their legal conflicts. Kant's historical descriptions of the positions of former philosophers are almost exclusively limited to the "prefaces," and they, too, do not go beyond a minimal reference to the history of philosophy. As long as the trial is shown to be necessary, it deals only with the decisive substantial questions: What is space? What is time? What is causality? Which role do they play in knowledge? These questions are both articulated and discussed in an immediately systematic fashion, without need for far-reaching knowledge of the history of philosophy. Even in the "history of pure reason," Kant does not sketch a history of philosophy; a "short sketch" is rather to be found in the *Logic* (IX 27–33). In line with the disparagement of all merely historical knowledge in the "Architectonic" (B 863f.), the first *Critique* is concerned with what is scientific as the idea underlying a history of pure reason (cf. Höffe 1998, 636ff.).

The *third antisolipsistic* and again *political aspect* of Kant's theory, namely, his notion of reason that consists in the "consent of free citizens," is, according to contemporary understanding, altogether democratic. A trial, if it indeed occurs, will have to take place in a court of lay assessors or of assizes, in which the lay judges are represented by the same votes as professional judges or academic philosophers. Reason itself, with respect to fundamental epistemic questions, is not the special resource of an academic profession but is a general competence. This Kantian insight tacitly breaks with Plato. In opposition to the aristocracy that is alluded to in the famous principle of philosopher-kings (*Republic* V 473c–d, cf. VII. *Letter* 326b) and underlined in the Platonic program of pedagogy, most clearly in the analogy of the cave (*Republic* VII 514aff.), Kant endorses democratization. Remarkably, he does not reserve democratic thought for the domains of ethics and politics, but incorporates it in theoretical reason as well.

One might object that the argumentation in the first *Critique* exceeds the intellectual capacity of the layman and that Plato's elitist understanding of philosophy is thus de facto confirmed. Kant even concedes that his work can "never become popular," for "just as little as the people want to fill their heads with fine-spun arguments for useful truths, so just as little do the equally subtle objections against these truths ever enter their minds" (B xxxiv, similarly in GMM IV 409f.). Yet the speculative philosopher "remains the exclusive trustee of a science that is useful to the public even without their knowledge" (B xxxiv).

12.5. A Juridical State of Reason

Kant's metaphor of the court of justice, along with the expressions "critique," "deduction," and "*quaestio juris/facti*," raise the question of who gives the laws to the court: Who is the legislator of (theoretical) reason? If we take reason in a wider sense, not as the principle faculty of knowledge but as the sum total of all faculties of knowledge, then it does not acquire its laws from external sources, but rather is endowed with them to begin with. The pure forms of intuition lie in intuition, the categories lie in understanding, and the ideas lie in reason in the narrow sense.

Reason's endowment with cognitive capacities is less of an accomplishment than its capacity for self-legislation, which is ascribed only to pure practical reason. The "Architectonic" no doubt seeks to extend reason; it contains the following *fourth antisolipsistic* and *political aspect* of the first *Critique*. The philosopher, so long as his ideal is represented as an archetype or as the idea of a philosopher, is a "legislator of human reason." To trace a characteristic profile of this widely neglected line of thought, two considerations are necessary: First, the philosopher is opposed to the mathematician, the naturalist, and the logician, who are "only artists of reason" (B 867), and thus, like technicians, merely employ reason as it is already given to us. Second, Kant does not have in mind the representatives of a specific profession, or "professional thinkers" (B 871), but is explicitly concerned with a legislation that "is found in every human reason" (B 867).

"Universal human reason" (B 780) is not restricted to the task of carrying out a trial in which it takes on all three roles of the prosecutor, defendant, and judge (on the judicial office of reason, cf. ibid.). It is also responsible for lawgiving. Since it additionally administers a "government" and with its help constructs a unity of a system out of the rhapsodic aggregate of knowledge (B 860 and 862f.), the sphere of knowledge presents us with a highly unusual situation: Reason takes over the competences of all three public powers.

In this way, the division of powers, as a fundamental element of the republic or constitutional democracy, seems to succumb to the establishment of a dictatorship of reason. If this were the case, there would be a direct democracy free from the division of powers in the epistemic community – precisely what Kant had rejected for the political community (*Peace*, "First Definitive Article"). For Kant, this direct democracy would be a dictatorship, the very opposite of a republic. But he emphatically renounces such an idea. In order for reason not to "have dictatorial authority," he demands that the "claim" of reason be "never anything more than the agreement of free citizens, each of whom must be able to express his reservations, indeed even his veto, without holding back" (B 767f.; cf. already A xi).

The democracy signaled by the "agreement of free citizens" may on no account be understood empirically, as though a majority ruling were relevant to reason and metaphysics. The first *Critique* does not endorse a democracy in the sense of a system of institutions, organizations, and procedures that gives rise to certain authoritative decisions determined by majority rule. Kant refers to the "agreement of free citizens" within the ambit of the "discipline of pure reason" and understands by a "discipline" not a scientific subject or a "teaching" [*Belehrung*], but a "disciplined training" [*Zucht*] (B 738). Discipline has to do with coercion or, in terms of political theory, with a ruling order.

Reason does make authoritative decisions. Since it is "concerned to prescribe its discipline to all other endeavors," Kant's refutation of private language is more fundamental than Wittgenstein's (*Philosophical Investigations*, §243). However, Kant's arguments are not taken from the philosophy of language. Wittgenstein appeals to the necessity of criteria (rules) for correct linguistic usage, which must be public, since in merely private arbitration "whatever is going to seem right to me is right. And that only means that here we can't talk about 'right'" (*Philosophical Investigations*, §258). The *Critique* explicitly dismisses all arbitrariness that allows for "free and unlimited movement" (B 738) by providing necessary rules for correctness. Whoever negatively thwarts one's "propensity to stray from certain rules" (B 737) advocates laws, and thus a legal order.

In the chapter on the "discipline," however, reason is not only a subject, but also an object. Its form of self-discipline is directed against its inherent penchant for overly ambitious claims. This obviously alludes to the second part of the transcendental logic, the dialectic. Kant does not spare pure reason from "humiliation" (B 738) through disciplined self-training in "constrain[ing] its propensity to expansion beyond the narrow boundaries of possible experience" (B 739) and, notably, in "prevent[ing] the devastations that a lawless speculative reason would otherwise inevitably perpetrate in both morality and religion" (B 877).

This negative contribution of the "discipline" precedes the positive achievement of a "doctrine." The agreement of free citizens, which Kant's first *Critique* depends on, consists in all insights gained from the aesthetic, analytic, and dialectic.

In order to avoid the misunderstanding hinted at, one should distinguish between an organizational and legitimizing concept of democracy. As a principle for organizing political decision-making processes, democracy is defined by majority rule. But as a principle of legitimation, democracy is the requirement that the people or subjects authorize all constraint. Transferred to the sphere of knowledge, the organizational concept of democracy would result in what is ruled out by Habermas's consensus theory of truth: A majority would decide on the objectivity of statements. Democracy as a principle of legitimation, on the contrary, would mean that there is no truth external to the subjects of cognition. This is in agreement with the Copernican revolution at the level of the fundamental questions discussed in the first *Critique.* The (a priori) truth conditions, namely, pure forms of intuitions, categories, principles, and ideas, lie in the theoretical subjects themselves. Kant denies the organizational understanding of "democracy" by instead using the term "republic," which he defines in the treatise on peace by means of freedom, dependence (on a common legislation), and equality. In the *Anthropology*, by way of contrast, it is linked to "authority, with freedom and law" (VII 331). Kant's republic is opposed to anarchy by its element of (public) authority, to despotism by freedom, and to barbarism by the coalescence of authority and lawfulness.

A democratic constitutional state is distinguished by three primary elements: democracy, human rights, and the division of powers. All three elements may be encountered again in Kant's epistemic republic. The principle of democracy in constitutional theory is predominant. Kant maintains that the understanding takes over "legislation for nature" (A 126) or prescribes "the law to nature" (B 159). This is also true of the a priori forms of knowledge, but not of the material of knowledge, which is received passively by the mind. All epistemic power is vested in the epistemic people, or in all subjects capable of knowledge.

The division of powers among the "objective" material and "subjective" forms is supplemented by a further division of power within the subjective realm among sensibility, understanding, and reason.

Moreover, there are epistemic principles that, like prepositive and suprapositive human rights, have a pre-empirical and supra-empirical

significance. Just as original sin is not to be understood as a histori-
cally first sin, but as the condition for the possibility of sin, the said
elements, according to their claims, belong to the original language,
namely, to the conditions for the possibility of every language. Just as
human rights belong to the core grammar of the social, the elements
Kant names belong to the core grammar of the epistemic. The constitutional principles of epistemic democracy, on the positive side, are called
pure forms of intuition, pure concepts, transcendental apperception,
pure schematisms, and above all, the principles of pure understanding or transcendental natural laws as the constructive apex of the first
Critique. The ideas may be added to this list. On the negative side, in
turn, there are the paralogisms, the antinomies, and further transcendental sophisms.

Besides the cited passage from the *Groundwork*, the *Critique of Judgment*
shows that Kant is familiar with the idea of an ideal exchange of roles
that is not an agreement among "free citizens." The focus, however, is
no longer on theoretical reason but on aesthetic judgment ("judgment
of taste"). For this reason one should be wary of interpreting the first
Critique and Kant's political philosophy by recourse to his theory of aesthetic judgment, as in Hans Saner (1967), Hannah Arendt (1982), and
Onora O'Neill (1989). The distinctiveness of aesthetic judgment is that
it is not objective but nevertheless "ascribes assent to everyone." This
is brought out by common sense, the fundamental principles of which
Kant articulates through three maxims of ordinary human understanding. The second of these maxims demands precisely what Habermas
takes up from G. H. Mead: We should "think in the position of everyone else," and its rationale lies in the fact that a universal standpoint
that disregards "the subjective private conditions of the judgment" can
be determined only "by putting himself into the standpoint of others"
(CJ §40). This maxim is evidently also valid for the first *Critique*. However, it does not play an explicit role therein, since its a priori assertions
from the very start set aside "subjective private conditions." Kant even
defines "asserting something" as "[pronouncing] it to be a judgment
necessarily valid for everyone" (B 849).

12.6. Beyond an Alternative

From the observations made up to this point, we may at least reject a
wholesale charge of solipsism. Reason, to the extent that it executes
the critique of knowledge, cannot be assimilated to the paradigm of a

monological consciousness. This becomes immediately apparent when the vague expression "rational subject" is refined by a distinction and when those faculties that are subjected to the critique of knowledge, namely, sensibility, understanding, and reason, are contrasted with the faculty that executes the critique. Thus Kant may no longer be taken as a principle source of the old paradigm. Rather with him begins at the latest the emancipation of the theory of knowledge from the paradigm of a monological consciousness. If previous sources are set aside, the birthplace of the paradigm of communication and discourse is not Frankfurt, and also not the "Cambridge Metaphysical Club" in which North American pragmatists assembled, but rather Königsberg.

A serious charge of solipsism can in the best case argue against the notion of reason that is the object of critique. However, even this charge is, as a rule, motivated by a selective reading of Kant. Instead of incorporating the transcendental aesthetic and transcendental judgment, it refers only to the doctrine of transcendental self-consciousness. Kant does consider it to be the "highest point to which one must affix all use of the understanding, even the whole of logic and, after it, transcendental philosophy" (B 134). But understanding is only one of two equally valid sources of knowledge. Moreover, transcendental apperception merely constitutes the highest point, not the constructive conclusion of the transcendental theory of understanding. This rather lies in the often-neglected "system of all principles of pure understanding."

Not only the selective reading but also its interpretation demand criticism. For the interpretation yokes the transcendental apperception to monologism and a private inner world in order to juxtapose this with a commonly shared, genuinely communicative linguistic and social world. The self of transcendental self-consciousness cannot, however, be regarded as monological in a straightforward way. This restriction of self-consciousness would be sensible only if there were an opening for the alternative of communication, that is, for the sphere of empirical subjects who relate either to themselves or to others. We should add that they relate "more or less" to themselves or to others, since an exclusive self-reference is just as impossible as an exclusive reference to others. Even in discourse, the validity claims of individual subjects are made problematic; individuals make suggestions for the sake of a new agreement and examine the suggestions, again as individuals, in order to find them correct or to reject them as unconvincing. The transcendental "I think" does not belong to the empirical ego as contrasted with an alter ego, but rather to those conditions of knowledge in general that are on a logically superior level to the alternative "ego or alter."

Since misunderstanding nevertheless is to be expected, Kant offers other options for expressing the "I think," including the symbol for the unknown: "x." He thus unambiguously gives us to understand that the transcendental "I think" has nothing to do with the conventional idea of a general, empirical I: As the paralogism chapter demonstrates, "through this I, or He, or It (the thing), which thinks, nothing further is represented than a transcendental subject of thoughts $= x$" (B 404).

Whoever directs the charge of solipsism even against the superior, transcendental apperception must be aware that he can maintain the charge only in a greatly weakened form. Otherwise, he would also have to attack the other superior elements, comprising the pure concepts of understanding, the schematisms, and the principles of pure understanding. For all of these elements belong to theoretical subjectivity and exceed the distinctive features of empirical subjects. Furthermore, as common elements of all subjects, they are intersubjectively valid in a well-determined sense, just like transcendental apperception.

One has recently put forward reservations about the assuredly high demands enunciated in the first *Critique*, on the grounds that human reason is barred from the divine perspective (e.g., Schnädelbach 2000). If the modesty this suggests is more than an arid assurance, it should not shy away from efforts to determine the exact point at which human and divine knowledge diverge. This is the very beginning of the unwelcome determination of a strict, not merely relative, but absolute a priori. And at least this aspect in Kant remains plausible, that human knowledge is not possible as exclusively spontaneous knowledge but also relies on receptive intuition outside of understanding. Intuitions, in turn, cannot be had outside of space and time.

It is thus at this point difficult to avoid coming to the following conclusion: The alternative pairs "subjective-intersubjective" and "monologue-dialogue" or "monological-communicative," which have already become accepted dogma, contribute little to understanding the first *Critique*. The components of the "transcendental doctrine of elements" do not require consensus, but they are capable of consensus and enable consensus. They are conditions, namely, that enable not just any common world but a common world in the strictest objective sense. At the same time, they enable consensus that refers to this world and, as the conditions of the possibility of consensus, deserve the "agreement of free citizens."

Apel's transcendental pragmatics, Habermas's universal pragmatics, and Rorty's pragmatics significantly do not broach the question as to whether knowledge in an emphatic sense would be possible if there were no pure forms of intuition, pure concepts, transcendental laws of nature, or elements equivalent to them. Nor are Apel, Habermas, and Rorty able to replace the first *Critique* as a "substantial theory" of mathematics and of natural science.

Pragmatics and pragmatism, in their various forms, attach importance to the openness of reason with respect to "history, tradition, language, social praxis, life, finitude, etc." (Kuhlmann 1987, 149). Kant, too, acknowledges this openness, but for different reasons. The precommunicative and unhistorical elements of his philosophy are very modest and often are of even less import than Kant himself and his interpreters assume. In the transcendental aesthetics, for instance, the pure forms of intuition prove to be much more formal, and thus of less material content than is suggested by the way in which Kant presents them. The transcendental concept of space merely denotes spatiality and not special determinacy as it is employed by mathematical geometry or, at Kant's time, by Euclidian geometry. Nor does it denote the special determinacy that distinguishes physical theories as the only correct interpretations of reality among the range of mathematically possible geometries.

This reference to the minimal implications of the transcendental allows us partially to acknowledge the criticism brought forward against the philosophy of subjectivity by thinkers ranging from Nietzsche to Heidegger and Foucault. These authors do not do justice to their intention of "dismissing the modern subject," since this would involve them in a pragmatic contradiction. They lay claim to objectivity and truth for their own assertions, as, for instance, Heidegger in *Being and Time* with respect to the existentials of *Befindlichkeit* (state of being/mind), thrownness, and care. They thus assume precisely what they wanted to challenge: an objective world and a subject capable of objective truth. On the other hand, they present reasons worth considering for the view that the scope of universal statements about the objective world and about the truth capacity of theoretical subjectivity is to be determined in a new and more clearly modest way.

Nevertheless, Kant emerges as a systematic alternative to recent favored attempts to understand objectivity merely as intersubjectivity or sociality. He might effortlessly agree with the thesis that the objective world is a commonly shared and thus social world. But the reason for this is its objectivity, not its sociality, and the conditions for objectivity coincide with the conditions for sociality in general. It is assumed that these conditions, and these alone, unite all human beings into one whole, regardless of their differences. Kant's *fifth antisolipsistic* and *political aspect* is as follows: On the transcendental plane, the human being is a subject (determined by rules) and constitutes a (regulated and thus legally organized) society.

12.7. The Cosmo-Political Concept of Philosophy

In the transcendental society, reason already demonstrates its regency in its search for unity, in contrast to a rhapsodic collecting of this and that. And it increases its ability to govern by ensuring unity on a higher or even supreme level. Unity is outlined not "empirically, in accordance with aims occurring contingently," but "in accordance with an idea, i.e., from the chief end of reason" (B 861). Inferior, technical unity arises for (1) external, (2) perhaps numerous, and (3) arbitrary ends (ibid.); moreover, it is (4) "in accordance with contingently perceived affinities" and (5) "as it were, established by good luck" (B 875).

Kant uses two variously rigid concepts for a superior, architectonic unity. The more modest concept refers to a plurality: Unity is "in conformity with . . . essential ends" (B 875). The more ambitious concept introduced before this passage concerns a singular superlative. Unity is derived "from a single supreme and inner end, which first makes possible the whole" (B 861). Toward the close of the first section of the "discipline," Kant writes: "Our reason itself (subjectively) is a system, but in its pure use, by means of mere concepts, only a system for research in accordance with principles of unity, for which *experience* alone can give the matter" (B 765f.).

According to a popular *topos*, a philosophy committed to ends or teleology is a relic of classical antiquity, notably of Aristotelian thought, which in modernity has become increasingly obsolete. That Kant, an indisputably modern thinker, frequently uses the concept of end or purpose gives us cause for revising the *topos*. According to arguments worth considering in the third *Critique*, both aesthetic and biological judgments are orientated toward an end. The philosophy of history discusses the end of the history of the human species (see above, chapter 9), and in the *Groundwork* there is a critique of happiness as the end of moral nature (IV 395, ll. 4ff.). In the first *Critique*, reason itself is ultimately oriented toward an end, and committed to unity and completeness. As a novelty in comparison with classical antiquity, however, the ends are not given in the things themselves, but rather, in agreement with the Copernican revolution, issue from the subject. (Cf. a passage from the "Progress...Metaphysics": "[T]he concept of purpose...[is] framed always by ourselves, and that of the ultimate purpose must be framed a priori through reason," XX 294f.).

Kant rightly sees that reason governs when its "essential ends" prevail (B 860). He first establishes the system as a necessary instrument for this purpose, and only later considers the ends themselves and the philosopher who is responsible for constructing them. The philosopher is put into relief again according not to the scholastic but to the cosmopolitan concept, which in turn is defined by the concept of the end. Philosophy according to its scholastic concept might, despite its subtleness and elegance, in the end turn out to be merely an intellectual glass bead game, for it is, by this concept, merely a "doctrine of skill" (*Logic* IX 24). According to its cosmological concept, it is a "doctrine of wisdom" (ibid.). And instead of a "cosmological concept (*in sensu cosmico*)" (ibid.), the *Logic* makes reference to "philosophy in this cosmopolitan meaning" two paragraphs further on (IX 25).

The "cosmopolitan" meaning of philosophy may be elucidated by means of four integral aspects. They are modest and do not yet reach back to draw on Kant's more detailed definition of the cosmopolitan concept of philosophy as "the science of the relation of all cognition to the essential ends of human reason" (B 867; cf. *Logic* IX 23f.). The four still modest aspects together constitute the *sixth antisolipsistic* and *political aspect* of Kant's *Critique*: (1) Instead of a mere intellectual glass bead game, cosmopolitan philosophy deals with the world, and as theoretical philosophy, with the sum total of what is: nature. (2) All human beings share this world-nature together. Even if they are not yet juridical world citizens, since cosmopolitan right in a proper, legal sense, which includes the right of nations, is still outstanding, they are already *epistemic world citizens*: All human beings are equally called on to cognize their common world and they are equally competent in doing so. (3) If there are other rational beings in other possible worlds, they are subject to the same epistemic conditions. (4) The corresponding world republic, however, does not rest content with the world of cognition and its correlate, the world-nature. According to Kant's famous three questions – What can I know? What should I do? What may I hope? (B 832f.; cf. *Logic* IX 25) – the field of philosophy in the cosmopolitan sense extends to three shared cosmopolitan worlds.

All human beings are equal members of (a) the world of cognition, (b) the world of moral action, and (c) the world of rational hope (for an in-depth cosmopolitan reading of the CPR, see Höffe, 2003).

12.8. The Self-Governance of Reason

The strict cosmopolitan concept of philosophy refers to the essential ends of reason. Kant does not enunciate all of them, but only the most important of the highest ends, "of which . . . there can be only a single one." The final end is none other than "the entire vocation (*Bestimmung*) of human beings" (B 868; cf. *Logic* IX 24f.). Contrary to one's expectations, the "architectonic" does not explain how this is to be understood, nor does it clarify the "vocation of human beings" or why it should be the final end. Moreover, Kant does not at any other place in the first *Critique* mention the *Bestimmung* of human beings.

In German, *Bestimmung* can mean "fixation," "demarcation," or "concept," and in this sense refers to determination [*determinatio*] and definition [*definitio*], or it denotes the destination [*destinatio*]: the direction taken, the assignment, vocation, or providence. Since in the passage in the "Architectonic" Kant is not concerned with the concept of the human being, the expression is to be understood in the sense of *destinatio*. But this still leaves open whether Kant has in mind obligation [*obligatio*], precept [*praeceptum*], or fate [*fatum*].

The vocation of human beings could lie in the completion of knowledge, as familiar from Aristotle's notion of *theôria*. Without even considering this option, Kant rejects it and turns directly to morals. In anticipation of his moral philosophy, he accedes priority to the domain of morals. The primacy of (pure) practical reason is suggested in other passages of the first *Critique* (e.g., B xxxiv), clearly articulated in the first section of the "Canon" (e.g., B 829), and corroborated in the discussion of the governance of reason.

Autobiographical experience serves as a backdrop to all this. Very similar to Aristotle's adulation of *theôria*, Kant writes of himself: "I am by inclination a scholar [*Forscher*]. I sense the unquenchable thirst for knowledge and the eager unrest to advance therein, as well as the satisfaction that accompanies progress." And he continues: "There was a time when I believed that all of this could be what constitutes the dignity of mankind." But "Rousseau brought me to my senses. This delusion of privilege has disappeared"; and I "would consider myself much less useful than the common workers if I did not believe that this view of things could give all else value, by establishing the rights of mankind" (XXI 273f.).

Outside the first *Critique*, Kant discusses the "vocation of human beings" in important works, but he does not use this expression: These include the works on the philosophy of history, the *Critique of Judgment*, the *Groundwork*, and the treatise on religion. In each of these cases he is also concerned with morals. In the philosophy of history, morals play a role to the extent that the complete and purposive "unfolding" of natural predispositions takes place in the legally ordered coexistence of persons at a global level, or in the state of cosmopolitan right, as required by legal morals (cf. chapter 9). In the *Critique of Judgment* (§42), Kant directly mentions the "moral vocation" that "constitutes the ultimate end of our existence" (V 301; V 298 similarly mentions the "ultimate end of humanity, namely the morally good"). Even in the treatise on religion, there is mention of the "moral vocation" (VI 50), and the *Groundwork* deals with morals from the very outset.

Among passages in the first *Critique*, one might add the first section of the "Canon," where Kant discusses the concept of the final end of pure reason. In anticipation of §42 of the *Critique of Judgment*, he calls what is moral "the ultimate aim of nature which provides for us wisely in the disposition of reason" (B 829). The "vocation" [*Bestimmung*] of human beings is thus to be understood as their final end. As in other places, Kant's first *Critique* also identifies the final end not with complete knowledge of *theôria*, as does Aristotle, but rather with morals.

Reason as a whole thus ultimately governs as pure practical reason, not as theoretical reason. But this governance is not external, even for theoretical reason, since this would provoke the danger of foreign rule or even dictatorship. Reason must remain bound to genuinely theoretical elements – ranging from the pure forms of intuition to pure concepts, pure schematisms, and transcendental laws of nature, and finally to the ideas. Therefore, its government is not exclusive, but complementary. And since this rule is justified by the concepts of system and end that belong to theoretical reason, there is an immanent extension of theoretical to practical reason or a self-transcendence of reason: Within reason, its theoretical side is compelled to pass over to its practical side.

This forceful self-overcoming of theoretical reason underscores that multilayered unity of reason that appears in both of the "prefaces" of the first *Critique* in the form of a double intention: In its theoretical employment, reason is motivated by the craving to overcome contradictions, whereas in practical respects it is motivated to overcome materialism, fatalism, and atheism. This duality is repeated at the end of the first *Critique*. The completion of theoretical reason in a "system," which implies Kant's cosmopolitan concept of philosophy, arises from the theoretical interest in unity, which in turn is extended and surpassed by the practical interest or the ultimate moral vocation of human beings.

Since right constitutes an essential part of morals, the following conclusion is inevitable. The final completion of right in a common, political cosmopolitanism, that is, in the right of nations and cosmopolitan right, is no more, and no less, than one aspect of Kant's radical anti-solipsism and comprehensive cosmopolitanism. And it can already be found in the first *Critique*.

BIBLIOGRAPHY

Primary Sources

Achenwall, Gottfried, and Pütter, Johann Stephan. *Elementa Iuris Naturae / Anfangsgründe des Naturrechts* [1750]. Latin/German. Translated and edited by J. Schröder. Frankfurt am Main, 1995.

Aristotle. *Nichomachean Ethics.* In *The Complete Works of Aristotle.* Vol. 1. The Revised Oxford Translation. Edited by Jonathan Barnes. Princeton, N.J.: Princeton University Press, 1984.

Aristotle. *Politics.* In *The Complete Works of Aristotle.* Vol. 2.

Austin, John. *The Province of Jurisprudence Determined* [1832]. Edited by H. L. A. Hart. London, 1954.

Descartes, René. *Discourse on Method* [1637]. Translated by E. S. Haldane and G. R. T. Ross, edited by D. Weissman. New Haven: Yale University Press, 1996.

Diels, Hermann, and Walther Kranz, eds. *Die Fragmente der Vorsokratiker.* Berlin: Weidmann, 1951–1952.

Durkheim, Émile . "Determination du fait moral." In *Sociologie et philosophie*, 1974. Pp. 51–83.

Fichte, Johann Gottlieb. "Zum Ewigen Frieden. Ein philosophischer Entwurf von Immanuel Kant." In *Philosophisches Journal einer Gesellschaft Teutscher Gelehrten* [1795]. Edited by F. I. Niethammer, vol. 4, no. 1. Neu-Strelitz, pp. 81–92. (Reprinted in J. G. Fichte, *Gesamtausgabe der Bayrischen Akademie der Wissenschaften*, edited by R. Lauth and G. Gliwitzky. Vol. I/3. Stuttgart and Bad Canstatt, 1966. Pp. 217–228.

Hegel, Georg Wilhelm Friedrich. "Natural Law: The Scientific Ways of Treating Natural Law, Its Place in Moral Philosophy, and Its Relation to the Positive Sciences of Law" [1803]. Translated by T. M. Knox. Philadelphia: University of Pennsylvania Press, 1975.

Hegel, Georg Wilhelm Friedrich. *Elements of the Philosophy of Right.* Edited by A. W. Wood, translated by H. B. Nisbet. Cambridge and New York: Cambridge University Press, 1991.

Hobbes, Thomas. *Leviathan or the Matter, Form and Power of a Commonwealth, Ecclesiastical and Civil* [1651]. Edited by R. Tuck. Cambridge: Cambridge University Press, 1991.

Kant, Immanuel. "An Answer to the Question: What Is Enlightenment?" [1784]. Translated by Mary J. Gregor. In *Practical Philosophy*. Cambridge: Cambridge University Press, 1996. (Academy edition, VIII: 33–42.)

Kant, Immanuel. *Anthropology from a Pragmatic Point of View* [1798]. Translated by Mary J. Gregor. The Hague: Martinus Nijhoff, 1974. (Academy edition, VII: 117–334.)

Kant, Immanuel. "The Conflict of the Faculties" [1798]. Translated by Mary J. Gregor and Robert Anchor. In *Religion and Rational Theology*, edited by Allen W. Wood. Cambridge: Cambridge University Press, 1996. (Academy edition, VII: 1–116.)

Kant, Immanuel. "Conjectures on the Beginning of Human History." Translated by H. B. Nisbet. In *Kant. Political Writings*. Cambridge: Cambridge University Press, 1991. (Academy edition, VIII: 107–123.)

Kant, Immanuel. *Correspondence*. Translated and edited by Arnulf Zweig. Cambridge: Cambridge University Press, 1999.

Kant, Immanuel. "Critique of Practical Reason" [1788]. Translated by Mary J. Gregor. In *Practical Philosophy*. Cambridge: Cambridge University Press, 1996. (Academy edition V: 1–163.)

Kant, Immanuel. *Critique of Pure Reason* [1781]. Translated by Paul Guyer and Allen W. Wood. Cambridge: Cambridge University Press, 1998. (Academy edition, A: IV: 1–252; B: III: 1–552.)

Kant, Immanuel. "Groundwork of the Metaphysics of Morals" [1785]. Translated by Mary J. Gregor. In *Practical Philosophy*. Cambridge: Cambridge University Press, 1996. (Academy edition, IV: 385–463.)

Kant, Immanuel. "Idea for a Universal History with a Cosmopolitan Purpose" [1784]. Translated by Hugh B. Nisbet. Second, enlarged edition. Cambridge: Cambridge University Press, 1970. (Academy edition, VIII: 15–32.)

Kant, Immanuel. "Immanuel Kant's Announcement of the Programme of His Lectures for the Winter Semester 1765–1766" [1765]. Translated by David Walford in collaboration with Ralf Meerbote. In *Immanuel Kant: Theoretical Philosophy, 1755–1770*. Cambridge: Cambridge University Press, 1992. (Academy edition, II: 303–314.)

Kant, Immanuel. *Kant on Education (Über Pädagogik)*. Translated by Annette Churton. Bristol: Thoemmes Press, 1992.

Kant, Immanuel. *Lectures on Ethics* [1775–80]. Edited by Peter Heath and Jerome B. Schneewind, translated by Peter Heath. Cambridge: Cambridge University Press, 2001.

Kant, Immanuel. *Lectures on Logic*. Translated and edited by J. Michael Young. Cambridge: Cambridge University Press, 1992.

Kant, Immanuel. "Metaphysical Foundations of Natural Science" [1786]. Translated by Michael Friedman. In *Theoretical Philosophy after 1781*. Cambridge: Cambridge University Press, 2002. (Academy edition, IV: 467–565.)

Kant, Immanuel. "The Metaphysics of Morals" [1797]. Translated by Mary J. Gregor. In *Practical Philosophy*. Cambridge: Cambridge University Press, 1996. (Academy edition, VI: 203–493.)

Kant, Immanuel. "On the Common Saying: 'This May Be True in Theory, but It Is of No Use in Practice" [1793]. Translated by Mary J. Gregor. In *Practical*

Philosophy. Cambridge: Cambridge University Press, 1996. (Academy edition, VIII: 273–313.)

Kant, Immanuel. *Opus postumum*. Edited by Eckart Förster, translated by Eckart Förster and Michael Rosen. Cambridge: Cambridge University Press, 1993.

Kant, Immanuel. "Proclamation of the Immanent Conclusion of a Treaty of Perpetual Peace in Philosophy" [1796]. Translated by Peter Heath. In *Theoretical Philosophy after 1781*. Cambridge: Cambridge University Press, 2002. (Academy edition, VIII: 412–422.)

Kant, Immanuel. "Prolegomena to Any Future Metaphysics That Will Be Able to Come Forward as Science" [1783]. Translated by Gary Hatfield. In *Theoretical Philosophy after 1781*. Cambridge: Cambridge University Press, 2002. (Academy edition, IV: 255–383.)

Kant, Immanuel. "Religion within the Boundaries of Mere Reason" [1793]. Translated by George di Giovanni. In *Religion and Rational Theology*, edited by Allen W. Wood. Cambridge: Cambridge University Press, 1996. (Academy edition, VI: 1–202.)

Kant, Immanuel. "Toward Perpetual Peace." Translated by Mary J. Gregor. In *Practical Philosophy*. Cambridge: Cambridge University Press, 1996. (Academy edition, VIII: 341–386.)

Kant, Immanuel. *Vorlesungen I. Abteilung. Vorlesungen über Enzyklopädie und Logik*. Edited by Gerhard Lehmann. Berlin: Akademie-Verlag, 1961.

Kant, Immanuel. "What Does It Mean to Orient Oneself in Thinking?" [1786]. Translated by Allen W. Wood. In *Religion and Rational Theology*. (Academy edition, VIII: 133–146.)

Kant, Immanuel. "What Real Progress Has Metaphysics Made in Germany since the Time of Leibniz and Wolff?" [1793/1804]. Translated by Peter Heath. In *Theoretical Philosophy after 1781*. Cambridge: Cambridge University Press, 2002.

Kierkegaard, Søren. *The Sickness unto Death*. Edited by Robert L. Perkins. Macon, Ga.: Mercer University Press, 1987.

Nietzsche, Friedrich. "Nachgelassene Fragemente 1885–1887." In *Kritische Studienausgabe*, edited by Giorgio Colli and Mazzino Montinari. Munich/Berlin/New York, 1980ff. Vol. XII.

Nietzsche, Friedrich. *Thus Spoke Zarathustra*. Translated by Reginald J. Hollingdale. New York: Penguin, 1969.

Nietzsche, Friedrich. *Unmodern Observations*. William Arrowsmith, general editor. New Haven and London: Yale University Press, 1990.

Plato. *Laws*. Translated by Trevor J. Saunders. In *Plato. Complete Works*, edited by John M. Cooper. Indianapolis and Cambridge: Hackett, 1997.

Plato. *Menon*. Edited and translated by R. W. Sharples. Warminster: Aris & Phillips, 1985.

Plato. *Republic*. Translated by George M. A. Grube and Rev. C. D. C. Reeve. In *Plato. Complete Works*.

Pufendorf, Samuel. *De iure naturae et gentium* [1672]. London.

Rousseau, Jean-Jacques. *The Social Contract* [1762] *and the Discourses*. Translated by G. D. H. Cole, revised and augmented by J. H. Brumfitt and John C. Hall. New York: Knopf, 1993.

Schiller, Friedrich. "Über Anmut und Würde." In *Schillers Werke. Nationalausgabe*, edited by v. L. Blumenthal and B. von Wiese, vol. XX. Weimar 1962. Pp. 251–308.

Schlegel, Friedrich. "Versuch über den Begriff des Republikanismus veranlaßt durch die Kantische Schrift zum ewigen Frieden" [1796]. In *Kritische Friedrich-Schlegel-Ausgabe*, edited by v. E. Behler. Munich, Paderborn, and Vienna, 1966. Vol. VII: 11–25.

Smith, Adam. "The Theory of Moral Sentiments" [1759]. In *The Glasgow Edition of the Works and Correspondence of Adam Smith*, edited by A. S. Skinner. Oxford, 1976. Vol. I.

Thomasius, Christian. *Fundamenta iuris naturae et gentium ex sensu communi deducta*. Halae: C. Salfeldii, 1718.

Thucydides. *Historiae*. Edited by Henricus Stuart Jones and Johannes Enoch Powell. Oxford, 1942.

Tocqueville, Alexis de. "De la démocratie en Amérique" [1835–41]. In *Oevres complètes*. Paris, 1979.

Wittgenstein, Ludwig. *Philosophische Untersuchungen*. Frankfurt am Main, 1977.

Secondary Sources

Ackrill, John L. "Aristotle on Eudaimonia." In *Proceedings of the British Academy* 60 (1974). Reprinted In Höffe 1995a, 39–62.

Allison, Henry. *Kant's Theory of Freedom*. Cambridge: Cambridge University Press, 1990.

Anagnostopoulos, Georgios. *Aristotle on the Goals and the Exactness of Ethics*. Berkeley: University of California Press, 1994.

Annas, Julia. *The Morality of Happiness*. New York: Oxford University Press, 1993.

Anscombe, Elizabeth. "Modern Moral Philosophy." *Philosophy* 33 (1958): 1–9.

Apel, Karl-Otto. *Transformation der Philosophie*. 2 vols. Frankfurt am Main, 1973.

Apel, Karl-Otto, ed. *Sprachpragmatik und Philosophie*. Frankfurt am Main, 1976.

Archer, Clive. *International Organizations*. London and Boston: Allen & Unwin, 1983.

Arendt, Hannah. *The Human Condition: A Study on the Central Dilemma Facing Modern Man*. Chicago: University of Chicago Press, 1958.

Arendt, Hannah. *Lectures on Kant's Political Philosophy*, edited and with an interpretive essay by R. Beiner. Chicago: University of Chicago Press, 1982.

Arendt, Hannah. *Eichmann in Jerusalem. Ein Bericht über die Banalität des Bösen*. Munich, 1986.

Aubenque, Pierre. *La prudence chez Aristote*. Paris: Presses universitaires de France, 1986.

Azouvi, François, and Dominique, Bourel. *De Königsberg à Paris: Le réception de Kant en France (1788–1804)*. Paris: Vrin, 1991.

Bachteler, Tobias. "Explaining the Democratic Peace: The Evidence from Ancient Greece Reviewed." *Journal of Peace Research* 34, no. 3 (1997): 315–322.

Baier, Kurt. *The Moral Point of View: A Rational Basis of Ethics*. New York: Random House, 1965.

Baker, Gordon P., and Peter M. S. Hacker, eds. *Wittgenstein: Rules, Grammar and Necessity*, vol. 2 *of an Analytical Commentary on the Philosophical Investigations*. Oxford and New York: Blackwell, 1985.

Barbey, Günther. "Der Status des Richters." In *Handbuch des Staatsrechts*, edited by Joseph Isensee and Paul Kirchhof. Vol. 4. Heidelberg, 1996. Pp. 815–857.

Bedau, Hugo Adam, ed. *Civil Disobedience: Theory and Practice*. New York: Pegasus, 1969.

Beiner, Ronald. "The Moral Vocabulary of Liberalism." *Nomos* 34 (1992): 154–184.

Beitz, Charles. *Political Theory and International Relations*. Princeton: Princeton University Press, 1979.

Berlin, Isaiah. "Two Concepts of Liberty." In *Four Essays on Liberty*. Oxford: Clarendon, 1969. Pp. 118–172.

Bien, Günther. "Ethik und Kantische Moraltheorie." In *Freiburger Universitätsblätter*, no. 73: *Aristoteles und die moderne Wissenschaft*. Freiburg i. Br., 1981. Pp. 57–74.

Bien, Günther. *Die Grundlegung der politischen Philosophie bei Aristoteles*. Freiburg i. Br. and Munich, 1985.

Bischof, Norbert. "On the Phylogeny of Human Morality." In *Morality as a Biological Phenomenon*, edited by Günther S. Stent. Berlin: Abakon-Verlagsgesellschaft, 1978. Pp. 53–73.

Bittner, Rüdiger. "Maximen." In *Akten des 4. Internationalen Kant-Kongresses, Mainz 1974*, edited by G. Funke. Berlin and New York (1974). Pt. 2.2, Pp. 485–498.

Blühdorn, Jürgen, and Joachim Ritter, eds. *Recht und Ethik. Zum Problem ihrer Beziehung im 19. Jahrhundert*. Frankfurt am Main, 1970.

Böckle, Franz, and Ernst-Wolfgang, Böckenförde, eds. *Naturrecht in der Kritik*. Mainz, 1973.

Bohrer, Karl-Heinz. "Die permanente Theodizee." In *Nach der Natur. Über Politik und Ästhetik*. Munich and Wien, 1988. Pp. 133–161.

Bollnow, Otto Friedrich. *Wesen und Wandel der Tugenden*. Frankfurt am Main, 1958.

Bostock, David. "Pleasure and Activity in Aristotle's Ethics." *Phronesis* 33 (1988): 251–272.

Brink, David O. *Moral Realism and the Foundations of Ethics*. Cambridge: Cambridge University Press, 1989.

Broadie, Sarah W. *Ethics with Aristotle*. New York: Oxford University Press, 1991.

Brown, Michael, Sean M., Lynn-Jones, and Steven E. Miller. *Debating the Democratic Peace*. Cambridge, Mass.: MIT Press, 1996.

Buhr, Manfred, and Steffen Dietzsch, eds. *Imanuel Kant: Zum ewigen Frieden. Mit Texten zur Rezeption 1796–1800*. Leipzig, 1984.

Busch, Hans J. and Horstmann, Alexander. "Kosmopolit/Kosmopolitismus." In *Historisches Wörterbuch der Philosophie*, vol. IV. Darmstadt, 1976. Pp. 1155–1167.

Cavallar, Georg. *Pax Kantiana. Systematisch-historische Untersuchung des Entwurfs "Zum ewigen Frieden" (1795) von Immanuel Kant*. Wien: Böhlau, 1992.

Chapman, John W., and William A. Galston, eds. *Virtue (Nomos 34)*. London, 1992.

Chaunu, Pierre, ed. *Les fondements de la paix: Des origines au début du XVIIIe siècle*. Paris: Presses Universitaires de France, 1993.

Conradt, Michael. "Der Schlüssel zur Metaphysik. Zum Begriff rationaler Hoffnung in Kants kritischer Moral- und Religionsphilosophie." Ph.D. dissertation, University of Tübingen, 1999.

Cramer, Karl. "Hypothetische Imperative?" In *Rehabilitierung der praktischen Philosophie*, edited by Manfred Riedel Vol. 1. Freiburg, 1972. Pp. 159–212.

Crisp, Roger, and Michael Slote, eds. *Virtue Ethics*. New York: Oxford University Press, 1997.

Czempiel, Ernst Otto. "Kants Theorem und die zeitgenössische Theorie der internationalen Beziehungen." In *Frieden durch Recht. Kants Friedensidee und das Problem einer neuen Weltordnung*, edited by Matthias Lutz-Bachmann and James Bohmann. Frankfurt am Main, 1996. Pp. 300–323.

Dahlstrom, Daniel O. "Kants politischer Kosmopolitismus." *Jahrbuch für Recht und Ethik* 5 (1998): 55–72.

Dancy, Jonathan. *Moral Reasons*. Oxford and Cambridge, Mass.: Blackwell, 1993.

Dietze, Anita, and Walter Dietze, eds. *Ewiger Friede? Dokumente einer detuschen Diskussion um 1800*. Leipzig and Weimar, 1989.

Dietze, Walter. "Abriß einer Entwicklungsgeschichte der Friedensidee vom Mittelalter bis zur Französischen Revolution." In Dietze and Dietze 1989, 7–58.

Dihle, Albrecht. *Die Vorstellung vom Willen in der Antike*. Gottingen, 1985.

Dobler, Phillipp. *Recht auf demokratischen Ungehorsam*. Fribourg (CH), 1995.

Doyle, Michael. W. "Kant, Liberal Legacies, and Foreign Affairs." *Philosophy and Public Affairs* 12 (1983): 205–235 and 323–353.

Doyle, Michael. W. "Die Stimme der Völker. Politische Denker uber die internationalen Auswirkungen der Demokratie." In Höffe 1995b, 221–244.

Duncan, Alastair R. C. *Practical Reason and Morality: A Study on Immanuel Kant's Foundations for the Metaphysics of Morals*. London and New York: Nelson, 1957.

Durkheim, Émile. *Sociologie et Philosophie*. Paris: Presses Universitaires de France, 1967.

Dworkin, Ronald. *A Matter of Principle*. Cambridge, Mass.: Harvard University Press, 1985.

Dworkin, Ronald. *Taking Rights Seriously*. London: Duckworth, 1977. Reprint, 1996.

Engstrom, Stephen, and Jennifer Whiting, eds. *Aristotle, Kant and the Stoics: Rethinking Happiness and Duty*. New York: Cambridge University Press, 1996.

Finnis, John. *Natural Law and Natural Rights*. Reprinted, with corrections. Oxford: Clarendon, 1982.

Foot, Phillippa. *Virtues and Vices*. Berkeley: University of California Press, 1978.

Freud, Sigmund. "Das Unbehagen in der Kultur." In *Gesammelte Werke*, vol. XIV. London, 1948.

Fromm, Erich. *Man for Himself: An Inquiry into the Psychology of Ethics*. New York, 1947.

Fromm, Erich. *The Anatomy of Human Destructiveness*. New York, 1973.

Gantzel, Klaus Jürgen, ed. *Kriege nach dem Zweiten Weltkrieg 1945 bis 1992: Daten and Tendenzen*. Münster, 1995.

Gauthier, René A., and Jean Y. Jolif. *L'Ethique à Nicomaque*. 4 vols. Löwen, 1970.

Geerlings, Wilhelm. "'De civitate dei,' XIX als Buch der Augustinischen Friedenslehre." In Horn 1997, 211–233.

Geismann, Georg, and Hariolf Oberer, eds. *Kant and das Recht der Lüge.* Würzburg, 1986.

Gerhardt, Volker. *Immanuel Kants Entwurf "Zum ewigen Frieden." Eine Theorie der Politik.* Darmstadt, 1995.

Gigon, Olof. *Aristoteles. Die Nikomachische Ethik, neu übersetzt, mit einer Einleitung und erkärenden Anmerkungen versehen.* Zurich and Stuttgart, 1991.

Gorres, Albert, and Karl Rahner. *Das Böse. Wege zu seiner Bewältigung in Psychotherapie und Christentum.* Fribourg, Basel, and Wien, 1982.

Grimm, Jacob, and Wilhelm Grimm. *Deutsches Wörterbuch.* 17 vols. Leipzig, 1854. Reprinted in 33 vols., Munich, 1984.

Guardini, Romano. "Tugenden. Meditationen uber Gestalten sittlichen Lebens" (1963). In R. Guardini, *Werke,* vol. 5. Paderborn, 1992.

Habermas, Jürgen. *Legitimationsprobleme im Spätkapitalismus.* Frankfurt am Main, 1973.

Habermas, Jürgen. "Was heißt Universalpragmatik?". In *Sprachpragmatik and Philosophie,* Frankfurt am Main, edited by K. O. Apel. 1976. Pp. 174–272.

Habermas, Jürgen. *Theorie des kommunikativen Handelns.* Frankfurt am Main, 1981.

Habermas, Jürgen. *Moralbewußtsein and kommunikatives Handeln.* Frankfurt am Main, 1983.

Habermas, Jürgen. *Faktizität and Geltung. Beiträge zur Diskurstheorie des Rechts and des demokratischen Rechtstaates.* Frankfurt am Main, 1994.

Habermas, Jürgen. "Kants Idee des ewigen Friedens – aus dem historischen Abstand von 200 Jahren." *Kritische Justiz* 28 (1995): 293–319. Also in J. Habermas, *Die Einbeziehung des Anderen. Studien zur politischen Theorie.* Frankfurt am Main, 1996. Pp. 192–236.

Haegerstrohm, A. "Kants kategorischer Imperativ als Kriterium des Sittlichen." *Zeitschrift fur philosophische Forschung* 31 (1902): 354–384.

Hart, Herbert Lionel Adolphus. *The Concept of Law.* Oxford: Clarendon, 1961.

Hartmann, Nicolai. *Ethik.* Berlin, 1926.

Hassemer, Winfried. "Rechtssystem and Kodifikation. Die Bindung des Richters an das Gesetz." In *Rechtsphilosophie and Rechtstheorie der Gegenwart,* edited by Arthur Kaufmann and Winfried Hassemer. Heidelberg, 1994. Pp. 248–268.

Heinaman, Robert. "Eudaimonia and Self-Sufficiency in the Nicomachean Ethics." *Phronesis* 33 (1988): 31–53.

Helmholz, Richard. "Trusts in the English Ecclesiastical Courts 1300–1640." In *Itinera Fiduciae: Trust and Treuhand in Historical Perspective,* edited by Richard Helmholz and Reinhard Zimmermann. Berlin: Duncker & Humblot, 1998. Pp. 153–172.

Hennies, Werner. *Politik and praktische Philosophie. Eine Studie zur Rekonstruktion der politischen Wissenschaft.* Neuwied and Berlin, 1963.

Herman, Barbara. *Morality as Rationality: A Study on Kant's Ethics.* New York: Garland, 1990a.

Herman, Barbara. "Obligation and Performance: A Kantian Account of Moral Conflict." In *Identity, Character and Morality: Essays in Moral Psychology,* edited by O. Flanagan and A. Oksenberg Rorty. Cambridge, Mass.: MIT Press, 1990b. Pp. 311–337.

Herman, Barbara. *The Practice of Moral Judgement.* Cambridge, Mass.: Harvard University Press, 1993.

Herman, Barbara. "A Cosmopolitan Kingdom of Ends." In *Reclaiming the History of Ethics: Essays for John Rawls,* edited by Andrew Reath, Barbara Herman, and Christine M. Korsgaard. Cambridge: Cambridge University Press, 1997.

Hildebrand, Dietrich v. *Sittliche Grundhaltungen.* Mainz, 1993.

Höffe, Otfried. *Sittlich politische Diskurse. Philosophische Grundlagen – politische Ethik – biomedizinische Ethik.* Frankfurt am Main, 1981.

Höffe, Otfried. *Ethik and Politik. Grundmodelle and – probleme der praktischen Philosophie.* Frankfurt am Main, 1987.

Höffe, Otfried. *Kategorische Rechtsprinzipien. Ein Kontrapunkt der Moderne.* Frankfurt am Main, 1990. (*Categorical Principles of Law: A Counterpoint to Modernity.* Translated by M. Migotti. University Park, Pa., 2002.)

Höffe, Otfried. *Politische Gerechtigkeit. Grundlegung einer kritischen Philosophie von Recht and Staat.* Frankfurt am Main, 1994.

Höffe, Otfried, ed. *Aristoteles: Nikomachische Ethik.* Klassiker Auslegen, vol. 2. Berlin, 1995a.

Höffe, Otfried, ed. *Immanuel Kant: Zum ewigen Frieden.* Klassiker Auslegen, vol. 1. Berlin, 1995b.

Höffe, Otfried. *Immanuel Kant.* Munich, 1996a. (*Immanuel Kant.* Translated by M. Farrier. New York, 1994.)

Höffe, Otfried. *Praktische Philosophie. Das Modell des Aristoteles.* Munich, 1996b.

Höffe, Otfried. *Vernunft and Recht. Bausteine zu einem interkulturellen Rechtsdiskurs.* Frankfurt am Main, 1996c.

Höffe, Otfried, ed. *Platon: Politeia.* Klassiker Auslegen, vol. 7. Berlin, 1997.

Höffe, Otfried. "Architektonik and Geschichte der reinen Vernunft." In *Immanuel Kant. Kritik der reinen Vernunft,* edited by G. Mohr and M. Willaschek. Klassiker Auslegen, vol. 17/18. Berlin, 1998. Pp. 617–645.

Höffe, Otfried. *Aristoteles.* Munich, 1999a.

Höffe, Otfried, ed. *Grundlegung zur Metaphysik der Sitten. Ein kooperativer Kommentar.* Frankfurt am Main, 1999b.

Höffe, Otfried, ed. *Immanuel Kant. Metaphysische Anfangsgrunde der Rechtslehre.* Klassiker Auslegen, vol. 19. Berlin, 1999c.

Höffe, Otfried. "Humanitäre Intervention? Rechtsethische Überlegungen." In Merkel 2000a. 167–186.

Höffe, Otfried. *Moral als Preis der Moderne. Ein Versuch über Wissenschaft, Technik and Umwelt.* Frankfurt am Main, 2000b.

Höffe, Otfried *Demokratie im Zeitalter der Globalisierung.* Munich, 2002a.

Höffe, Otfried, ed. *Immanuel Kant. Kritik der praktischen Vernunft.* Klassiker Auslegen, vol. 26. Berlin: Akademie-Verlag, 2002b.

Höffe, Otfried. *Kants Kritik der reinen Vernunft: Die Grundlegung der modernen Philosophie.* Munich, 2003. Reprint, 2004.

Höffe, Otfried, and Christof Rapp. "Tugend (Neuzeit)." In *Historisches Wörterbuch der Philosophie,* vol. 10. Basel, 1999.

Holzhey, Helmut "Das Böse. Vom ethischen zum metaphysischen Diskurs." *Studia Philosophica* 52 (1993): 7–27.

Holzhey, Helmut, and Jean-Pierre Leyvraz, eds. "Die Philosophie und das Böse; La philosophie et le mal." *Studia philosophica*, vol. 52. Basel, 1993.

Horn, Christoph. "Augustinus and die Entstehung des philosophischen Willensbegriffs." *Zeitschrift für philosophische Forschung* 50 (1996): 113–132.

Horn, Christoph, ed. *Augustinus: De Civitate Dei*. Klassiker Auslegen, vol. 11. Berlin, 1997.

Hruschka, Joachim. "Rechtfertigungs – und Entschuldigungsgrunde: Das Brett des Karneades bei Gentz and Kant." *Goldtammers Archiv für Strafrecht* 138 (1991): 1–10.

Irwin, Terence. "Who Discovered the Will?" *Philosophical Perspectives* 6 (1992): 453–473.

Isensee, Josef. *Das legalisierte Widerstandsrecht. Eine staatsrechtliche Analyse des Art. 20 Abs. 4 Grundgesetz*. Bad Homburg, 1969.

Jankelevitch, Vladimir. *Traité des vertus*. Paris: Bordas, 1949.

Janssen, Wilhelm. "Friede." In *Geschichtliche Grundbegriffe. Historisches Lexikon zur politisch-sozialen Sprache in Deutschland*, edited by Otto Brunner, Werner Conze, and Reinhart Koselleck. Vol. 2. Stuttgart, 1975. Pp. 543–591.

Jaspers, Karl. *Philosophie II. Existenzerhellung*. Berlin, 1973.

Jenisch, Daniel. *Die Ethik des Aristoteles in 10 Büchern, mit dem Anhang: Kritische Übersicht des aristotelischen Moralsystems*. Danzig, 1791.

Jhering, Rudolf von. *Der Zweck im Recht*. 2 vols. Leipzig, 1877/1893.

Jones, Neil. "Trusts in England after the Statute of Uses: A View from the 16th Century." In *Itinera fiduciae: Trust and Treuhand in Historical Perspective*, edited by R. Helmholz and R. Zimmermann. Berlin, 1998. Pp. 173–205.

Kain, Patrick P. "Self-Legislation and Prudence in Kant's Moral Philosophy: A Critical Examination of Some Constructivist Interpretations." Ph.D. diss., University of Notre Dame, 1999.

Kelsen, Hans. "The Strategy of Peace." *American Journal of Sociology* 49 (1944): 381–389.

Kelsen, Hans. "Was ist die Reine Rechtslehre?" In *Demokratie and Rechtstaat. Festschrift für Z. Giacometti*. Zurich, 1953. Pp. 143–162.

Kelsen, Hans. *Reine Rechtslehre*. 1934. Wien, 1960.

Kenny, Anthony. *The Aristotelian Ethics*. Oxford: Clarendon, 1978.

Kenny, Anthony. *Aristotle's Theory of the Will*. London: Duckworth, 1979.

Kenny, Anthony. *Aristotle on the Perfect Life*. Oxford: Clarendon, 1992.

Kersting, Wolfgang. *Wohlgeordnete Freiheit. Immanuel Kants Rechts – und Staatsphilosophie*. Frankfurt am Main: Suhrkamp, 1993.

Kleger, Heinz. *Der neue Ungehorsam. Widerstände und politische Verpflichtungen in einer lernfähigen Demokratie*. Frankfurt am Main: Campus Verlag, 1993.

Kleingeld, Pauline. "Kants politischer Kosmopolitismus." *Jahrbuch für Recht und Ethik* 5 (1998): 333–348.

Kluxen, Wolfgang. *Ethik als Ethos*. Freiburg i. Br. and Munich, 1974.

Korsgaard, Christine. *Creating the Kingdom of Ends*. Cambridge: Cambridge University Press, 1996a.

Korsgaard, Christine. *The Sources of Normativity*. Cambridge: Cambridge University Press, 1996b.

Koselleck, Reinhart. "Vom Sinn and Unsinn der Geschichte." *Merkur* 51 (1997): 319–334.

Kraut, Richard. *Aristotle on the Human Good*. Princeton, N.J.: Princeton University Press, 1989.

Krings, Hermann. "Die Grenzen der Transzendentalpragmatik." In *Prinzip Freiheit – Eine Auseinandersetzung um Chancen and Grenzen transzendentalphilosophischen Denkens*, edited by Hans Michael Baumgartner. Freiburg: Alber, 1979.

Kripke, Saul. *Wittgenstein über Regeln und Privatsprache*. Frankfurt am Main, 1987.

Kühl, Kristian. *Eigentumsordnung als Freiheitsordnung. Zur Aktualität der Kantischen Rechts– and Eigentumstheorie*. Freiburg i. Br.: Alber, 1984.

Kuhlmann, Wolfgang. "Tod des Subjekts? Eine transzendentalpragmatische Verteidigung des Vernunftsubjekts." In *Tod des Subjekts*, edited by Herta Nagl and Helmuth Vetter. Wien: R. Oldenbourg, 1987. Pp. 120–136. Reprint in Wolfgang Kuhlmann. *Kant und die Transzendentalpragmatik*. Würzburg: Königshausen & Neumann, 1992. Pp. 147–187.

Kuhn, Helmut. "Der Mensch in der Entscheidung: Prohairesis in der Nikomachischen Ethik." In *Das Sein and das Gute*, edited by H. Kuhn. Munich: Kösel-Verlag, 1962. Pp. 275–295.

Kuhn, Helmut. "Aristoteles und die Methode der praktischen Wissenschaft." *Zeitschrift für Politik* 12 (1965): 101–120.

Laberge, Pierre. "Das radikale Böse and der Völkerzustand." In *Kant über Religion*, edited by Friedo Ricken and François Marty. Stuttgart: Kohlhammer, 1992. Pp. 112–123.

Laberge, Pierre. "La définition de la volonté comme faculté d'agir selon des lois." In Höffe 1999, 83–96.

Larmore, Charles. "The Heterogeneity of Practical Reason." In *Einheit als Grundlage der Philosophie*, edited by G. Kloy and E. Rudolph. Darmstadt, 1985. Pp. 322–337.

Larmore, Charles. *Patterns of Moral Complexity*. Cambridge: Cambridge University Press, 1995.

Lorenz, Konrad. *Das sogenannte Böse. Zur Naturgeschichte der Aggression*. Vienna, 1998.

Lorenzen, Paul, and Oswald Schwemmer. *Konstruktive Logik, Ethik und Wissenschaftstheorie*. Mannheim, Wien, and Zurich: Bibliographisches Institut, 1973.

Lübbe, Hermann. *Philosophie nach der Aufklärung. Von der Notwendigkeit pragmatischer Vernunft*. Düsseldorf: Econ Verlag, 1980.

Lübbe, Hermann. *Politischer Moralismus. Der Triumph der Gesinnung über die Urteilskraft*. Berlin, 1987.

Ludwig, Bernd. "Kants Verabschiedung der Vertragstheorie. Konsequenzen für eine Theorie sozialer Gerechtigkeit." *Jahrbuch für Recht und Ethik* 1 (1993): 221–254.

Luhmann, Niklas. "Soziologie der Moral." In *Theorietechnik und Moral*, edited by N. Luhmann and St. Pfürtner. Frankfurt am Main, 1978. Pp. 8–116.

Luhmann, Niklas. *Ausdifferenzierung des Rechts. Beiträge zur Rechtssoziologie und Rechtstheorie*. Frankfurt am Main, 1981.

Luhmann, Niklas. *Rechtssoziologie.* Opladen, 1987.

Luhmann, Niklas. *Das Recht der Gesellschaft.* Frankfurt am Main, 1993.

Lundstedt, Vilhelm. "Law and Justice: A Criticism of the Method of Justice." In *Interpretations of Modern Legal Philosophy,* edited by P. Sayre. New York: Oxford University Press, 1947. Pp. 450–483.

Lutz, Dieter S., ed. *Der Kosovo-Krieg. Rechtliche und rechtsethische Aspekte.* Baden-Baden: Nomos-Verlag, 2000.

MacIntyre, Alasdair C. "Is Patriotism a Virtue?" In *The Lindley Lecture.* University of Kansas, Department of Philosophy, March 26, 1984. Pp. 3–20.

MacIntyre, Alasdair C. *After Virtue.* London: Duckworth, 1987.

MacIntyre, Alasdair C. *Whose Justice? Which Rationality?* London: Duckworth, 1988.

MacIntyre, Alasdair C. *Three Rival Versions of Moral Enquiry: Encyclopedia, Genealogy, Tradition.* London: Duckworth, 1990.

Maôz, Zeev, and Bruce Russett. "Normative and Structural Causes of Democratic Peace, 1946–1986." *American Political Science Review* 87 (1993): 624–638.

Marquard, Odo. *Apologie des Zufälligen. Philosophische Studien.* Stuttgart: Reclam, 1986.

Marquard, Odo. "Drei Phasen der medizinethischen Debatte." In *Anfang und Ende menschlichen Lebens,* edited by Odo Marquard and Hugo Staudinger. *Medizinethische Probleme.* Paderborn: Fink, 1987. Pp. 111–115.

Mayer-Maly, Dorothea, and Peter M. Simons, eds. *Das Naturrechtsdenken heute und morgen. Gedächtnisschrift für René Marcic.* Berlin: Duncker & Humblot, 1983.

McDowell, John. "Virtue and Reason." In *Wittgenstein: To Follow a Rule,* edited by Steven Holtzman and Christopher Leich. London: Routledge & Kegan Paul, 1981. Pp. 141–162.

McDowell, John. "Deliberation and Moral Development in Aristotle's Ethics." In *Aristotle, Kant and the Stoics: Rethinking Happiness and Duty,* edited by Stephen Engstrom and Jennifer Whiting. Cambridge: Cambridge University Press, 1996.

McDowell, John. "Are Moral Requirements Hypothetical Imperatives." In *Mind, Value and Reality.* edited by John McDowell. Cambridge, Mass.: Harvard University Press, 1998. Pp. 77–94.

McNaughton, David. *Moral Vision: An Introduction to Ethics.* Oxford: Basil Blackwell, 1988.

Merkel, Reinhard, ed. *Der Kosovo-Krieg und das Volkerrecht.* Frankfurt am Main: Suhrkamp, 2000.

Merkel, Reinhard, and Roland Wittmann, eds. *"Zum ewigen Frieden": Grundlagen, Aktualität und Aussichten einer Idee von Immanuel Kant.* Frankfurt am Main: Suhrkamp, 1996.

Merle, Jean-Christoph. "Funktionen, Befugnisse und Zwecke der Staatsverwaltung. Zur Allgemeinen Anmerkung zu § 52, B-D." In Höffe 1999c, 195–212.

Meulen, Jelle van der. *Der Gedanke der Internationalen Organisation in seiner Entwicklung.* Vols. 1, 2/1, 2/2. Den Haag, 1917–1940.

Mitchell, Brian R. *International Historical Statistics, Europe, 1750–1988.* London: Macmillan, 1992.

Morgenthau, Hans J. *Politics among Nations: The Struggle for Power and Peace.* New York: A. A. Knopf, 1948.

Muirhead, John H. *Rule and End in Morals*. London: Oxford University Press, 1932. Reprint Freeport, N.Y., 1969.

Mulholland, Leslie Arthur. *Kant's System of Rights*. New York: Columbia University Press, 1990.

Nagler, Michael. *Über die Funktion des Staates and des Widerstandsrechts*. St. Augustin: Academia-Verlag, 1991.

Nancy, Jean-Luc. *L'impératif catégorique*. Paris: Flammarion, 1983.

Nozick, R. *Anarchy, State and Utopia*. Oxford: Blackwell, 1974.

Nussbaum, Martha. "Non-Relative Virtues: An Aristotelian Approach." In *The Quality of Life*, edited by Martha Nussbaum and Amartya Sen. Oxford: Oxford University Press, 1993. Pp. 242–276.

O'Brien, Denis. "Plotinus on Evil." In *Le Néoplatonisme*, edited by Pierre-Maxime Schuhl and Pierre Hadot. Paris: Editions du Centre national de la recherche scientifique, 1971. Pp. 113–146.

O'Brien, Denis. *Théodizée plotinienne-Théodizée gnostique*. Leiden, 1992.

Oelmüller, Willi. "Das Böse." In *Handbuch philosophischer Grundbegriffe*, edited by Hermann Krings et al. Munich: Kösel, 1973. Pp. 255–268.

O'Neill, Onora. *Constructions of Reason: Explorations of Kant's Practical Philosophy*. Cambridge: Cambridge University Press, 1989.

O'Neill, Onora. *Towards Justice and Virtue: A Constructive Account of Practical Reasoning*. Cambridge: Cambridge University Press, 1996.

Paton, Herbert James. *The Categorical Imperative: A Study in Kant's Moral Philosophy*. Philadelphia, 1971 (1947).

Pieper, Annemarie. "Der Ursprung des Bösen – Schellings Versuch einer Rekonstruktion des transzendentalen Anfangs von Geschichte." In *Festschrift für H. A. Salmony. Philosophische Tradition im Dialog mit der Gegenwart*, edited by Andreas Cesana and Olga Rubitschon. Basel, Boston, and Stuttgart: Birkhäuser, 1985.

Pieper, Annemarie. *Einführung in die Ethik*. Tübingen, 1991.

Pieper, Joseph. *Über den Begriff der Sünde*. Munich: Kösel, 1977.

Plack, Arno. *Die Gesellschaft and das Bose: Eine Kritik der herrschenden Moral*. Frankfurt am Main: Fischer-Taschenbuchverlag, 1991.

Pleines, Jürgen-Eckardt. *Praxis and Vernunft. Zum Begriff praktischer Urteilskraft*. Würzburg: Königshausen & Neumann, 1983.

Portmann, Franz. *Einheit aus der Metaphysik. Eine alternative Rekonstruktion der Kantischen Lehre*. Freiburg i. Br.: Alber, 2000.

Puhl, Klaus. "Regelfolgen." In *Ludwig Wittgenstein. Philosophische Untersuchungen*, edited by Eike von Savigny. Klassiker Auslegen, vol. 13. Berlin: Akademie-Verlag, 1998. Pp. 119–142.

Radbruch, Gustav. *Rechtsphilosophie*. Leipzig, 1932. Reprint: Heidelberg, 1999.

Radbruch, Gustav. "Fünf Minuten Rechtsphilosophie." *Rhein-Neckar-Zeitung*, September 12, 1945. Reprint in G. Radbruch, *Rechtsphilosophie*. Heidelberg, 1999. Pp. 209–210.

Rapp, Christof. "Freiwilligkeit, Entscheidung und Verantwortlichkeit (III 1–7)." In Höffe 1995b, 109–134.

Raumer, Kurt von. *Ewiger Friede. Friedensrufe und Friedenspläne seit der Renaissance*. Freiburg and Munich: Alber, 1953.

Rawls, John. *A Theory of Justice*. Cambridge, Mass.: Belknap Press of Harvard University Press, 1971.

Rawls, John. *Political Liberalism*. New York: Columbia University Press, 1993.

Reeve, C. D. C. *Practices of Reason: Aristotle's Nicomachean Ethics*. Oxford: Oxford University Press, 1992.

"Rezension von Kants Rechtslehre." [1797]. In *Tübinger Gelehrte Anzeigen, 39. Stück, 15*. 5: 305–310, and *40. Stück, 18*. 5: 316–320.

Ricken, Friedo. "Wert and Wesen der Lust (VII 12–15 and X 1–5)." In Höffe 1995b, 207–228.

Ricoeur, Paul. "La symbolique du mal." In Paul Ricoer, *Finitude et culpabilité*, vol. 2. Paris: Aubier, 1969.

Ricoeur, Paul. *Du texte à l'action: Essais d'herménetique II*. Paris: Le Seuil, 1986.

Riley, Patrick. *Kant's Political Philosophy*. Totowa, N.J.: Rowman and Littlefield, 1983.

Rippe, Klaus Peter, and Peter Schaber, eds. *Tugendethik*. Stuttgart: Reclam, 1999.

Risse-Kappen, Thomas. "Demokratischer Frieden? Unfriedliche Demokratien? Überlegungen zu einem theoretischen Puzzle." In *Frieden und Konflikt in den internationalen Beziehungen*, edited by Gert Krell and Harald Müller. Frankfurt am Main: Campus-Verlag, 1994. Pp. 159–189.

Ritter, Joachim. *Metaphysik und Politik. Studien zu Aristoteles and Hegel*. Frankfurt am Main: Suhrkamp, 1969.

Robinson, Richard. "Aristotle on Akrasia (VII 1–11)." In Höffe 1995b, 187–206.

Rosen, Allen D. *Kant's Theory of Justice*. Ithaca, N.Y.: Cornell University Press, 1993.

Rosenau, James N., ed. *Governance without Government*. Cambridge: Cambridge University Press, 1992.

Saner, Hans. *Kants Weg vom Krieg zum Frieden*, vol. 1: *Widerstreit and Einheit. Wege zu Kants politischem Denken*. Munich: Piper, 1967/1983.

Sartre, Jean-Paul. *L'existentialisme est un humanisme?* Paris: Nagel, 1946.

Schaber, Peter. *Moralischer Realismus*. Freiburg im Breisgau: Alber, 1997.

Scheler, Max. "Zur Rehabilitierung der Tugend" [1913]. In M. Scheler, *Gesammelte Werke*, vol. 3: *Vom Umsturz der Werte*. Bonn: Bouvier, 1972.

Scheler, Max. *Der Formalismus in der Ethik und die materiale Wertethik* [1916]. Bonn: Bouvier, 2000.

Schmidt-Biggemann, Wilhelm. "Vorwort. Über die unfaßliche Evidenz des Bösen." In *Das Böse. Eine historische Phänomenologie des Unerklärlichen*, edited by Carsten Colpe and Wilhelm Schmidt-Biggemann. Frankfurt am Main: Suhrkamp, 1993.

Schnädelbach, Herbert. "Der Fluch des Christentums. Die sieben Geburtsfehler einer alt gewordenen Weltreligion." *Die Zeit* 20(2000).

Schroth, Ulrich. "Philosophie and juristische Hermeneutik." In *Rechtsphilosophie und Rechtstbeorie der Gegenwart*, edited by Arthur Kaufmann and Winfried Hassemer. Heidelberg: Müller, 1994. Pp. 344–370.

Schuller, Alexander, and Wolfert von Rahden, eds. *Die andere Kraft. Zur Renaissance des Bösen*. Berlin: Akademie-Verlag, 1993.

Schulte, Christoph. *Radikal böse. Die Karriere des Bösen von Kant bis Nietzsche*. Munich: Fink, 1988.

Schulz, Walter. *Philosophie in der veränderten Welt*. Pfullingen: Neske, 1972.

Schulz, Walter. *Grundprobleme der Ethik.* Pfullingen: Neske, 1989.
Schumpeter, Joseph A. "Zur Soziologie der Imperialismen" [1919]. Reprinted in Joseph A. Schumpeter, *Aufsätze zur Soziologie.* Tübingen: Mohr, 1952. Pp. 72–146.
Schwan, Gesine. "Der nichtutopische Frieden." *Geschichte in Wissenschaft and Unterricht* (1985): no. 1: 1–21 and no. 2: 75–100.
Schwemmer, Oswald. *Ethische Untersuchungen. Rückfragen zu einigen Grundbegriffen.* Frankfurt am Main: Suhrkamp, 1986.
Sherman, Nancz. *The Fabric of Character: Aristotle's Theory of Virtue.* Oxford: Clarendon, 1989.
Sherman, Nancz. *Making a Necessity of Virtue: Aristotle and Kant on Virtue.* Cambridge: Cambridge University Press, 1997.
Singer, J. David, and Melvin Small. *The Wages of War 1816–1965: A Statistical Handbook.* New York: Wiley, 1972.
Singer, J. David, and Melvin Small. *Resort to Arms: International and Civil Wars; 1816–1980.* Beverly Hills, Calif.: Sage, 1982.
Slote, Michael. *From Morality to Virtue.* Oxford: Oxford University Press, 1992.
Soloviev, Vladimir S. *Kurze Erzählungen vom Antichrist.* Translated and edited by Ludolf Müller. Munich: Wewel, 1900/1984.
Spaemann, Robert. *Glück and Wohlwollen. Versuch über Ethik.* Stuttgart: Klett-Cotta, 1989.
Spiro, David E. "The Insignificance of the Liberal Peace." *International Security* 19, no. 2 (1994): 50–86.
Strauss, Leo. *The City and Man.* Chicago: Rand McNally, 1964.
Taylor, Charles. *Sources of the Self: The Making of Modern Identity.* Cambridge, Mass.: Harvard University Press, 1989.
Taylor, Michael. *Community, Anarchy and Liberty.* Cambridge: Cambridge University Press, 1982.
Trianosky, Gregory. "What Is Virtue Ethics All About?" *American Philosophical Quarterly* 27 (1990): 335–344.
Tugendhat, Ernst. *Probleme der Ethik.* Stuttgart: Reclam, 1984.
Tugendhat, Ernst. "Die Hilflosigkeit der Philosophie angesichts der moralischen Herausforderungen unserer Zeit." *Information Philosophie* 18 (1990): 5–15.
Überweg, Friedrich. *Grundriss der Geschichte der Philosophie der Neuzeit.* Berlin: Mittler, 1914.
Voegelin, Eric. *Order and History,* vol. 3: *Plato and Aristotle.* Baton Rouge: Louisiana State University Press, 1957.
Vollrath, Ernst. *Die Rekonstruktion der politischen Urteilskraft.* Stuttgart: Klett, 1977.
Vorländer, Karl. "Einleitung." In *I. Kant, Grundlegung zur Metaphysik der Sitten.* Hamburg: Meiner, pp. v–xxvii, 1965 (1906).
Vorländer, Karl. *Immanuel Kant. Der Mann und das Werk.* Hamburg: Meiner, 1992.
Waltz, Kenneth Neal. *Theory of International Politics.* Reading, Mass.: Addison-Wesley, 1979.
Walzer, Michael. *Spheres of Justice.* New York: Basic Books, 1983.
Wassermann, Rudolf. *Die richterliche Gewalt. Macht und Verantwortung des Richters in der modernen Gesellschaft.* Heidelberg: Müller, 1985.

Weber, Max. "Politik als Beruf." In Max Weber, *Gesammelte politische Schriften*, edited by J. Winckelmann. Tübingen: Mohr (Siebeck), 1971. Pp. 505–560.

Weber, Max. "Die Protestantische Ethik and der Geist des Kapitalismus" [1904–1905]. In Max Weber, *Gesammelte Aufsätze zur Religionssoziologie*. Tübingen: Mohr, 1986. Pp. 17–206.

Wehler, Hans-Ulrich. "Die Hybris einer Geschichtsphilosophie." In *Rechtshistorisches Journal*, vol. 18. Frankfurt am Main: Löwenklau-Gesellschaft, 1999. Pp. 540–547.

Welte, Bernhard. *Über das Böse. Eine thomistische Untersuchung*. Freiburg: Herder, 1959.

Wieland, Wolfgang. *Aporien der praktischen Vernunft*. Frankfurt am Main: Klostermann, 1989.

Wieland, Wolfgang. "Kants Rechtsphilosophie der Urteilskraft." In *Zeitschrift für philosophische Forschung* 52, no.1. Frankfurt am Main: Klostermann, 1998. Pp. 1–22.

Willaschek, Marcus. "Why the 'Doctrine of Rights' Does Not Belong in the 'Metaphysics of Morals.' On Some Basic Distinctions in Kant's Moral Philosophy." In *Jahrbuch für Recht und Ethik*, vol. 5. Berlin: Dunker und Humblot, 1997. Pp. 205–227.

Williams, Bernard Arthur Owen. *Ethics and the Limits of Philosophy*. Cambridge, Mass.: Harvard University Press, 1985.

Williams, Howard. *Kant's Political Philosophy*. New York: St. Martin's Press, 1983.

Wolf, Ursula. *Die Philosophie und die Frage nach dem guten Leben*. Reinbeck bei Hamburg: Rowohlt-Taschenbuch-Verlag, 1999.

Wolff, Robert Paul. *In Defense of Anarchism*. New York: Harper & Row, 1970.

Wright, Quincy. *A Study of War*. Chicago: University of Chicago Press, 1971 (1941).

Zancarini, Jean-Claude, ed. *Le droit de résistance*. Fontenay-aux-Roses: ENS, 1999.

INDEX